You'll Know When You Get There

You'll Know
When
You Get There

Herbie Hancock and the Mwandishi Band

Bob Gluck

The University of Chicago Press

Chicago and London

Bob Gluck is associate professor of music and director of the Electronic Music Studio at the State University of New York, Albany.

The University of Chicago Press, Chicago 60637
The University of Chicago Press, Ltd., London
© 2012 by The University of Chicago
All rights reserved. Published 2012.
Printed in the United States of America

21 20 19 18 17 16 15 14 13 12   1 2 3 4 5

ISBN-13: 978-0-226-30004-7   (cloth)
ISBN-10: 0-226-30004-8   (cloth)

Library of Congress Cataloging-in-Publication Data

Gluck, Bob.
    You'll know when you get there : Herbie Hancock and the Mwandishi band / Bob Gluck.
        pages ; cm
    Includes bibliographical references, discography and index.
    ISBN-13: 978-0-226-30004-7 (cloth : alkaline paper)
    ISBN-10: 0-226-30004-8 (cloth : alkaline paper)   1. Hancock, Herbie, 1940–
2. African American jazz musicians.   3. Hancock, Herbie, 1940—Criticism and interpretation.   4. Herbie Hancock Sextet.   5. Jazz—1971–1980—History and criticism.   I. Title.
    ML417.H23G58 2012
    781.65092—dc23
                                                              2011046241

♾ This paper meets the requirements of ANSI/NISO Z39.48-1992 (Permanence of Paper).

Contents

v

Preface

The year was 1970, and the Mwandishi band was coalescing into the musical force that captivated the imagination of many musicians. I was fifteen years old. My musical and political awareness were taking shape, and I, a conservatory student at the time, was in search of music that mattered. I, like many of my generation, was feeling the turmoil and promise of the era, and I was shaped—as a musician, educator, writer, and rabbi—through my experience of its politics and music. Central to my own story and, as I have discovered, the story of others, was Herbie Hancock's Mwandishi band. Their story encapsulates themes of weight and import: the place of the musician to forge new and unpredictable musical paths rather than perform standard repertory, race, the use of music as a vehicle to explore personal and musical identity, the role of the collective in music making, the interplay between musical expression and religious experience, how to engage new technologies, how music with a message can survive in the commercial world. This was a band with something to say, and as I emerged from a period of training where music was performed strictly for its own sake, I was seeking music with impact on the world around it.

I spent my younger years in Queens, New York City, dividing my time between studying piano in a conservatory setting and playing baseball. My parents were civil rights activists whose commitment was an expression of our family's Jewish identity. As I moved into young adulthood, my focus in one area was clear: I affirmed my family's political legacy by marching in Black Panther protests and attending antiwar rallies. But musically I felt adrift and perceived a growing gap between my political and musical commitments. Particularly at issue was my conservatory's affirmation that classical music was the sole indicator of cultural value. The personal conflict I experienced, although uncomfortable and unwelcome, opened me to new musical experiences and sounds. I encountered the irresistible appeal of the music of first Jimi Hendrix, followed by King Crimson, Frank Zappa, and Emerson, Lake and Palmer, and then the Herbie Hancock Sextet.

My encounter with Hancock's music came entirely by chance. My uncle Milton Schubin, the family's pied piper, regularly brought my cousins, brother, and me on wild adventures. Most were in the woods, but one, in summer 1970, placed me in the audience of my first two rock concerts, both at the Schaefer Music Festival in Central Park, New York City. The headliner for one of these was Iron Butterfly, but sharing the bill was an exciting ensemble that I later discovered was the Herbie Hancock Sextet.

Roiling in this perplexity, once I began college, I met two important mentors, Donald Funes and Philip Royster. As these devoted musician/educators helped me explore the depths and intricacies of musical cultures that were new to me—black, popular, avant-garde, and international—I became inspired by the realization that everything I learned also reinforced the significance of my own cultural and personal identity and obligations. Writing this book returned me to the musical journey of my younger life and presented an opportunity to more fully understand a body of music that has, in myriad ways, entranced and inspired me ever since.

Donald Funes was my teacher at the Crane School of Music at the State University of New York at Potsdam. Don nurtured what he called his "tribe" on a wild romp through Indian ragas, Stravinsky, Subotnick, Wagner, Coltrane, Zappa, Cage, and Wonder, as we engaged in collective improvisation and learned to compose and perform electronic music with Buchla, Arp, and Moog synthesizers; magnetic tape splicing blocks; and tape loops. It was within the context of Don's "tribe" that I met pianist Mitchel Forman, on whose car stereo I discovered "Sleeping Giant" from Herbie Hancock's *Crossings* while driving to New York City through the snow banks of New York State's North Country. Our shared appreciation of *Crossings* came not just from our collective love of electric jazz, but also from Don Funes's vision of the essential unity of electronics, jazz, and every form of dance and abstract music.

I was subsequently mentored at SUNY Albany by writer, educator, and drummer extraordinaire Professor Philip Royster while taking his courses covering a wide array of arts and letters from the perspective of black culture: the essay, drama, music, and literature. Professor Royster used music and literature to explore how artistic forms of expression become modes of self-discovery. One of the effects (or maybe tools) of oppression, he has always believed, is to limit people's self-knowledge. His pedagogy has become my own as a college professor. Dr. Royster has also been an invaluable resource in helping me navigate the geography and musical culture of the South Side of Chicago, where both he and Herbie Hancock were raised. Having lost Don Funes in 1999 and Milt Schubin in 2010, I have become increasingly aware of how fortunate I am to have Phil as a continuing presence in my life.

Another important mentor has been my college professor and subsequent friend and collaborator, Joel Chadabe. I greatly appreciate Joel's encouragement in the evolution of my writing about music history, and particularly electronic music. Joel has been an important mentor as I've learned to write in a manner that merges musical and historical sensibilities.

I have been fascinated to see how many musicians, whether part of or influenced by the Mwandishi band, have jumped at the chance to speak with me about this ensemble. An important part of the development of this book was a series of interviews I conducted with the various members of the Mwandishi band. An opening came through connections made by Don Preston, whom I had invited to perform at my university, and Andre Cholmondeley. They introduced me to Patrick Gleeson, from whom Preston had purchased a Moog III synthesizer. Pat Gleeson subsequently connected me with Bennie Maupin, Buster Williams, Billy Hart, Julian Priester, and producer David Rubinson. This project might have never gotten off of the ground had Andre not connected me with Pat Gleeson and had Pat not been so generous with his time and opened his life to me.

I offer thanks to Herbie Hancock, surely one of the busiest creative forces on the planet, for taking the time to converse on the phone, in person, and by e-mail, and to Jessica Hancock, who has been gracious in her assistance. I offer my gratitude to the members of the Mwandishi band and to Garnett Brown, a member of the original Herbie Hancock Sextet. Billy Hart continues to freely share his wisdom about all things musical. Buster Williams has been incredibly generous with his time and personal support, providing me a window into Buddhism. Bennie Maupin has offered encouragement and valuable connections. Eddie Henderson opened his home to me, where I had one of the most enjoyable and engaging conversations. Julian Priester has been an absolute pleasure to speak with. David Rubinson has generously given of his time and has shared thought-provoking ideas about music, the music business, politics, and food. David led me to Herbie Hancock. Natsuko Henderson and Nashira Priester have been supportive boosters throughout.

My gratitude goes to Steven F. Pond, author of the one previously published book about the work of Herbie Hancock, *Headhunters: The Making of Jazz's First Platinum Album*. While the focus of his work is the group that followed the Mwandishi band, the author's discussion of the Mwandishi band's music, electronic textures, Afrocentric sensibilities, postproduction, and improvisatory nature are praiseworthy and helpful. Very special thanks to Max Schlueter, whose background research documenting the band's history has been invaluable at every step along the way. Kirk Degiorgio, whose work briefly paralleled mine, provided a bouncing board for my thinking (see Degiorgio 2008). George E. Lewis and many others have provided information or connections with colleagues. Several readers have provided helpful feedback, among them Shira Gluck, David Katz, James Keepnews, Elisa Meredith, Philip Royster, David Rubinson, Max Schlueter, and James Weidman. Assisting with translations has been Francoise Chadabe, Mark Dermer, and Anne Legeene.

I greatly appreciate those musicians who have taken time from their busy schedules to offer reflections, advice, and information, among them Steve Bach, Thurman Barker, Bill Bruford, Ndugu Leon Chancler, Billy Childs, Pete Cosey, Kirk Digiorgio, Gregory Applegate Edwards, Ellery Eskelin, Douglas Ewert, Alvin Fielder, Mitchel Forman, Onaje Allan Gumbs, Skip Hadden, Harold Jones (via Reggie Willis), Ernie Krivda, Victor Lewis, Christian McBride, Bobby McFerrin, Pat Metheny, Jason Miles, Ras Moshe, Bob Musso, Mike Ning, Vernon Reid, Wallace Roney, Patrice Rushen, Michael Stern, Richard Teitelbaum, Henry Threadgill, Miroslav Vitous, John Wetton, and Reggie Willis. Many thanks to the musicians with whom I have played Mwandishi band repertoire: Dean Sharp, Michael Bisio, Christopher Dean Sullivan, Jay

Rosen, and David Katz. Conversations with Jeff Tamarkin helped me clarify my thinking, as he interviewed me for his own article (2010).

Journalists, editors, scholars, and music business professionals who have been of assistance and support include Frank Alkyer, Tom Atkins, Harriet Choice, Ken Engel, Tony Herrington, Jim de Jong, Bob Koester Sr., John Litweiler, Katie Malloch, Howard Mandel, Chuck Mitchell, Dan Morgenstern, Bob Musso, Chuck Nessa, Matt Robin, Paul Steinbeck, and Ron Wynn. Thanks also to David and James Marienthal for their reminiscences and materials; to photographers Veryl Oakland, Jan Persson, Don Nguyan, Tom Copi, and Herb Nolan; and to Danny Goodwin for his digital photo magic. Thanks also to Nashira Priester and Natsuko Henderson for their assistance searching for and locating photographs.

Many thanks to my editor, Elizabeth Branch Dyson, for her graciousness and intelligence, which has continually kept me on the right course. Thanks to her assistants Anne Summers Goldberg and Russ Damian, and to my manuscript editor Lisa Wehrle, for their assistance in every manner of detail.

Finally, I offer my deep gratitude to my parents, my spouse Pamela, and daughter Allison. Pamela has been an ever-patient, supportive, and encouraging life partner, intellectual compatriot, adept reader, and fellow traveler. She has been willing to embark on nearly every crazy idea I have generated for my life and our lives together. Pamela has journeyed with me through radical changes from my life as a rabbi, to a renewed life as a musician and educator. I could hardly ask for more. Allison was raised singing Frank Zappa tunes and attending all sorts of concerts and multimedia exhibitions I've given. Her love is musical theater, but recently she told me how she now understands that the sounds of birds and the wind rushing through trees is no less musical than her favorite tunes. I have been overjoyed to watch her grow as a musician and thinker, quickly becoming part of this book's target audience.

The experience of writing this book has been a joyride for me. It has brought together many of the topics and issues that interest me most. Writing about music in depth requires repeated listening, and this has been a pleasure. Doing so offered insight not only to the musical mind of Herbie Hancock, but also to the deeply creative impulses of all the members of the Mwandishi band. This book is thus their story as much as it is his. I hope you enjoy the ride as much as I have.

It is to the memory of my uncle Milton Schubin that this book is dedicated.

Introduction

This is a book about the music of pianist and composer Herbie Hancock during the first decade of his professional career. At its center is Hancock's work with the remarkably creative ensemble informally known as the Mwandishi band. The Mwandishi band emerged from Hancock's original 1968 Sextet, which in 1969 became his first touring ensemble as a bandleader. As that band became increasingly exploratory and underwent a change of personnel, its Mwandishi incarnation became the experimental laboratory in which Hancock first integrally joined the core musical elements that would form the building blocks that have served his musical creativity throughout his career.

My goal is to consider how this forward-looking young musician developed the stylistic, aesthetic, technological, and cultural ingredients that together represented the underlying musical values of his new endeavor. To do so requires paying close attention to attributes of Hancock's various projects as a young man, from his work as a sideman with Donald Byrd, Jackie McLean, Eric Dolphy, and of course, Miles Davis, to the early Blue Note recordings under his own name. After considering how the various sides of Hancock's musical approach each take shape, the narrative shifts to exploring how Hancock drew on them to craft a style appropriate to this endeavor. I trace the development of the highly unusual and rarely predictable band that forms, to some degree by serendipity, as their work unfolded on the road and in the studio, and then consider why it came to an end. My primary evidence is the music itself, supported by reminiscences by the people who made the music or learned from it, and published accounts in the press. I seek to generalize about the nature of the music and, equally important, the process by which it unfolded, by looking at musical examples, sometimes comparatively.

What defined the Mwandishi band was a constellation of features. None of them alone explain the nature of Hancock's project. Among these are collective improvisation and the careful listening it requires; open musical forms; the primacy of timbre (tone color) and rhythm over and above melody and harmony; black cultural identification and representation; and the integration of acoustic, electric, and eventually electronic sounds as part of a single sonic tapestry. It was with all of these musical attributes in hand that Hancock drew on the Mwandishi band as a dynamic vehicle for his compositions. Each of these musical attributes is treated, along with its evolution within Hancock's earlier work. I then consider how together they came to define a distinct and unified musical approach that can be identified as the Mwandishi sound.

This book begins with the first opportunity the band had for these musical ingredients to percolate in depth. This came during an unusually long month's residency at the London House, a steak house and jazz club in Chicago. The black cultural values of the band are introduced in this opening chapter by discussing a 1969 pre-Mwandishi recording that includes Herbie Hancock, where some of these elements are prefigured. Among other features, this is the place where Hancock first assumed the name Mwandishi.

In chapter 2, I turn to Hancock's early biography and the beginnings of his development as a jazz musician. I discuss two parallel but distinct musical worlds in which he participated during his first decade as a professional: Hancock's work within the context of hard bop, an amalgam of bebop, gospel, and the blues; and his membership in the Miles Davis Quintet. I explore what Hancock learned from Davis's use of intuition and emotion as formal musical principles, as an alternative to the primacy of elaborate chord changes. To understand this requires looking at sources of abstraction within Hancock's playing, among them early performances with Eric Dolphy and Hancock's use of tone clusters as an alternative to chords or modal configurations.

Chapters 3 and 4 examine Hancock's music in 1969 and 1970, which helped prepare the stage for the Mwandishi band. Herbie Hancock's first Sextet represented a bridge between the Miles Davis Quintet and the Mwandishi band by furthering the use of intuition as a means of structuring musical form and providing a laboratory for Hancock's exploration of the electric piano. Lacking a recording of that band, we consider Sextet saxophonist Joe Henderson's recording *Power to the People* (1969) as evidence of the musical interaction between Hancock and Henderson that may have been displayed in the work of Hancock's Sextet. Other influences during that period included Davis's electric sessions, Hancock's engagement with rhythm and blues on *Fat Albert Rotunda* (1969), and his further exploration of the electric piano as a rhythm instrument on Freddie Hubbard's *Red Clay* (1970). It was at this point that the diverse, full range of Hancock's playing to date, considered in chapter 2— lyricism, rhythmic intensity, abstraction, and sensitive listening—begin to coalesce within an integrated form of expression that is simultaneously exploratory and funky, electric and collectivist in its conception.

The live performances and recordings of the Mwandishi band represent the core of this book. Chapter 5 focuses on the band's road performances of the material that would be recorded on *Mwandishi* (1971); chapter 6 considers the recording and role of postproduction in that project; chapter 7 features the introduction of Patrick Gleeson's electronic sounds on *Crossings* (1972), which led to the focus of chapter 8, the incorporation of Gleeson's synthesizers and sound design in the touring band and the recording *Sextant* (1973).

Chapter 9 addresses special topics that defined the Mwandishi band's musical approach: their collective approach to music making and use of open forms in place of conventional song structures commonly found within idiomatic jazz. It is only after considering the developments discussed in chapters 6 through 9 that in chapter 10 we can meaningfully pick up the thread left off in chapter 5, the band's life on the road. At this point in the band's development, its performances reflect the full embrace of the studio and of electronic sounds. The book concludes in chapter 11, which discusses the business of operating an exploratory band like Hancock's Mwandishi and some of the causes of the band's demise. These are treated within the context of broader issues in the music business and in the personal narrative of Hancock's evolving career. An epilogue provides evidence of the band's continued importance and contains reminiscences by younger musicians who consider the Mwandishi band pivotal to their own musical development. The epilogue concludes with band members' memories identifying aspects of their time together that mattered most to them.

The story of the Mwandishi band and its predecessor Sextet must be placed within its historical context, that tumultuous and creative era when the 1960s gave way to the early 1970s. Hancock's 1968 departure from the Miles Davis Quintet and the founding of his Sextet was the same year as the horrific assassinations of Martin Luther King Jr. and Robert Kennedy. Black power was ascendant, symbolized in the international arena by the raised-fist salute given by two black Americans at the Olympic games in Mexico City, and in Chicago by Fred Hampton founding a local chapter of the two-year old Black Panther party. The antiwar movement was growing, symbolized by protests at the Democratic National Convention in Chicago.

The cultural amalgam included Stanley Kubrick's futuristic film *2001* (including music by Gyorgy Ligeti, symbolic of the aesthetics of the European avant-garde), and James Brown's "Say It Loud—I'm Black and I'm Proud." The Jackson Five released their first single and signed with Motown Records. This was the year of Sly and the Family Stone's "Dance to the Music," Otis Redding's "(Sittin' On) the Dock of the Bay," The Temptations' "Cloud Nine," and Aretha Franklin's "Chain of Fools." For some people, it was the era of psychedelia, drugs, and rock and roll, and for others, poverty and a combination of despair, hope, and empowerment. Woodstock was a year away, as was the first moon landing, the emergence of the Weathermen from Students for a Democratic Society, the premiere of *Sesame Street* and the first artificial heart to be transplanted into a human being. And the following year, Funkadelic, one of the most eclectic, musically radical, and funky bands to ever appear on the scene, would release *Free Your Mind . . . And Your Ass Will Follow*.

The members of the Herbie Hancock Sextet assumed Swahili names and sometimes performed wearing dashikis. Their music was infused with a wide range of influences, many but by no means all of them from black culture. It is impossible to listen to their recordings without feeling the political and cultural sensibilities of the time: the deep grooves, buoyed by Hancock's funky, wah-wah–inflected electric piano, the unpredictable qualities of the collective improvisation, the hand percussion instruments, the political implications of the song title "Ostinato: Song for Angela," honoring black activist Angela Davis, and the African sensibilities in the imagery of the cover art on the final two albums. That mix profoundly resonates with black identity and political consciousness during the early 1970s.

Despite the Afrocentric political symbolism, for most of the band's members, the band's racial identity was first and foremost about feeling like family and with pride of self and pride of place in the world. Even after the entrance of white Irish Catholic Patrick Gleeson, blackness was a given, a core identity through which many influences could be freely refracted and explored. Like musicians within the Chicago-based Association for the Advancement of Creative Musicians, African American musical forms provided a lens capable of refracting a multiplicity of influences, among them the Euro-American avant-garde. For Hancock, this could result in the merging of an atonal flight of fancy with the feel of funk that characterized his opening solo on "Sleeping Giant," the suite that opens the second Mwandishi recording, *Crossings*. As always, Hancock followed his muse. During the Mwandishi period, his muse included a group of like-minded, fascinating fellow musicians each with ideas of his own.

Hancock's work has rarely remained static, but there has never been a more sustained period during which the title of his tune, and of this book, "You'll Know When You Get There," has been more true than his time with the Mwandishi band. Ironically, the end point of this book is precisely the moment when Hancock was fortunate enough to gain the recognition he deserved, with the advent of the Headhunters band.

Herbie Hancock has modeled how a musician can continually adapt and explore in ways that embrace new learning. He has shown the wisdom of collapsing conventional musical categories, from what is considered avant-garde to the most popular, failing to find meaningful distinctions between music that moves the heart and toes and music that engages the cerebral. Is that not the very essence of jazz? Why not offer Karlheinz Stockhausen a place at the table alongside Jackie McLean, with Claude Debussy sitting shoulder to shoulder with Sly and the Family Stone? And we forget how radical were some earlier musical developments we take for granted, such as Charlie Parker's angularity and speed of musical line, as he navigated the chord changes of popular songs. For Hancock, diverse musical influences belong together and the synthesis deserves a broad audience. To this listener, the results echo the teaching of the Jewish mystic Rav Kook that our task is "to make the old new and the new holy." I suspect that Hancock would agree. The music of the Mwandishi band is prime evidence.

Right Band Members for a Special Setting

Five musicians who, with Herbie Hancock, constituted the Mwandishi band in fall 1970 would remain together for the balance of the band's time together. Each, like Hancock, adopted a Swahili name, which appears with its translation in the sections that follow.

Bassist Buster Williams, Mchezaji (The Player of the Art)

Buster Williams's association with Herbie Hancock, Mwandishi (The Composer), dated back several years:

> I first met Herbie and Wayne [Shorter], Tony [Williams], George Coleman, Miles [Davis] and Ron [Carter] on the French Riviera in 1963. I was touring with Sarah Vaughan. We were staying at the same hotel. We were playing the Jean Lapon jazz club. Miles Davis was performing, as was Sarah Vaughan. That's when I first met them. Then, in 1967, I joined the Miles Davis Quintet. I got a phone call from Herbie that Miles wanted me to join them in San Francisco at a club called the Both/And. So I went there to join them. I was with Nancy Wilson at that time, but Nancy was taking a hiatus for six weeks. So for a time I was with Miles. I was living in California; I moved to Los Angeles when I joined Nancy in 1965 and she was moving her operation out to the West Coast.
>
> During the time with Miles, we were all friendly and got along well and it was a good musical marriage. It was not easy stepping into Ron's shoes because the band had really become a family. Ron, Tony, Herbie and Wayne, along with Miles. They were breaking new ground and they had their own way of doing things. So for me to step in there and try to take the place of an ensconced family member was not easy to do. They welcomed me and supported me and in no time it was like being at home. I guess I fit in because I had that kind of mentality and I was prepared, musically.[1]

In addition to the live dates, Williams recorded one studio session with Miles on May 9, 1967, on the tune "Limbo":

> I came back to New York at the end of 1968. When Herbie decided to form his Sextet, he was leaving Miles, and he called me for that, in 1969. The thing we learned from Miles was possibilities and to think outside the box. When

Herbie formed the Sextet, that's where we started from day one. It became a great exploration from that point.

Drummer Billy Hart, Jabali (Energy)

Drummer Billy Hart had prior connections with several members of the band: "I first met Bennie [Maupin] when I met Buster [Williams], in Detroit, because Bennie was living in Detroit." Being of the same generation and all moving to New York, they experienced a confluence of influences, as Hart observes:

> This whole Afro-American revolution was going on sociologically or politically. It was the so-called beginning of intellectual African-American [culture]: Archie Shepp, Cecil Taylor, all of those meetings of those kinds of minds; to say nothing of Coltrane and Ornette Coleman and the way they mixed Leonard Bernstein, Gunther Schuller, John Lewis, Tanglewood. All of that was in the mix, just at the time when all of us were hitting there.

Hart grew up in Washington, D.C., a few blocks from a jazz club, the Spotlite Room, where he heard Miles Davis's first quintet and the John Coltrane Quartet. Coltrane proved to be a major musical influence, particularly in the saxophonist's late period. Hancock and Hart first met in the early 1960s, at the Village Vanguard shortly before Hancock joined Davis's band. "When I worked with Shirley Horn, I was a teenager in Washington, D.C., where Shirley lived. Wynton Kelly was the piano player. We used to play opposite Miles at the Vanguard because Miles loved Shirley so much. A bunch of times I got off the bandstand and I saw Herbie just standing there. He must have been 18 or 19, maybe 20." In an interview with Ethan Iverson, Hart added: "Herbie was standing in sort of the same area as Freddie Hubbard and Joe Henderson, but they didn't know each other yet. . . . I remember telling Herbie how great he sounded on this Donald Byrd record with Billy Higgins. He seemed surprised that I knew it and was really grateful for the compliment."[2]

Hart first played with Hancock in a trio with Miroslav Vitous, informally at bassist Walter Booker's place. Around the time he joined the Sextet, Hart had a regular gig in New York City with pianist Marian McPartland. Hart shared something important in common with Buster Williams: pivotal experiences accompanying singers. "I met Buster, in Detroit on Betty Carter's gig. That's how we became friends." Hart didn't want to leave Shirley Horn, so he returned to Washington to play with her rather than continuing with Carter (and Williams) at Birdland in New York. Sarah Vaughan, with whom Buster was playing, "took Betty's whole rhythm section to California and that's when Buster made that record 'Live in Copenhagen' with Sarah Vaughan. Then, after that, Nancy Wilson took Sarah's rhythm section. And Buster played with Dakota Staton after that. So, we're all singer's drummers; I'm still a singer's drummer."

Hart proved to be an excellent choice for the Mwandishi band, in part because of the eclectic mix of his early professional experiences, which included rhythm and blues and jazz. His early collaborations, in addition to Horn, included guitarist Wes Montgomery; saxophonists Buck Hill, Eddie Harris (including the saxophonist's work using electronics), Stan Getz, and Sonny Rollins; and more than three years with organist Jimmy Smith. Tootie Heath, whom Hart knew from school, was an early drumming influence. The addition of Billy Hart meant that three members of the Mwandishi band were consummate accompanists, sharing an ability to flexibly support as well as lead.

Reedist Bennie Maupin, Mwile At Akya (Body of Good Health)

Bennie Maupin's major influences as a young adult were Yusef Lateef, Eric Dolphy, and John Coltrane. Dolphy once gave him an informal flute lesson, and Coltrane, whom Maupin encountered at jam sessions in his home city of Detroit, was personally warm and supportive. Maupin also studied formally at the Detroit Institute of Musical Art. "Where I was growing up in Detroit, you were automatically exposed to all that church music, blues, the beginnings of R&B and all those things that came out of Motown. Classical musicians came there; they had emigrated from Europe. . . . It was a place to get some good training, so I kind of came up through that." Among the many bandleaders who hired Maupin were Roy Haynes, Horace Silver, Lee Morgan, McCoy Tyner, and Marion Brown.

After moving to New York City, Maupin played in 1965–66 and again in 1970 with saxophonist Marion Brown, one of several young saxophonists in Coltrane's orbit during the mid-1960s. Maupin also joined saxophonist Archie Shepp, another member of this circle, on two 1966 recording sessions led by drummer Sonny Murray. These experiences helped shape Maupin's musical imagination. The first two of Maupin's three sessions with Marion Brown's Quartet (1965, on a tune titled "Exhibition," and in 1966 on "Juba-Lee") are musically related to Coltrane's *Ascension* (1965, released in 1966), on which both Brown and Shepp had played.

Maupin reflects on how these experiences changed him:

> [Brown's] support of what I was doing really enabled me to have a completely different outlet. I hadn't played music with any kind of free form like that, no real chord changes. We were working around some kind of rhythmic motif, some kind of melodic idea, and then we just did some kind of theme and variations improvisational things. My earliest recordings, I'm very proud of them. That enabled me to break free of the tyranny of a sequence of chords.[3]

What really placed Maupin on the map were his sinewy, serpentine bass clarinet lines that grace Miles Davis's *Bitches Brew* (1970). Maupin told interviewer Rex Butters: "I met Miles through Jack De Johnette. I used to play a lot with McCoy [Tyner], for a couple of years. Miles would be around New York sometimes making the rounds. Miles used to pop into a joint we used to play in on the Lower Eastside called Slug's." Davis, well dressed and with his Ferrari on the street, would say hello to people and quickly leave. But he heard Maupin play bass clarinet there. Soon his friend Jack De Johnette joined Miles, along "with Chick [Corea] and Dave [Holland], and everybody's working with Miles. So when the thing started coming up, I got that call. Miles wants me to come."[4] Maupin continued to be a central figure in sessions Miles recorded over the next few years, among them sessions on June 12, 1972 (released as part of *Big Fun*, 1974) and on July 7, 1972, joined by Herbie Hancock (released as part of *On the Corner*, 1972).

Maupin first met Hancock standing outside a gig by Sonny Rollins at the Half Note. "I look down to my left, I see Sonny carrying his horn, coming this way. I look to my right and there's Herbie. Both coming at the same time. Amazing. They both arrived there at the same time; I'm standing there. Sonny looks at Herbie, he looks at me, and says, 'Herbie, do you know Bennie?'" Later, "Joe Henderson was beginning to make his own records and not so interested in being a sideman in Herbie's band. The opportunity came, and Buster Williams said, 'Hey, you need to call Bennie Maupin.'"[5]

Trombonist Julian Priester, Pepo Mtoto (Spirit Child)

Julian Priester, like Herbie Hancock, was from Chicago, and five years older. Like many up and coming Chicago musicians, Priester studied with Capt.

Walter Dyett at DuSable High School. His early musical experiences were with blues musicians Muddy Waters and Bo Diddley, and he landed his first important sustained gig in 1954 with the eclectic big band pioneer Sun Ra, then in Chicago. Even though the gig came prior to Sun Ra's more experimental music, the experience proved useful for the creative, open-ended style Priester would encounter later with the Herbie Hancock Sextet:

> Sun Ra gave us very little concrete information or music that we were performing and we had to depend upon our ears to grasp the sounds and make sense out of the sounds that the band created, that Sun Ra dictated. He would point to individuals and indicate to just start playing, without any guidelines. And he left it up to each individual to create music from the palate that was created instantly on the spot, right there. There were no lead sheets, there were no . . . he might dictate a melody, a fragment of a melody that we had to use, but when it came to improvising, we had only the sounds that we could identify as a foundation. So we had to use that foundation, we had to relate to that foundation and build solos based on the music happening on the spot. Of course, my training demanded that it have musical qualities; that means that my interpretation of the sounds that were presented to me had to fall into categories, you know. When I hear a sound I have to associate it with a tonality. Once I identify that tonality, I can improvise a solo, a part of a solo. The training I received performing with Sun Ra prepared me for performing with the Sextet.

Priester left the financially unstable Sun Ra Arkestra in 1956 to tour with vibraphonist Lionel Hampton, and then moved to New York to play behind jazz singer Dinah Washington. There, Priester joined the stable of musicians who recorded on the Riverside label and, in the early 1960s, Blue Note, playing on sessions by Joe Henderson, McCoy Tyner, and Freddie Hubbard, whose Quintet he joined. He also played in pit orchestras for musical shows. Priester's more exploratory interests were expressed by playing with John Coltrane and Sam Rivers, and by joining Max Roach's band, playing on the influential recording *We Insist! Freedom Now* (1960). Roach introduced him to odd meters (7/4, 9/4 . . .), polyrhythms, and the incorporation of African drumming into a jazz setting. In 1969, Priester spent several months on the road with Duke Ellington's Orchestra. He also participated in improvisatory sessions with New York avant-garde poets and musicians, excellent preparation to join the Mwandishi band since "with Herbie, the difference is that we didn't have pre-determined directions. We had to sort of react on the spot to the changes in directions that the music [took]." When Garnett Brown, initial trombonist in the Herbie Hancock Sextet, called to ask if Priester could sub: "I wasn't working at the time. I had left Duke Ellington after a few months. I was in New York, rehearsing with my own band and, well, my bank account was feeling the effects of trying to put together a band in New York City."

Trumpeter Eddie Henderson, Mganga (Doctor of Good Health)

Eddie Henderson honed his skills as a trumpeter over many years, and, while in school, he found significant mentors:

> I always wanted to play, just always, always. When I got exposed to jazz, it touched a root, a nerve in me, and I just fell in love with music, no matter what. . . . My first big influence musically was Freddie Hubbard and Lee Morgan. Then I stopped trying to be influenced by just trumpet. I tried to get phrasings and stuff from Charlie Parker, John Coltrane; make "short-term loans" from Herbie's style. I played all through undergraduate school at UC Berkeley. After I met Miles Davis, I decided: "that's what I want to do!" I played all the way through medical school [at Howard University, in Washington, D.C.]. I had a little group in medical school, you know, and I used Billy Hart. And I would come up to New York every weekend for four years. Every Saturday I'd be at Freddie Hubbard's house. Every Sunday at Lee Morgan's house. I was playing on the same bill. I'd come up to New York and sit in with the guys . . . learning how to play.

Billy Hart recalls that "Eddie was always a good reader; that's how I knew him as a musician. When I was in the Howard theater band, Eddie was in it too: We played behind all the rock and roll acts. I played with Joe Tex, the Isley Brothers, Sam and Dave, Patti LaBelle, Otis Redding, Smokey Robinson, and the Miracles."

Eddie Henderson's career path was personally challenging and required persistence and courage. While in college, he decided to become a doctor like his stepfather, whom he describes as competitive, bitter, and negative. Henderson recalls that his stepfather thought he would never get anywhere in life and "bet my mother his medical license that I would never become a doctor." Although his stepson was accepted at his alma mater, the stepfather sought to interfere with his attending. Henderson bravely and maybe stubbornly continued to pursue his dual career as a doctor and a musician. "I just loved music. So I did it to spite him." He would attend class "every day from 8:00 to 5:00 in medical school, come home, study every day from 5:15 to 9:30, go out and play until 2:00 in the morning. Come back and study until I'd go to sleep about 4 or 5 in the morning, and then wake up at 7:30 and go back to school. Every day. I never missed a class!"

By 1969, Henderson was in the midst of a residency in psychiatry, in San Francisco, at the same clinic as jazz pianist Denny Zeitlin. Hancock recalls: "I'd known Eddie since '64 because his father is a good friend of Miles. I'd never heard him play, but everybody I spoke to recommend[ed] him. I had a rehearsal one day, and he read all the music off just like that, with feeling and everything . . . he scared the shit out of me."[6] Henderson believed that in hiring him for the initial week, Hancock "took the attitude 'OK, I'll bite the bullet; I'll just make it through this week,' but I'd heard the band and studied the music, the playing, for years, the repertoire." Thus, during the rehearsal, Henderson wasn't really sight-reading. It took a while for the trumpeter to grow in confidence, but as Hancock recalls, "after a few days I could hear his strength growing, so I asked him to come with us for three months, until January."[7]

Henderson, although still in his psychiatry residency, yearned to stay with the band. On Billy Hart's advice, "I called Herbie and said: 'Well, look, Herbie, I really want to be in the band if it's possible.' He said: 'Don't you want to continue to be a doctor?' I said 'Hell, no!' And so, when I joined Herbie Hancock, I was already a doctor, got my license and everything. . . . Danny Zeitlin asked me 'how did you make that decision?' I said: 'No question! I'll always be a doctor, but if I let this opportunity go, I'll hate myself forever.' There was no reluctance at all on my part." Henderson ended up staying the entire duration, even though it meant leaving psychiatry for an extended period.

The teasing of the young trumpeter, however, didn't cease for quite some time. "On the first record that I was ever on, *Mwandishi*, I had the music right here, a blank piece of music paper with all the ledger lines and, you know, [just] the staff lines. In the middle of two staff lines he has an eighth note, a tiny little eighth note, and at the top a bird's eye. I said: 'what do you want me to play?' Herbie said: 'Well, if you don't know, maybe I should call Johnny Coles!' I said: 'Wait, wait, wait, give me one shot.' And so I just had to play the way I played." Despite the continued ribbing, "Herbie said: "Just play the way you play." Isn't that something? He never told anybody how to play or what to do."

When the personnel changed, there was a whole new spiritual feeling with the band that opened up the veins, expanded the playing, the veins of the lifeblood of the playing of the band, into more intuitive playing than had happened with the previous band.

HERBIE HANCOCK, 2008

1

A Defining Moment
November 1970

Herbie Hancock traveled a long distance musically from the closing days of his membership in Miles Davis's renowned second Quintet. As his first touring band as leader began to coalesce, Hancock was assimilating much from the panoply of new musical experiences he accumulated during his first decade as a professional musician. From 1963 through 1968, Davis's band had provided an extended opportunity for Hancock to channel the flexibility and openness that Davis sought into his own performance practice. Davis's band had assimilated a decade of explorations by John Coltrane, Ornette Coleman, Chicago native Sun Ra, Cecil Taylor, and others within its own framework. Hancock was keenly aware of Coleman's and Coltrane's advances, enhanced by his early experiences performing with Coltrane associate Eric Dolphy. Hancock's synthesis helped shape Davis's musical direction. As Mike Zwerin observes, "this pillow of tense, ambiguous sound Hancock devised was the perfect bridge to bring Davis out of bebop toward more open forms."[1] The fruits of these efforts helped fuel the direction of Hancock's new Sextet.

Hancock's first band briefly premiered in November 1968 and went on the road six months later, touring through 1969 and into the late summer of 1970. Its music is explored in chapter 3, as the band's developments on the road fused what could be gleaned from Davis's Quintet with Hancock's growth as an orchestrator whose music deepened harmonically and lyrically, as can be heard on *The Prisoner* (1969).

During this period, Herbie Hancock was also giving deeper voice to personal and musical implications of black political and social awareness witnessed in at least two manifestations. One was the recording of the rhythm and blues–influenced *Fat Albert Rotunda* (1969). The second was Hancock's adoption in 1969 of the Swahili name Mwandishi (The Composer). This occurred within a social and musical context whose fruit included a little-known recording named *Kawaida* (Tradition), to which we will soon return. The sessions for both recordings took place in early December 1969. To fully appreciate the Mwandishi band, one must consider each of these sessions, the earlier musical directions in Hancock's career that pointed to them, and the nature of the unusual bond that was about to occur. Describing these experiences and their salient musical features is the task of the opening chapters of this book.

By the second half of 1970, Hancock's band had begun a dramatic evolution in personnel. Only two members of the Sextet that Herbie Hancock had fronted at the Village Vanguard in November 1968 remained: bassist Buster Williams, who had subbed for Ron Carter during part of that week,[2] and Hancock himself. David Rubinson, soon to be named Hancock's producer, felt the palpable change during the new band's first weeklong engagement at the Both/And in San Francisco: "The music was becoming both tighter and looser. Band members would just start playing. Anyone could start something," and the others would coalesce into an increasingly elastic musical fabric. Williams had just purchased an electric bass, a large body Fender, and was playing it in addition to his acoustic. Hancock himself was playing more electric than acoustic piano. Sparks were beginning to fly. The band continued to bond personally and musically at their next stop, Vancouver.

Hancock immediately realized that something unusual was unfolding. It lay deep in the connection between the band members, a dynamic that could not be described in simple musical terms: "From the first piece I felt something special, something profound, spiritual. The way that the music was moving extracted something that was eminently spiritual. I believe that this was one of the major characteristics of this group, this spiritual element that was evident from the first night."[3] That connection was about a sense of family, of shared musical purpose, of a collective intent to break down barriers. There was something deeply religious, albeit not in conventional terms, that brought them together.

The time was approaching for a defining moment, which occurred during an unusually lengthy month-long November gig[4] at the London House steak house in Chicago. The duration of the stand and future months on the road would help cement the feeling that the band was a family. But this perception was also grounded in the decision of the entire group to follow Hancock and Williams's lead by assuming Swahili names. This act simultaneously affirmed a shared black identity and created a family bond. To understand that decision, it helps to return to the context of Herbie Hancock's thinking back in December 1969 in the context of recording *Kawaida*.

Kawaida (Tradition)

Percussionist James Mtume, a disciple of Maulana Ron Karenga, is credited with naming *Kawaida*.[5] Karenga at the time was chairman of the Black Studies Department at California State University, Long Beach, and founder of the Los Angeles–based black nationalist US organization.[6] Karenga encouraged black identification with African culture, identity, and spiritual values, as witnessed by his invention of the festival of Kwanzaa. Most of the personnel on *Kawaida* accordingly assumed Swahili names, among them two members of Hancock's future Sextet, pioneering bebop drummer Kuumba Albert "Tootie" Heath and bassist Mchezaji Buster Williams. Also appearing were two members of Ornette Coleman's quartet: trumpeter Msafari Don Cherry and percussionist Ed Blackwell. Other participants included percussionist Mtume on conga, Tayari Jimmie Heath on tenor and soprano saxophone, and future Mwandishi band soundman and driver Fundi Billy Bonner, who played flute and percussion on one track. Herbie Hancock, playing exclusively acoustic piano, is listed as Mwandishi Herbie Hancock.[7] Two years later, Hancock's band would be referred to informally after his Swahili name, testimony to that ensemble's future identification with Africanism.

Kawaida draws on musical tendencies pioneered by various elements in the jazz avant-garde of John Coltrane and members of the black experimental music organization, the Chicago-based Association for the Advancement of Creative Musicians (AACM),[8] founded five years earlier. The opening tune

"Baraka" opens with quartal[9] harmonies reminiscent of Coltrane's pianist Mc-
Coy Tyner, despite the catchy melody and relaxed beat that follows. "Dunia"
follows an opening trumpet phrase with an open-ended improvisation featuring an interwoven saxophone and trumpet duet over driving percussion that
calls to mind Elvin Jones's playing with Coltrane. A percussion jam forms the
backbone of the solos that close out the tune. "Maulana" is a free form textural improvisation for flute and bells, over which speakers call out and chant
Swahili texts. After 1:30, Hancock and Williams's arco bass take an elegiac
tone, leading to a six-note rhythmic riff, again calling to mind Coltrane. Next
we hear an expansive saxophone solo, a more melodically oriented trumpet
solo, and then another percussion jam and hand clapping. Ever so briefly,
a singing voice adds a layer of complexity over the drums, bass, and bells.
"Dunia" and "Maulana" look ahead to musical elements—collective improvisation, textural emphasis, extended solos, and little instruments, particularly
percussion—that would play a role in the Mwandishi band.

The final composition and maybe the most distinctive on the recording is
a recitation of the seven guiding principles (Nguzo Saba) of Kwanzaa, read
by each of the band members in sequence.[10] The backdrop for the recitations
is a textural fabric of interwoven flute melodies presaging improvisatory moments in the Mwandishi band.

Kawaida and *Fat Albert Rotunda* display very different musical leanings, yet
share black cultural affinities. When one considers the sensibilities of these
two recordings and Hancock's experiences with the Miles Davis Quintet, it is
clear that a constellation of new ideas was coalescing to shape Hancock's current musical conception. It is not a tremendous conceptual leap from many
aspects of *Kawaida* to the music, however far more open-ended, played a year
later by the Mwandishi band. As Hancock later described the music to come:

> What we were looking for was to play a music that was based essentially on
> intuition. We had melodies and a certain number of chords at our disposal
> but we used them as little as possible. . . . [Thus] our music became more
> and more spontaneous, different from one night to the next. Sometimes we
> prepared ourselves to play certain themes and we started with an improvised
> introduction, but we found that having done that, we went so far that the in-
> troduction lasted three quarters of an hour! After a while I would realize that
> we had never played the melody in question . . . [or] not exposed the melody
> until the end, having made an incredible voyage. When this group was func-
> tioning at full tilt, when the different intuitions were harmonious with one

another, it was magic, pure and simple. The music that we were playing was thus so powerful that it literally transported the listener on the same voyage. It was a sort of fantasy.[11]

The London House

The Herbie Hancock Sextet played the London House for four weeks, five days a week, with Mondays and Tuesdays off. The club was located in a downtown Chicago apartment building on Michigan Avenue and catered mainly to a business crowd during the dinner hour time slot assigned to Hancock's band. Formal dress was expected, and dinner was expensive. Typical bookings included Barbara Carroll, Eddie Higgins, Oscar Peterson, Errol Garner, George Shearing, Mel Torme, Sarah Vaughan, Jim Hall, and vibraphonist Cal Tjader.[12] Pianist Ramsey Lewis played there often; Peterson and Vaughan recorded there.

Hancock recalls that the two club owners, the Marienthal brothers, were expecting to hear songs from Hancock's lush, melodious recording *Speak Like a Child* (1968), "a much softer, more gentle kind of sound. [For that album,] I was trying to come out of a Gil Evans influence." The club owners "knew I had a sextet with that basic instrumentation and they thought it was going to be that kind of thing," yet "[by the time we came to London House] we were already into the avant-garde, into playing sounds and exploring new sonic territories."

The shows at the London House were certainly not what the owners anticipated, as Hancock explains:

> We played "Maiden Voyage" and those tunes, but we had some other tunes, too! We didn't play any of it like what he had heard on the record. We were much further out than that. And he wanted us to play a dinner hour! And I said: "I don't recommend it!" So, we did a first day and he understood what we were talking about and he said: "OK, you don't have to play the dinner hour."

Hancock recalls the owners sounding "kind of disappointed we weren't playing what he expected. But . . . we were all determined to somehow break through to that audience." Despite their surprise, the owners adapted and kept the band on for a full month. Co-owner George Marienthal treated the booking as an opportunity: "Herbie's music doesn't appeal to the usual cocktail crowd. And he mystifies many of my dinner customers. But we have a lot more people of all ages coming out late at night to hear him. And that's a good sign." Marienthal added: "Now I'm looking for other talented groups like Herbie's."[13]

The *Chicago Tribune* offered a positive report, with hints from reviewer Harriet Choice that something unusual was taking place: "They are a tight and happy group, and even if diners are a little bewildered by the free form music . . . [they are] a combo that swings—and that's the essence of jazz."[14] The sharp contrast with the conservative nature of most London House bookings meant, as drummer Thurman Barker relates, that "when Herbie was going to be there, it was a hell of an event. I know the night I was there, all the tables were filled. I had to stand at the bar." Chicago-based bassist Reggie Willis remembers, however:

> It was unusual for a supper club like the London House to have such a musically expansive and experimental group as the Mwandishi band. I'm sure their music was a little ear shattering for audiences who were used to sitting and eating steak and lobster. Herbie's band was one of the most experimental bands of the time, demanding serious listening and attention. Herbie and the members of the band were really stretching the sound barrier.

Drummer Alvin Fielder, like Willis and Barker, was an original AACM member. Fielder, who had befriended and played with Hancock a decade earlier, recalls:

> I was in Chicago to visit my in-laws while Mwandishi was at the London House. I knew Billy Hart was with the group and Billy was a good friend. I had heard him with Jimmie Smith and Wes Montgomery and I was in admiration of his looseness and his conception. I went to see Mwandishi and sat on the bandstand near Billy to watch it. The music was special, different and right on the edge. The music covered many bases touching on bebop, post-bebop, avant-garde, Latin, colors [a broad sound palate], and so forth. What I heard from Mwandishi was new to me, and my ears. The music was everywhere and the flow was just phenomenal. Everyone in the group was strong, precise and creative, which is what happens when all the musicians are in synch. I especially remember the sound of Billy and his floating feel, his touch and how he would stretch rhythms. His time was like a rubber band. In any musical situation, I knew I would love his swing, feel and conception. Also, he's such a warm and humble person.

Trumpeter Eddie Henderson, however, remembers London House regulars "gagging" and not returning, and the composition of the audience shifting toward a more receptive group: "We brought all these jazz enthusiasts and a lot of the black avant-garde musicians from Chicago. They were there every night."

Word must have spread that an unusual band was playing at the London House, but many of the more experimental musicians in Chicago seemed unaware that the shows were ongoing. Barker adds: "If I had known, there was no way I wouldn't have come back often. For instance, when Miles was at the Plugged Nickel, I went out four nights." Apparently, Barker, Fielder, and Willis were among very few AACM members to attend these shows. This may seem surprising since AACM members were among the most forward-looking musicians in Chicago, except that the London House had a reputation for conservative bookings and it was an expensive club. Barker points out: "AACM members were pretty opinionated about a lot of the music at the time. I know this from being a teenager listening to the older guys talking about the music and about who they would go hear." Some AACM members had also left for New York and so were no longer in Chicago for the London House shows.

Members of the Sextet, however, regularly went out to see AACM groups perform on their nights off. Barker remembers: "Julian Priester and Billy Hart were always there when they were in town. Bennie Maupin came one or two times. . . . I knew Billy Hart from when he came to Chicago with the Montgomery Brothers in the early 60s. Julian Priester and Roscoe Mitchell go way back in Chicago." Fielder recalls: "I first met Billy Hart at an AACM concert. I was working with Anthony Braxton and Kalaparusha and Charles Clark. He'd come by a concert and I'd let him play. He'd let me play at his gigs with Wes Montgomery." The impact of the AACM on Hancock himself seems indirect since the organization was formed four years after he relocated to New York. Hancock was familiar with the key players prior to their more experimental stage, among them "Malachai Favors, Richard Abrams—when I knew him he was Richard [and not yet Muhal Richard] Abrams—[as well as Sun Ra associate] John Gilmore. I played with some of them in jam sessions. When I knew Richard Abrams, he was more a bebop player." Elements of the AACM musical approach and cultural concerns had permeated the musical avant-garde, and its influence can be heard in the music of *Kawaida* and on recordings of the Sextet in live performance. Important features in common included the use of little percussion instruments and flutes, increasing attention to timbre, extended instrumental techniques, a collective approach to music making, and a celebration of African cultural roots.

Thurman Barker describes what he witnessed at the London House in greater detail:

> I had been following Herbie as much as I could, especially when he came to Chicago. . . . I saw his Sextet twice, once at London House and once, a year later, when they played at Joe Siegel's Jazz Showcase. Fortunately the personnel were the same on both occasions. There are many things that I remember about the music at the London House show; clearly, it was very different from what Herbie had been playing with Miles.
>
> First of all, Billy Hart was playing rhythms that had a defined beat, different from a jazz beat. It was a very elastic rock beat or a boogaloo beat. It was like jazz over this boogaloo beat that was very loose. This was all new, a sound that I heard Jack [De Johnette] doing, along with some other guys like Billy Cobham. It had a backbeat but it wasn't always on two and four. It was disjointed, but the rhythms were really elastic, and it was very smooth. Billy Hart, being the musical drummer he is, really knows the drum kit. His playing was not flamboyant, but he was always there in the pocket. If it were Tony Williams, it would have been a totally different sound; it would have been clear that everything was coming from the drums. The feeling that Billy plays with really went into the band. Billy never overshadowed anybody; he'd always play at a level that you could hear everybody in the band. Billy and Buster were really connected musically and as New Yorkers, as they were at the time. I also got the feeling they all knew they were doing something special.
>
> Number two, the music was very open and there were lots of vamps; they were improvising off of vamps. There was a totally different dynamic from *Bitches Brew*. Miles Davis sort of dominated *Bitches Brew*, and on that recording you never really heard the horns do anything together. It was Miles, and then somebody else would take a solo. With the Sextet at London House, even though this was Herbie's band, Herbie didn't play like it was his band. While the music was very open, Herbie, being the director and composer that he is, he was like the choreographer, the guy who made it all happen. Being a keyboard player, he was always in the center of the mix, but the horns all played together. The band came across really together as organized and professional, but new and fresh.
>
> There were these long, long compositions and all the solos seemed to overlap each other. All of this to me was unexpected. I liked it. The bass clari-

net playing of Bennie Maupin, bass clarinet in a live jazz setting, was new to me; I had never heard Eric Dolphy live. The sound of the flugelhorn and bass clarinet gave it a nice texture. The flugelhorn is a mellower sounding instrument than trumpet. And to me, the way the playing went down, it seemed to fit the room. It was nice hearing that music in that room; the music became the center of attraction, certainly not their meals.

Third, it was very clear that Herbie was doing something experimental. And whatever he was doing, it was working. I liked it. The real bottom line was that they had taken jazz into this electronic sound, loose yet well reorganized, compositional yet open.

A Numinous Musical Experience

Mwandishi band trumpeter Eddie Henderson noticed subtle shifts that were emerging in the music that audience members like Barker detected, as Henderson recalls: "It just happened so organically and it was like an [unconscious] change; I couldn't put my finger and say it started here and it happened here. We knew something was going on, but we never talked about it decisively like this: 'When do we make the change?' We knew it was happening."

And this is when the band first started making the change. That's an "everybody talking at once!" you know, those sounds all at once. And we did say "Wow, that's kind of what we wanted to do." Other than that, I don't think we really ever talked about it concretely. There wasn't a concrete line. That band, at that time, you know, in any field there's like an ocean, there's like many currents, little tiny currents, and then all the sudden you might have a mega tsunami . . . it opened doors. It opened the scope of what jazz was then.

The band had started listening to music from the European avant-garde. Henderson remembers Karlheinz Stockhausen being one example. During the third week, Herbie Hancock remembers, something unexpected took place:

We started playing and I felt totally focused but yet I wasn't in control. And it almost felt to me that everything was integrated and we were so in synch with each other. It felt like the musicality of all of the guys was coming through me. All of our inner self-wisdom and musicality was expressing itself collectively through every individual. It was like all of the guys were in me. All of the guys were in Buster. All of the guys were in Bennie Maupin. It was like that. And I was watching my fingers and everything just worked perfectly. Like it was some symphony. And it was totally spiritual.

When we finished playing, I looked out at the people [but] I couldn't move at first. I couldn't move. None of us could. There was no applause. Nothing. And slowly I got up from the piano and I started to walk, but I couldn't feel my feet. And I looked and it was like my feet were twelve feet below me, like they were way below me. And I felt some kind of elevation, and then we slowly walked off the stage. Still no applause, but I looked at the faces and people were like their mouths were open, like dumbfounded and amazed.

We had to walk through the audience to get to the back of the room and to the elevators that took us to the musicians' room. We got halfway through the room and the applause started, and kept going and going. . . . Maybe fifteen, twenty minutes go by and somebody came up and said, "the people are still applauding." We couldn't go back downstairs when they said people were applauding. They must have applauded at least twenty minutes or thirty minutes. It just went on and on. We couldn't go back on. I couldn't go out there and play another [note]. What would we do after that?

The band was essentially living together on the road, developing a deep level of intimacy. Julian Priester observes, "You have great musicians performing together and you get a bunch of individuals contributing to the overall sound of the group. And then you get those special groups who live, eat and sleep on the same schedule. And when they get together to perform, well, I call it magic, but it's uncanny that they perform as one, if that makes any sense." Given greater permission to explore than one would find in most jazz ensembles, what developed, as Priester explains, was a "group concept where what we were performing was really based on what everyone else was performing. Everyone was contributing to this unique sound. Everyone was listening to each other [as] we used to describe it, leaving our egos out of the process; just responding to what the overall group invents. The sound that came from the band is a result of each person contributing to the whole. And that whole was unified." The growing intimacy, the level of permission to be guided by intuition, and the clearly positive results engendered a depth of mutual musical solidarity.

The musical possibilities that became clear during the London House engagement continued to open and expand. Julian Priester elaborates:

There were no restrictions. Everyone in the band was pretty much of the same mind. Even when we went in opposite directions, it was all right. I'm talking about musically, artistically. Everybody had [the freedom] to be as expressive as they wanted to be. And because everyone was of the same mind, everything worked. Everything we attempted to do musically was fruitful. . . . I believe that kind of magic is special. It doesn't happen every day.

Herbie Hancock recalls that the numinous experience didn't end after the close of the night's third and final set that so shook the audience and band members. "We went to someone's house after that" listening to recordings of the shows, along with two regular attendees, both named Jerry. One of the two "went into a kind of trance, listening to the tapes. He had been to the gig, too." The second Jerry, who had been unable to attend the evening's performance "went into a catatonic trance. He fell over in a chair. He fell over and he was in the same seated-position on the floor. It, like, took him completely out. It was transcendent. It was amazing." Hancock continues:

I think this was the third week [of the month at the London House]. We had one more week there. But you know what? The essence of that was still there. And then we went to Detroit, where we played the Strata Music Gallery.[15] (We did so other times later, once for a full week.) The essence of that was *still* there, although it was tapering off. Little by little it was tapering off. We were listening to these tapes every night. It was nothing boastful. It wasn't like we were listening to "our great achievement." It was like something happened. We wanted to learn from it.

Somehow, the band needed to find a way to sustain and expand what transpired during that remarkable night. A recalled "feeling" wouldn't suffice. What replaced it was the recurrent experience of shared intuition and deep listening. During a show in Seattle, shortly before the London House gig, Buster Williams had stunned his fellow band members with a shift in his playing occasioned, he said, by his discovery of Nichiren Buddhism.[16]

Williams's encounter with Nichiren Buddhism was a chance occurrence. His sister introduced his wife Ronnie to its practice of chanting the Japanese phrase *Nam-myoho-renge-kyo*. Ronnie was recovering from a car accident. Williams noticed the positive effect this was having on both women, and so he adopted the practice himself and had his sister chant it for the band members, who liked its rhythmic qualities. Williams recalls, "We were in Seattle. Everybody was tired. We came to the gig; this was the opening night. We had to set up. But I had been doing my morning and evening prayers every day, which we call *Gongyo*, and I was feeling refreshed. After doing this a month, it was having a tremendous effect on me." Hancock picks up the narrative:

> So the bassist Buster Williams starts playing this introduction. And what came out of him was something I'd never heard before. And not only had I not heard it from him, I'd never heard it from anybody. It was just pure beauty and ideas and—it was magical. Magical. And people were freaking out, it was so incredible what he was playing. I let him play for a long time, maybe 10, 15 minutes. He just came up with idea after idea, so full of inspiration. And then I could feel myself waking up just before we really came in with the melody for the song. And I could tell that the whole band woke up, and there was some energy that was generating from Buster. We played the set and it was like magic. When we finished, many people ran up to the front of the stage and reached up their hands to shake ours. Some of them were crying they were so moved by the music. The music was very spiritual, too.

Williams remembers:

> I came off the bandstand, Herbie grabbed me by the shoulders and said, "I've never heard you play like that before. What was that? What is going on with you? I've been noticing some changes in you. What is happening?" So I said, "Herbie, man, remember when I brought my sister over, had her do that chant for us?" He said, "Yeah." I said, "That's what I've been doing. That's what I've been doing. I've been chanting Nam-myoho-renge-kyo and you got to try it.

The chanting practice caught on briefly with some band members and longer term with others. Either way, Buddhism became a part of the group's inspiration and a metaphor for the spontaneity and freshness the band sought to discover. It became an unanticipated parallel to the musical experiences in which they were already engaged as an emerging creative unit.

Becoming a Culturally Pan-African Family

Another way the band sustained their musical collectivity was by joining Herbie Hancock and Buster Williams in adopting Swahili names, as Priester explains, "for the unifying effect in that when everyone adopted those names it had the effect on each individual joining. They became a unit. It was like we became a family, you know? We had something in common, as families do. It wasn't like a traditional family where everyone shares the same name. . . . [The name given me] Pepo Mtoto is a name that means 'Spirit Child.' Pepo is a name that's interpretation; the English would be 'spiritual.' Mtoto is a name for a child." Bassist Buster Williams adds, "Mtume gave me my name, Mchezaji. It means the Player, the player of the Art. . . . Herbie's name became Mwandishi, the Composer. . . . And Eddie Henderson is a doctor, and his name became Mganga, Doctor of Good Health. Bennie Maupin's name became Mwile At Akya, which means Body of Good Health. Bennie was the vegetarian in the band. He was the one who made us all vegetarians. And Billy Hart became Jabali, which means Energy." As Hancock noted in a 1971 interview, "using both a Swahili and American name indicates that I am a black man as well as an American. I believe the blacks should get credit for what they create. Every group should get credit for its contributions."[17]

There was a circle of people around the Mwandishi band who also adopted African names. Pianist Onaje Allan Gumbs remembers:

> I adopted the name "Onaje" while living in Buffalo. I found it in a book of African Names compiled by Amiri Baraka, then still known as Leroy Jones. It is Nigerian in origin and means "the sensitive one, owner of the feeling." I feel that the "Mwandishi Period" of cats having African names influenced my own decision to also adopt an African name that I tacked on to my given name.

The music of the Mwandishi band struck a course that showed little deference to musical categories, borrowing from every conceivable source, affirming that its music was an authentic expression of the collective members of the band. The band was proudly black identified (even with the addition, in mid-1972, of Patrick Gleeson), exemplified by its racial composition, use of Swahili names, wearing of dashikis, and black musical signifiers, among them rhythmic multiplicity and complexity, contrasting timbre, call-and-response patterning.[18] Their awareness grew within the strengths of each individual, tapping into the mysterious chemistry that naturally evolved within the group. In a multiplicity of ways, the band was becoming an integral unit, looking ahead to a remarkable musical journey.

2

Becoming Herbie Hancock

Beginnings

Wayman Hancock Sr., Herbie Hancock's father, once recalled in an oral history:

> [Herbie] was crazy about music. He always liked music. If he was crying or if something was bothering him, music would stop him. We could tell that right from the very first . . . my wife [Winnie], she played music at church, and she recognized that Herbie was musically inclined. . . . He was seven years old when he started (formal lessons). He started on piano. I found a guy who sold me a piano. What happened was that I was a meat peddler back then. I was selling meat out of an old truck. That truck was insulated, and I had a barrel in it that I used to fill up with ice to keep the meat cold, and I would buy meat from the Yards, and sell it to stores and restaurants. Well, one day I went

by this church and this fellow who at that time was the bass fiddler with
Nat King Cole . . . sold me a piano for twenty-five dollars. It came out of his
father's church, or something like that. [Laughter] [It was] an upright, and
I paid some guys a couple of dollars apiece, and we all moved it over to our
apartment.[1]

At the time, Herbie was at Forestville Elementary School, on East 45th Street,
on the South Side of Chicago. When Herbie was nine, his father went to work
for the Agriculture Department as a meat inspector. Wayman Hancock was
proud of his son's continued accomplishments as a pianist:

When [Herbie] was eleven—after four years—he won a contest given by
the Chicago Symphony Orchestra. The prize was to appear with the Chicago
Symphony Orchestra, and that's what he did. He appeared with them, and
he played Mozart's "Coronation" Concerto. . . . I was in the hospital when he
played. I was in the hospital with undulant fever. At that time I had started
work as a federal meat inspector for the Department of Agriculture at the
stockyards, and I had contracted undulant fever. . . . I was in the hospital, and
I had to be in there five or six weeks while they gave me streptomycin and
all those sorts of drugs. I had been in there for about two or three weeks, but
they let me out to go to that concert, and Herbie played with that hundred-
piece orchestra. The lights went down and when they came up, he was standing there by the piano. . . . [It was in] Orchestra Hall."[2]

As a child, Herbie Hancock was trained in classical piano, but as he told Ira
Gitler in 1963: "As a teenager, I went through my rhythm and blues days. . . .
R&B may have been simple in harmony but it has a feeling that was close to
the everyday."[3] Jazz didn't interest the young Hancock until one day when he
heard a fellow thirteen year-old schoolmate's trio play at a variety show. In fact,
as Hancock related the story to Joy Williams,[4] he became interested in jazz
records by George Shearing and Earl Bostic. These were ironically the same
ones that his mother had given him for Christmas and that he had disliked at
first. But now, Hancock was intrigued to see someone his age improvising, a
skill that classically trained pianists typically lack:

I was wondering: "How could this kid create music?" I was fascinated and I
said, "I've got to learn how to do this. That's my instrument, and he can do it.
Why can't I?" So, he taught me how to play a simple riff and I somehow found

a couple of other notes to play, then I learned how to watch his left hand and I learned where the notes were. I could read, you see, so I would watch his left hand and kind of find what notes to play. Then I would watch him improvise, and I would be fascinated by what he was doing. And I was always grabbing him and saying, "Hey, man, let's have a little jam session."

Hancock's friend played in the thick block chord style of Shearing, which Hancock wanted to emulate. Herbie listened closely, transcribing passages that interested him, and in that way picked up elements of Shearing's harmonic and melodic style. His learning approach was inductive at first:

When I got to the fifth bar [of "I Remember April"] I noticed there was something similar about the way the fifth bar sounded and the way the fourth bar sounded. And I began to notice that some of the notes were the same and I said, "What is this?" That's when I began to be aware of voicings and of inversions. And then I started to find out what it is that is holding these two things together. That's when I began to understand what a chord is. So I learned theory to find a shorter method to take things off a record.[5]

In this way, Hancock's inductive method gave way to a more considered theoretical approach. He continued to practice four-handed with his schoolmate pianist, each taking a turn improvising with the right hand, while the other one played left-hand chords. Hancock attended Hyde Park High School, despite Chicago's strict rules tying school district assignments to neighborhood residency. This should have meant that Hancock would attend DuSable High School, where his music teacher would have been Captain Walter Dyett, mentor to Eddie Harris and to many of the musicians who formed the Association for the Advancement of Creative Musicians (AACM). But the family felt that Hyde Park would be stronger academically. Although his family lived on East 45th Street, attending a school in another district was made possible by using his uncle's address on Maryland Street, where he babysat for his cousin every day after school. During this time, he also worked at a grocery store.

Things moved quickly once Hancock entered Hyde Park High School, and he began playing locally around Chicago with a band of his own. Hancock also began to transcribe Bill Evans's recorded solos, pointing toward another important influence on Hancock's playing, the reduction of chords to smaller fragments and coloristic voicing. It was one thing for a classically trained musician to absorb and replicate harmonic concepts. But it was something else to appreciate the intricacies of syncopated rhythms, including the idea of un-evenly played eighth notes. "At first I sounded like any stiff classical musician, trying to play that stuff." But Hancock was a quick learner, and he "also noticed that sometimes things were playing right after the beat. 'Cause I noticed that I'd plan out the notes and then I'd try to play it and I'd have to say, 'It doesn't sound the same. What's the difference?' And I'd notice, 'Well, this note's lon-ger than that other one. Or, he [Shearing] delayed this one.' And it fascinated me the way George Shearing could lay back like that."[6]

Hancock expanded his rhythmic concept by listening to records by Oscar Peterson. These records were "more bluesy kind of things, which I really like; then I had to learn to feel." Hancock recalls: "I tried to copy his solos or his phrases off of various [of Peterson's] records early on. His sense of swing, I loved that. I loved the intelligence in his playing, the lyricism, and the blues el-ement that's there."[7] Hancock memorialized Peterson at the time of the older pianist's death in 2007:

> I consider him to be the dominant piano player that established my foun-dation. . . . I had started off as a classical pianist, and I was dazzled by the precision of his playing. But it was primarily the groove that moved me about Oscar. The groove and the blues, but with the sophistication that I was used to from classical music.[8]

Attending the academically challenging Hyde Park High School paid off because it prepared Hancock to spend four years at Grinnell College in Iowa, the first two as an engineering major before graduating in 1960 with a degree in music composition. Hancock played all sorts of music while at Grinnell, including with a fellow student who was a guitarist, noting, as he told Gitler, that he not only played jazz, but "we played for the farmers—western, rock and roll."[9] Musical boundaries seemed to hold little interest for Hancock, even as a teenager and young adult in college.

Coming of Age as an Empathetic Player

Herbie Hancock was clearly a gifted and rapidly developing pianist, composer, and jazz musician. But he had to travel a long distance from his early promise to become the leader of a dynamic ensemble whose musical process would be guided by intuition. While strongly acknowledging the crucial contribution of Hancock's band members, the *Chicago Daily Defender* points to the breadth of his gifts, as witnessed by audiences during November 1970 at London House: "He is considered as one of the great contemporary composers because of his ability to capture the imagination with beautiful tone painting or blow one's mind with his dissonances. He plays with great conviction and the result is a tremendous artistic impact. He is powerful and dynamic and for contrast can be enhancingly lyrical. Regardless of whatever means employed, the pianist is sure to exhibit a thorough virtuosity."[10] Yet the most important feature of Hancock's leadership of this particular band was not his inarguable virtuosity but his empathy as an accompanist and skills as a listener. This required the cultivation of rare and quite specialized talents.

Philip Royster, director of the African American Cultural Center at the University of Illinois, Chicago, suggests that the very nature of growing up in Chicago's Bronzeville neighborhood on the South Side in the 1940s and '50s could have helped cultivate Hancock's innate empathetic gifts. Many important fellow musicians were raised there, among them Muhal Richard Abrams and other members of the AACM, Charles Stepney, and Maurice White. Royster describes Bronzeville as

a deeply complex, highly intricate, and vastly diverse environment during this period because it was an urban, Negro ghetto that was both slowly expanding and slowly deteriorating . . . [yet] continuing to thrive with astonishing vitality. As a boy growing up in this environment, Herbie crossed paths with an extremely diverse concentration of black folk and black cultures. . . . [S]ome folks carried books home from the Hall Branch Library on Michigan Avenue. Others carried keloid scars from their fights in local taverns. Some would tour the world displaying their genius; others would be found dead some morning on the cobblestones of a South Side alley, and everything and anything in between.

Herbie learned to play this world and to play out of this world. Herbie knew how to live with all this, how to take of some, wave at others in passing, cross the street to avoid a forming crowd, listen to the sounds of the cars and streetcars, the children fighting or the grown folks partying at a family reunion, the foghorn blowing from Lake Michigan. . . . As well, he had to live with the knowledge that there were pianists and organists in those South Side churches who couldn't read a note but yet could transpose any gospel, hymn, spiritual, or anthem into any key the singer broke out in and play an accompaniment suited not merely to the vocal personality but also the mood prevailing in the moment of the religious service. Mastering well the unusual diversity of cultural experiences, expressions, and "languages" in his own background prepared Herbie to listen, absorb, and respond in accompanying dialog and conversation to the creations of other people from around the world.

Over the ensuing decade, Hancock used every musical opportunity available to develop as a musically empathic, close listener, one who cultivated his intuitive skills. Combined with openness to a wide range of influences and embrace of stylistic eclecticism, Hancock would embark on a musical course that prepared him to found his ensembles of the late 1960s and early 1970s.

Embarking on a Professional Journey

After graduation from Grinnell College, Hancock returned home to Chicago for one year, in 1960. It was during that year that Hancock befriended and began to play with professional musicians. Drummer Alvin Fielder recalls: "Herbie and I met in 1960. He had just gotten home from college. I don't remember how we met but we became friends. We put together a group that included my brother William, Reggie Willis and Reuben Cooper. We would audition for club owners to get jobs. After a while that group broke up and we joined [trombonist] John Hines' group." Hancock subsequently played in a second group with Fielder and Willis, as Reggie Lewis remembers:

> Herbie was the first pianist in our band, the Jazz Disciples. The band included Billy Brimfield on trumpet, Skip James on tenor sax, Harold Jones on drums, myself on bass, and initially, Herbie Hancock on piano. We played one or two nights at the Wonder Inn, on the South Side, and also at the Sutherland Hotel, home at that time of Joe Siegel's Modern Jazz Showcase, at 47th Street and Drexel Boulevard. I might have met Herbie in the summer, when he had just graduated from Grinnell. He was taking classes at Roosevelt University for a short time. He worked briefly for the post office, as did I.

Hancock's first big break came that year when he was invited to back visiting musicians. As Hancock tells it: "My first gig with a name group was a two-week engagement in Chicago with Coleman Hawkins." A chance snowstorm during winter 1960–61 left visiting trumpeter Donald Byrd searching for a local rhythm section to fill in for his regular musicians.[11] Although he was unknown, Hancock got the gig, replacing pianist Duke Pearson. Harold

Jones filled the drum chair. Things went so well that Byrd asked Hancock to join his Quintet with Pepper Adams. "Donald Byrd brought me to New York, and he and I were sharing an apartment [in the Bronx]. It was actually his apartment. He took me under his wing. He introduced me to Miles. He kind of showed me the ropes of New York because I was really green." During that time, Hancock also played with Phil Woods and Oliver Nelson and with the Al Grey/Billy Mitchell, Phil Woods/Gene Quill, and Clark Terry/Bob Brook-meyer bands.

In 1961, Hancock recorded first sessions with Byrd and with three other leaders, all with Blue Note Records with which he signed an exclusive con-tract. In addition, Hancock began a master's degree in composition at the Manhattan School of Music.[12] He also expanded his musical horizons as he had during high school, by listening to records; this time it was Bud Powell, Charlie Parker, and a variety of classical music.

Hancock's mentor Donald Byrd was a central figure in the jazz movement that became dominant during Hancock's young adulthood: hard bop. When Byrd brought Hancock to New York City to live in the Bronx and work in Manhattan clubs, the young pianist became placed in the geographical cen-ter of this music. Hancock was gaining a breadth of experience by playing not only with Byrd and, starting in 1963, with Miles Davis, but also within a circle of musicians at the core of the hard bop movement,[13] many of whom recorded on each other's sessions for Blue Note Records.[14] The recordings most often took place at the Rudy Van Gelder Studio in Englewood Cliffs, New Jersey.

Musical Influences on the Developing Pianist

Oscar Peterson

The approach taken by Oscar Peterson, Herbie Hancock's first major jazz in-fluence, included a precise sense of time, melodies played in thick chords in the style of Errol Garner, strong blues inflections, and a technique that dazzled like Art Tatum's, highlighted by rapid runs and melodic filigree. For the young pianist, listening to Oscar Peterson must have been like experiencing an en-cyclopedia of jazz piano styles, interwoven within a single player's imagina-tion. Peterson's 1945 recording of "I Got Rhythm" provides an excellent ex-ample: The tune is played in thick block chords, syncopated yet rhythmically rock solid. A stride piano section appears thirty seconds in, Peterson's right hand playing ragtime-like melodic patterns, somewhat reminiscent of Teddy Wilson. Peterson then falls into a stuttering riff, a steadily and rapidly repeating note in one hand and, in the same register, a repeated syncopated note rhythmic pattern. After comping with the bass and drums, and briefly returning to the stuttering pattern, he plays a downward-moving boogie-woogie bass line,[15] on which a melodic solo is constructed in the right hand. Variations of these patterns prepare the return of the head, this time accompanied by the continuing boogie-woogie riff, before ending.

While Peterson's *Night Train* (1962) was released after Hancock was already playing professionally with Donald Byrd, the recording shows some of the features that must have already captured Hancock's imagination. These include the oscillating octaves in "Georgia on My Mind," a technique that has appeared at moments of climax in Hancock's solos ever since. On "Band Call," a tune played with Errol Garner-like thick chords, an equally dense, repeated chordal riff like a clarion call appears, echoed years later in passages in Hancock's "Sleeping Giant." On the title track, "Night Train," Peterson opens with blues-inflected passages and then makes use of the broad expanse of the keyboard, encompassing several registers, suggesting an orchestral sensibility. Sweeping, shaking chords call to mind a big band shout. On "Easy Does It," Peterson makes use of the entire dynamic range from nearly inaudible to moderately loud, reminiscent of Nat King Cole. As Hancock has acknowledged, Peterson provided an exemplary model of an eclectic pianist, able to integrate a range of styles and sensibilities into a coherent whole, with an impeccable sense of time and rhythmic detail.

Hard Bop: Bop, Gospel, and the Blues

In some ways, hard bop—the music championed by Hancock's early employer Donald Byrd, Art Blakey, Horace Silver, and others—represented a new way to play bebop.[16] The pace was often less breakneck than the bebop revolution of the 1940s. Hard bop continued the drive and creativity of bebop, but it was grounded in the rhythmic earthiness of rhythm and blues and the emotional and harmonic flavor of the blues.[17] It drew on gospel music of the sanctified church, a form that injected spirituals and church hymns with syncopated rhythms and blues forms. The practitioners of hard bop sought to meld the free-blowing aesthetic and angularity of bebop with these more popular and accessible forms of music that black people were listening to at home, in clubs, in dance halls, and at church.[18] In this sense, it was a populist movement, particularly in black communities,[19] and is well represented among the best-selling jazz recordings of the era.

A keen rhythmic feel coupled with blues-rooted phrases infuse Hancock's comping in his earliest recordings with Byrd, for instance, on the tune "Pentacostal Feeling," from *Free Form*, Hancock's third recording with Byrd (recorded on December 11, 1961). Here, Hancock taps into the gospel roots of this tune rhythmically and harmonically. Hancock's solo, beginning at 4:00, is rhythmically precise and tuneful, based on a simple riff, repeated and expanded, emphasizing the rhythmic pattern of the tune. "French Spice" is a quintessential hard bop tune in its blend of bebop lines, blues-feel melody, syncopated beat, and gospel-influenced piano comping elements, rhythmic and appending blues licks at the end of phrases.[20]

Hancock's rhythmic, percussive approach to comping also echoes the work of hard bop pianist Horace Silver. Examples include Silver's playing on two 1954 recordings, Miles Davis's *Bag's Groove*, particularly "Airegin," and "Room 608" from *Horace Silver and the Jazz Messengers*, where Silver's percussive-attacked comping chords emphasize the rhythmic feel. His rhythmic, chordal ostinati behind Hank Mobley's solo simulate horn section articulations, but approximate a locked groove that we will often hear in Hancock's Mwandishi-era playing. Silver's syncopated, rhythmic chord patterns behind Junior Cook's tenor solo on the title cut of Silver's *Blowin' the Blues Away* (1959) includes an ascending three-chord riff of the sort that Herbie Hancock will draw on later. This appears during Cook's second chorus.

Example 1. Opening passage of Hancock's solo in "Pentacostal Feeling" (Byrd)

Example 2. Horace Silver's comping for the second chorus of Junior Cook's saxophone solo, second chorus, "Blowing the Blues Away"

First Recordings as a Leader

Hancock's inaugural recording as a leader, *Takin' Off* (1962), showcases elements of gospel and the blues, integrated within a broader conception. "Watermelon Man" would soon become his most famous tune, thanks to a highly popular cover by Latin percussionist Mongo Santamaria.[21] Hancock's solid and steady chordal comping sets the stage from the opening vamp, continuing through the confident yet relaxed trumpet solo by Freddie Hubbard and Dexter Gordon's gut-bucket-influenced blues tenor saxophone solo. The opening vamp of "Watermelon Man" displays a gospel influence in its harmonic flavor, particularly the Dominant 7—IV—I chord progression. Throughout the tune, including Hancock's piano solo, the pianist draws on simple and direct blues lines. One detects in this tune the influence of Horace Silver, for instance, Silver's churchy blues gospel tune "Sister Sadie" from *Blowin' the Blues Away*. Similar Silver touches appear in Hancock's later tune "Cantaloupe Island" (1964).

On *Takin' Off*, two other tunes place an easygoing groove in the forefront, "Empty Pockets" (without the gospel feel) and "Driftin'," which features an extended Hancock solo whose opening calls to mind the logical consistency of Bud Powell's melodic lines. The solo begins with a simple statement, extended and elaborated across long melodies, calling and answering one another in a stately, nonliteral way. Hancock then stitches the solo together with a complex upward two-handed figure that presses toward the solo's emotional climax, followed by an easier, more blues-inflected section. Then, short melodic fragments bring the listener back to the expansive Powell-like lines, this time even longer than before, landing at more blues-inflected statements, after which both approaches merge and interpenetrate. A tightly woven groove brings us to oscillating octaves. A chorus powered by thick chords and occasionally extended lines brings the solo to its conclusion. Similar blues connotations are featured on Hancock's slow blues tune "Yams," on Jackie McLean's *Vertigo* (recorded on February 11, 1963), where the pianist's block chords tightly enforce the beat, calling to mind Wynton Kelly. A similar rhythmic drive and precision and exquisite sense of syncopation is found in Hancock's chordal comping on Donald Byrd's up-tempo riff-driven "Dusty Foot," from the same session. Hancock's solo opens with a jigsaw puzzle rhythmic interplay between his left-hand chords and a simple bluesy riff. Throughout the solo, Hancock's left-hand chords land precisely on nearly every beat; in some bars, the chords shift tonality ever so slightly, taking on increased dissonance to build tension, and then resolving to the next chord change. Chords moving upward stepwise will continue to be a technique Hancock draws on to increase the harmonic tension.

Hancock's second recording as a leader, *My Point of View* (recorded March 19, 1963), shows how a gospel and blues sensibility, refracted through the highly rhythmic hard bop movement, continues to play an important role in the pianist's musical development. The tunes "Blind Man, Blind Man" and "And What If I Don't" are easygoing, rhythmically charged gospel blues tunes in which Hancock's solos emphasize simply stated blues lines. While much of his third album, *Empyrean Isles* (1964), moves more decisively in a more lyrical and harmonically complex direction, the tune "Cantaloupe Island" remains firmly in this rhythmically finger-popping, foot-tapping gospel blues vein. The rhythmic feel of this tune ticks along as if it were a moderately paced locomotive engine, its multiple parts interlocked to form a single groove. Hancock's solo offsets variants of the opening rhythmic figure with syncopated accented notes and speedier off-kilter sixteenth note runs. The result is a deeper affirmation of the groove, a direction that will appear in a more directly rhythm and blues format on *Fat Albert Rotunda* (1970). And they form a basis for his 1970s funky playing, which begins during the Mwandishi period and continues with *Head Hunters* (1974).

With the Miles Davis Quintet

Hancock's work with the Miles Davis Quintet, 1963–68,[22] reflects a different side of his musical aesthetic. The repertoire for the Quintet during 1963–65 focused on standards, show tunes, and popular songs from the 1930s, '40s, and '50s. This music, organized on a melodic and harmonic foundation, was increasingly supplemented by Davis's own tunes.[23] After this more conventional period, the music of Davis's new band gradually extended the more open ideas of Davis's *Kind of Blue* (1959) into freer territory on which Hancock would build. We will soon turn to this topic.

An excellent example of Hancock's pianistic approach during his first two years with Miles Davis comes not from the Davis recordings but from a lesser-known session from the same period. Hancock's solo on Donald Byrd's assertive "Marney" on Jackie McLean's *Vertigo* (recorded on February 11, 1963) begins just after 3:30 with two repetitions of a riff played in fourths, a variant of a chordal pattern he has used to comp during McLean's solo earlier in the tune. A third repetition breaks down midstream into an extended figure. A

Example 3. Opening passage of Hancock's solo in "Marney"

call-and-response pattern leads to the kind of single-note passage that characterizes so much of Hancock's soloing with the Miles Davis Quintet, straight
eighth notes running upward, out of which grows a figure that takes a hairpin
downward turn for half an octave, then reaching back up to a note below the
top from which he propels down a variant of that line.

Another upward-moving call-and-response line leads to chromatic transpositions of the figure and then spins additional musical threads, sometimes
breaking them down into two-note phrases, varied in their direction of movement and size of intervals. The chords he uses to comp tend toward chromaticism and fragmentation.[24] This will increasingly be Hancock's approach while
playing with Davis. The chromatic transpositions, extensions, and variations,
integrated with the rhythmic qualities found in his own recordings, represent
important building blocks of Hancock's style during the Mwandishi period.

Hancock's playing during his time with Davis could be quite lyrical.
While this would not represent the most central aspect of his playing during
the Mwandishi period, it bears mention here. Hancock's lyrical side is most
dominant on his fifth recording, *Maiden Voyage* (1965), particularly on the
title track and on the rich harmonies of "Dolphin Dance." Both tunes display
Hancock's inclination toward slowly evolving melodic invention, in which an
idea is extended and varied, shifting chromatically in subtle ways, but always
noticeable for its strikingly beautiful turns of phrase. But Hancock played lyrically as early as his own "Night Flower" on Donald Byrd's *Free Form*. His solo
begins just after 2:30 with a thrice-repeated note, which then shifts downward
a step and repeats twice. The melodic line continues downward two more
notes, leading upward again, continuing with a slow, tuneful line, and moves
onward to explorations of the harmonic possibilities of the chord changes.
After a series of variants of descending line, Hancock, at 3:30, contrasts this
slower motion with a rapid-fire line, after which he briefly alternates the
slow and the fast, returning to a lyrical passage, before closing out the solo.

Hancock's solo on his "Tribute to Some," from the second recording under his own name, *My Point of View* (1963), is another melodically tuneful and rhythmically solid construction of complex melodic lines. Like Bud Powell, each phrase provides material from which the ensuing phrase seemingly spins forth.

A major influence on the maturing Hancock was Bill Evans.[25] Evans's approach to comping was spare and often harmonically ambiguous. This was due to his reducing chords to their most essential elements, selecting component notes that provide color and often only hint at harmonic function. There is often no bass note included, and the resulting chord, a fragment, can be identified in different ways depending on what note is played by the bassist and in what harmonic direction, if any, a solo points. This perspective is well suited to the modal approach championed by George Russell,[26] is central to Miles Davis's *Milestones* (1958), and is more fully released on the tunes on which Evans plays on *Kind of Blue* (1959), among them "Blue in Green" and "Flamenco Sketches." The core modal concept is the replacement of chord changes with collections of groupings of sequential notes ("modes") to form the materials for improvisation. Hancock's solo on "French Spice" (from Donald Byrd's *Free Form*) reflects Evans in its use of chords and chord fragments as melodic elements. Similarly, his solo on Byrd's up-tempo, lilting "Nai Nai," which follows an intense, moving Wayne Shorter solo, initially brings to mind Evans soloing on *Waltz for Debby* (recorded at the Village Vanguard, earlier that same year, 1961) in its alternation between straight and syncopated eighth notes, heightening the swing of this tune.[27]

While Hancock's Sextet performances would continue to include ballads like "Maiden Voyage" and the newer "Toys" as staples, his lyricism is not what most clearly defined his musical evolution with Davis or his own Sextet. Having already introduced Hancock's rhythmic approach, we turn to the topic of abstraction, more pivotal for the Mwandishi band, yet often misunderstood.

Abstraction and Emotion as a Musical Guide

While playing with Miles Davis, Herbie Hancock came to understand that a soloist can shape phrases to capture emotion, by "using dynamics in playing your melodies no matter how jagged or how weird they'll be, that can stimulate some inner feelings within yourself as a listener . . . even though you may not be able to relate to the notes or the chords or the sounds that are being played in a way that you're used to relating to them, you still react because that emotional element is there."[28] The movement away from more conventional melodies, chords, and even modes toward an intuitive, more emotive approach is "abstraction."

Musical abstraction, like abstraction in visual art, can be understood as reducing forms to their basic elements: shape, color, and texture. Such is the nature of Claude Monet's famous "Water Lilies," which over time ceased to represent actual objects but rather objects transformed—abstracted—into shapes, colors, and textures. Henri Matisse once said: "Slowly I discovered the secret of my art. It consists of a meditation on nature, on the expression of a dream which is always inspired by reality."[29] Similarly in music, in the works of Claude Debussy[30] and his fellow impressionist composers, melody supported by harmony could give way to tone color, nonmelodic series of notes, musical textures, and densities of sounds, creating musical abstraction. Their goal was to capture sense impressions, to tap into the unconscious and offer not representation but reflection and imaginative refractions of external and internal reality. In the work of postimpressionist artists and composers, forms and shapes stand on their own, not representing anything outside themselves.[31]

For Hancock, the techniques of abstraction sometimes begin with functional harmony, but through reduction of those chords to one or more notes, their identity becomes blurred and rendered obscured. But other times, Hancock draws on practices located outside of functional harmony, even the extended harmony of bebop. In this sense—and we will explore his use of tone clusters as one example—Hancock is not directly referencing harmonic function at all. Because of his exposure to a wide range of musical forms and compositional techniques, which include not only the French impressionists but a wide range of representatives of the twentieth-century avant-garde, among them Olivier Messiaen, Igor Stravinsky, Pierre Schaeffer, and Karlheinz Stockhausen, Hancock's frame of reference afforded him great flexibility in how to approach a musical idea.

Hancock recalls that the drummer in Davis's band, Tony Williams, conveyed ideas for his first recordings not "in terms of notes or chords but . . . a bit like we could address the making of a painting, in terms of shapes, colors"[32] or, as Hancock told Len Lyons, "appreciating [music of the avant-garde] like a piece of sculpture."[33] "For the saxophonists, he wanted one to constantly play from high to low and low to high while the other stayed at the same level. . . . As a result, when I made these albums with Tony, I listened while having in my head the making of a canvas with lines, colors, as well as everything that was in the emotional framework. At times the enthusiasm for what was going on musically was so strong that I couldn't hold back from responding. At other times I did things to provoke a response from my partners."[34] Williams also opened his eyes to how drumming can propel more subtle aspects of a band's playing and serve as something of an energy source that stokes all aspects of collective music making, as he observes: "The energy level sustains the interest of the audience."[35]

Abstraction—through the use of color and texture to capture emotion and sense impressions—begins to play a central role in his work with Davis beginning in 1965. Like Bill Evans, Hancock of the Miles Davis Quintet generated "shapes, colors" by extending and fragmenting identifiable chordal structures. This represented a move beyond chord extensions, a core element within modern jazz history beginning with the bebop revolution. Hancock's, like Evans's, goals differed from those of Charlie Parker and Dizzy Gillespie, who explored more complex chords to harmonically support musical notes previously heard as dissonant. Hancock was keenly aware of how more adventuresome successors of bebop like John Coltrane and Ornette Coleman sought to transcend the expanded bebop harmonies, rendering the very idea of conventional harmony irrelevant.[36] But Hancock continued to draw on functional harmony as an oblique reference point. Detailed analyses, beyond the scope of the present work, can be found in the writing of Keith Waters.[37]

What one detects in Herbie Hancock's playing with Miles Davis during that era is harmonic ambiguity that maintains the affective nature of a harmonious sound. Clearly, French impressionist composer Claude Debussy[38] had made an impact on Hancock equal to that of Bill Evans and Oscar Peterson. During the Mwandishi period, Hancock's coloristic conception moved him further in the direction of abstraction and away from functional harmonic moorings. There, the goal has diversified, varying between capturing sense impressions and creating sonic textures that have no particular emotional reference point: sounds for sounds' sake.

Hancock's Earliest Consideration of Abstraction

Hancock began to draw on abstract elements in his playing prior to joining the Miles Davis Quintet. He began to explore alternatives to conventional chords during his live performances with Eric Dolphy's quartet in 1962–63, and in some of his otherwise straight-ahead hard bop work with trumpeter Donald Byrd in 1961–63. With Dolphy, Hancock straddles a fine line between fractured functional harmony and sound on its own terms, mirroring Dolphy's angular solo lines. On Byrd's title track on *Free Form*, his playing is more textural than chordal and the function of abstraction appears to be a display of sense impressions. Hancock began to assimilate some of these influences within his own recordings as early as the tune "The Egg" on Hancock's third recording, *Empyrian Isles* (1964).

When Hancock began to play with Dolphy and on Byrd's tune "Free Form," he found himself with a dilemma. It wasn't at all clear what he should play. "I hadn't paid that much attention to the avant-garde scene, except lip service more than anything, no more than that. It was a curiosity that I had. But I wasn't curious enough to really actively pursue finding out about it." Hancock describes having received an offer from Dolphy to do a few shows with him, including one at the Village Gate in New York, and accepting in part out of curiosity: "I remember asking him [Dolphy]—because I didn't know—I said to him: 'You know, I've never really played the avant-garde scene before, do you have tunes?' He said: 'Err, yes!' And I said: 'You have charts with chords and stuff?' He said: 'Yeah, we do!' So I said: 'OK, fine.'" Hancock realized that despite the fact that the charts had chords, he needed to do something unfamiliar:

> I said to myself: "I wonder if I broke some of the rules I normally use for playing, could that lead me to a doorway for some out playing?" That's what I decided to try and it seemed to work. That was like an entry point. Everything that happened after that was totally experimental stuff. So that experience, coupled with meeting Tony Williams [leads right into what I started doing with Miles; like fracturing and fragmenting the chords].

In a 1979 interview with a French jazz magazine, Hancock added: "Sometimes, in order to cross into the forbidden, I found myself completely lost; I then realized that there was nothing wrong with that. The important thing is to listen closely to what the others are playing and to work to create something that could integrate into the context without worrying about the rest, the foundational structures of the piece."[39] These proved to be important lessons that guided Hancock's approach with the Mwandishi band.

Tone Clusters

One thing Hancock discovered was the use of tone clusters, groupings of harmonically unrelated notes played as if they are a chord. Clusters may also be found in the work of Thelonious Monk and in some of Horace Silver's call-and-response passages, when he plays sounds in the lowest register of the piano. Unlike even the most complex chord, a cluster is built from contiguous notes, major and minor seconds. It is inherently dissonant. A cluster may be described by its lower and uppermost notes and by its relative note density.[40]

Monk uses tone clusters in a variety of ways: as more colorful alternatives to conventional chords or to add variety, depth, and shape to his sound materials, as if saying to the piano, "please let me stretch your sonic limitations." And there are times when Monk appears just to land on a cluster of piano keys for affect or punctuation, as if to offer personal extra-musical commentary. In his 1957 septet recording of "Well, You Needn't" from *Monk's Music*, the pianist's accompaniment rhythmically and harmonically punctuates the tune, but the chords eventually thicken into clusters and increase in density. Part way into his solo, Monk pauses, seeming to ponder where to go next and then plays a long descending run. After repeating two three-note higher-register major seventh-chord fragments, he heads in a more atonal direction, landing on a sustained seventh chord with an audible added sixth, sufficiently ambiguous to be called a cluster.[41]

Hancock's interest in using tone clusters appears to be sonic and intuitive, particularly his attraction to their harmonic ambiguity, parallel to his chord fragmentation, and in the way they allowed the piano to be utilized as a percussive instrument.

Miles Davis and Abstraction

As the music of the Miles Davis Quintet progressed in 1965, the trumpeter began to simplify the tunes, stripping away chords and leaving more open space within which the musicians could explore. The improvisations slowly ceased to be as literally guided by chord changes, incrementally shifting the musical concept. Ian Carr quotes Hancock as saying that "by the time we got to *E.S.P.* [1965], Miles said, 'I don't want to play chords anymore.' . . . " Davis, like Ornette Coleman before him, and gradually also Hancock, began to construct his solos based neither directly on the melody nor, like beboppers, on rapid and complex scales and arpeggios over the chords. Instead, the model was what has been termed musical "gestures."[42] Like a dancer's physical gestures, these could be based on the direction, up or down, of melodic fragments, intervallic relationships, rhythmic cells, chromatic elements, repetition of rhythmic fragments, or newly invented musical motifs. For Hancock, this also meant frag-mentation of chords and thus harmonic ambiguity. Freely walking bass lines by Ron Carter, at least on up-tempo tunes, juxtaposed with Tony Williams's steady, unaccented pulse in the drums, adds to the replacement of harmonic surety with a *sense* of a tonality. Hancock reflects:

> A composition is an example of a conception, so Miles, rather than play the composition, he wants to play the conception that the composition came from. . . . That's why you hear melody fragments and you kind of hear the momentum and the sound of the tune somewhere—something that distin-guishes that tune from another one . . . but maybe the chords are not there. Even when we were playing "Walkin'" or any of those other [familiar] things, he didn't want to play the chords after we played the melody.[43]

Hancock points out that there was a direct connection between Davis's new musical directions and what Davis was hearing from Ornette's band. "The avant-garde was a major influence on the Miles Davis band we had at that time. I remember one time, Miles finishing a solo, I don't remember where we were, and he leaned over to Tony Williams: 'That sounded like Don Cherry, didn't it.' Tony said: 'Yeah, yeah.' Even Miles was looking for new directions, and . . . I think Miles felt like what Don was reaching for and how he went about it was interesting, and worthy of pursuit." Guitarist Pat Metheny adds: "To me Ornette's thing involves a certain kind of poetry and imagination that goes beyond what is actually 'there,' a kind of implied content that sits along-side the thing itself. I totally see how that affected Herbie, maybe more so than it ever did even Miles or Wayne. Tony too had that connection."

This shift begins to become noticeable on the early 1965 recording *E.S.P.* and really comes to the fore on *Live at the Plugged Nickel* (1982). Wayne Shorter biographer Michelle Mercer narrates:

> On the third night at the Plugged Nickel . . . even a Miles classic like "So What" sounded reborn. Usually it was Tony who kicked things into high gear, juggling polyrhythms you just couldn't quantify punctuated by good-natured rim shot tantrums. Ron leapt over bar lines in a single bound. For his part, Herbie would key in on the melody, then change his mind and follow Wayne's smeared path of saxophone into a chromatic never-never land.[44]

Mercer quotes Hancock's analysis:

In music, if you're going up a ski slope, you usually slide down on the other side. But here, resolution wasn't just delayed, it was sometimes abandoned altogether. You'd go up the ski slope and all of a sudden there'd be nothing there. Tony would make a crash and it would just be with the cymbal, without the bass drum as usual. Or I would build up to a big chord and Ron would do nothing. Everything we did was the opposite of what everyone expected us to do.[45]

The tune "If I Were a Bell" from the first night's set, opening the multidisc *Plugged Nickel* recordings, exemplifies the musical textures Hancock contributed to the band during this period. His accompaniment is most often spare and at times entirely silent. Despite periodically providing recognizable two-chord cadential figures, Hancock regularly abstracts these motifs, relieving them of their harmonic function. He treats them as rhythmic or coloristic material, sometimes repeated in rising or falling patterns, repeated as if they were ostinati. Chord patterns take on the quality of rhythmic patterns, albeit brief and fractured.

During Davis's solo, brief piano interpolations, sometimes a two-chord figure and single staccato note, emerge out of silence. At an early point, Hancock follows a three-chord ascending figure with six chromatically descending chords. As we approach 3:00, he inserts three chromatically ascending chords. Shortly after that, Hancock plays a more active and conventional accompaniment, but then inserts a short two-chord interpolation and then again lays out. The pianist reappears with an ascending series of thirteen chromatic two-chord descending figures, followed by a more conventionally harmonic two-chord cadence. This becomes material for playful repetition and rhythmic variation, followed toward the end of Davis's solo with spare chordal interpolations. The function of Hancock's choices when they are not obviously chordal in nature can be variously interpreted. I hear them not within a functional harmonic context but as shapes and textures, the shaping of sounds as objects that offset and challenge Davis's more melodic inventions.

During Shorter's solo, Hancock initially limits himself to an occasional highly chromatic chordal gesture, and two two-note atonal chord fragments and angular phrases. Just before 10:00, Hancock arrives at a rhythmic chordal sequence that he repeats and expands. After a period of brief mutual imitative gestures and the pianist's angular contrapuntal line, Hancock plays a quick four-chord descending motif, which he seizes onto, repeating it ten times before altering it to ascend, and repeating it one more time before it morphs into more chordal comping. During the conclusion of the saxophone solo, Hancock insistently repeats a chromatic chord briefly, raising it one chromatic step, and then down for two final assertions. Here, one can listen for the density, shape, and direction of Hancock's creations above and beyond their possible harmonic function.

Hints and occasional use of these devices described here may be found on the title track to *E.S.P.*, but they are only fully realized during the *Plugged Nickel* sessions, nearly a year later. While Hancock often uses functional harmony on *E.S.P.*, his chord usage eleven months later has become fragmented and at times highly chromatic, blurring the line between chords and tone clusters. Harmonic analysis often ceases to be meaningful. Instead, as we've now seen on "If I Were a Bell," Hancock leads us on an unfolding adventure, the future never easily predictable, albeit with regular references to where he has already taken us. The overall sensation is one of a rational, articulated, spare, and percussively oriented whole. The same holds true of Hancock's playing on Sam Rivers's *Contours* (1965). During the opening tune, "Point of Many Returns," Hancock's accompaniment emphasizes and broadens the tune's ascending highly chromatic chords. Again, Hancock often makes use of rhythmically charged chord fragments and tone clusters, repeated, sometimes emphatically as if to punctuate the proceedings. The function here is akin to collage. His sound juxtapositions are not random but serve to frame the soloist within a sonic framework defined by shape, color, texture, and direction.

During this period, Hancock gradually sought to find his own voice: "I wanted to find out about me, where am I coming from, where is my individuality." The bifurcation in his playing style between his work with Miles Davis and on his own recordings was diminishing as a discernable "Herbie Hancock" sound became detectable in 1965. Davis was encouraging, having "told us to work outside of the comfort zone. He paid us to explore new territory and to go outside of the areas that we knew and to go into the areas we didn't know." The exploratory vein of the Miles Davis's Quintet increased in 1966 and 1967. Strains of rock beats begin to appear, supported in 1968 by the sounds of an electric piano.

During this period, Hancock was becoming a consummate ensemble player, using his own sound to respond to soloists in the moment, pulling together tiny shreds of melodic, rhythmic, and motivic material to provide coherence and spice to the proceedings. The soloists are alternately supported and challenged. These are qualities that helped create the delicate fabric of the Miles Davis Quintet, at its best when on the edge of musical disintegration, and they would suit Hancock well when it came time to form his own band. By that point, Hancock was ready to integrate the varying elements of his maturing style: the rhythm-driven gospel-blues approach from the early recordings under his own name that would soon morph into funk, plus his lyricism and abstraction. That integration was showing early buds as the initial incarnation of the Sextet took shape.

When I left Miles I put together a sextet. . . . [I]t was a much softer, more gentle kind of sound. I was trying to come out of a Gil Evans influence.

HERBIE HANCOCK

3

The First Sextet

After five years with Miles Davis's influential second Quintet, newly married at age 28, and back from a honeymoon in Brazil, Herbie Hancock was ready to explore new horizons as a composer, pianist, and, for the first time, leader of a working band. The year was 1968, and the new band would be a sextet. With a few personnel changes, some of them immediate, the Sextet would tour throughout 1969 and into 1970. Over a period of six months beginning in spring 1970, Hancock rebuilt his band, nearly piece by piece, transforming it into what became informally known as the Mwandishi band.

Hancock had already made five recordings under his own name, beginning in 1962, even before joining Davis. In addition to touring with Davis's band, individual performances had begun to take place under his leadership.[1] He had long been composing music for television commercials, some of which became the starting point for a number of his tunes, like "Maiden Voyage,"

"Tell Me a Bedtime Story," and "I Have a Dream,"[2] and he had composed and recorded the soundtrack for the Michelangelo Antonioni film *Blow Up* (1966). During his final six months with Davis, Hancock was steadily engaged as a session musician for Creed Taylor's CTI records, a new label that emphasized lushly arranged and orchestrated studio sessions, and he joined a cast of well-known jazz musicians on a little-known Jewish liturgical recording the same year.[3] Hancock's interest in Brazilian music is reflected in his playing on Milton Nascimento's *Courage*, for which recording was completed in late February 1969. His studio work also continued in 1969 with several Atlantic recordings by Steve Marcus, Roy Ayers, and Attila Zoller.

Even after leaving Davis's touring band, Hancock continued to record on Davis sessions, not fully leaving Davis's immediate orbit as a session participant until 1970. Between November 1968—six months after leaving Davis's touring band—and February 1969, Hancock was an integral element in Davis's first heavily electric studio sessions,[4] some of them involving multiple electric pianists. Hancock's electric piano on "Dual Mr. Anthony Tillmon Williams Process," a tune with a distinct rock beat, shows some of the funky style he was beginning to discover and adapt in his playing on that instrument. As we will see, those sessions left an important impression on Hancock.

Speak Like a Child, The Prisoner, and the Birth of the Sextet

Paradoxically, Hancock's post-Davis period began during a period while he continued to record with Davis. Hancock recorded *Speak Like a Child* in early March 1968.[5] This recording departed from Hancock's previous work by featuring a lush horn section and arrangements with affinities to Gil Evans's settings for Davis, including *Miles Ahead* (1957), *Porgy and Bess* (1958), and *Sketches of Spain* (1960). Hancock chose an unusual grouping of horns for coloristic purposes: on top was a flugelhorn, and then two lower, darker-sounding members of the brass and wind families: bass trombone and alto flute. The arrangements freely made use of these instruments in their various possible ranges and combinations, contributing to the rich, slightly unconventional sound of the ensemble. In the rhythm section, Hancock's piano was joined by former Miles Davis Quintet bassist Ron Carter and by drummer Mickey Roker. The Miles Davis Quintet had recorded two of the tunes, "Riot" and "The Sorcerer." "Toys" became a staple of Hancock's live performance sets throughout the life of his Sextet. Hancock chose a simple, direct approach to his soloing and piano voicings; beautifully melodic, almost vocal in quality.

The debut of the Herbie Hancock Sextet took place six months later, during an extended November 1968 stand at the Village Vanguard, a premiere jazz club in Greenwich Village. The initial personnel for Hancock's live band featured saxophonist Clifford Jordan, trumpeter Johnny Coles, trombonist Garnett Brown, drummer Pete La Roca, and bassist Ron Carter. The personnel began to change even during that initial stand. Buster Williams replaced Carter, and Mickey Roker subbed for Pete La Roca. Jordan remained with the band for several of its dates in 1969, although Eddie Daniels subbed on one occasion. Many years later, after the death of Coles in 1997, Hancock recalled of the trumpeter, "Johnny moves by the moment. . . . He plays things with such sheer beauty that I wonder where it's coming from."[6]

The band member with the longest tenure, aside from Williams and Hancock himself, was trombonist Garnett Brown. Brown's memories of the band are vivid and warm:

> I can't say for sure why Herbie called me to join his first gig at the Vanguard. But putting two and two together, I had been playing with Thad Jones' band before that, [and] at some point after that, Thad played on Herbie's album *Speak Like a Child*, which had just come out. I don't know, but maybe some conversations about me had gone on between Herbie and Thad during that period . . . although I wasn't fond of traveling, I wasn't married and had no kids. But, playing with both Thad's group and Herbie's at the same time, I loved it! Some of the guys who made *Speak Like a Child* were players in New York and didn't tour much. . . .
>
> Two things stand out most for me about playing with the Sextet. The first is that Herbie was very encouraging and open to everybody's participation. This could include writing (although we never did any of my stuff), giving criticism and listening to his insights into things I was doing. I could see him putting what he heard into action. The other is the performance, the feeling that I had on the bandstand. It was most electric for me when I could just listen to the trio [Herbie, Buster, and Albert "Tootie" Heath, who became the drummer] playing without me or the other two horns. Just to see the three of them go through a piece and reinvent things along the way! I said "wow!" When I was playing, they might reinvent something on what I was playing, something I was not even conscious of; but they had consciously felt its effects no less. Getting to listen to them when I wasn't playing could be even more fun than when I was playing. . . .
>
> Every night it happened. The moment of taking what comes, emanating

from a place beyond me was exhilarating. It's really inexplicable. It doesn't come from the conscious mind. As for Herbie, the man's talent is something. He isn't just intuitive; he could be very analytical, too. He can speak in terms that the guy around the corner will understand just as he can talk to a student in class on the same subject, but adjust his technical use of language accordingly. He's got so much, you wonder where all of that comes from—but it all coalesces into a single, unified experience.

In early March, the Sextet played at the Fillmore East, as part of the "Sunday Nights Jazz at the Fillmore" series.[7] In anticipation of an upcoming recording session, Hancock returned with the band to the Village Vanguard at the end of the month, on a double bill with Tony Williams Lifetime.[8] The Sextet played a second Vanguard stand, this time alongside the Keith Jarrett Trio, during the weekend of April 18, 1969,[9] at the same time that *The Prisoner* was being recorded. Although Joe Henderson appears on *The Prisoner*, Garnett Brown recalls that Clifford Jordan joined them for the Vanguard shows.[10]

The Prisoner features a horn ensemble melding six voices, double the size of *Speak Like a Child*.[11] The basic sextet lineup included Coles on flugelhorn, Henderson on tenor saxophonist and flute, and Brown on trombone. A second horn trio varied between the two main sessions, including bass clarinet, flute, and bass trombone. For the first time on one of Hancock's own recordings, he used electric piano in the mix to add some darker colors, particularly on "I Have a Dream"[12] and "He Who Lives in Fear." Williams offered a solid anchor on bass, complementing Heath's complex but direct drumming. Brown doesn't

recall any rehearsals with the full orchestration. It seemed chancy because Herbie knew it was totally unlike what he had done before. His sights were set very high, but he appreciated the expression of something more that wasn't essentially concerned with its perfection. Charles Mingus had once written something for a baritone player who told him: "I can't do that." Mingus said: "That's alright; all I want to hear is the struggle." . . . With Herbie, he can make music out of struggle as well as from myriad aspects of human emotion and natural phenomena.

The Prisoner is a thematic recording, tied to issues of black identity and freedom. In his linter notes to the original release, Herb Wong comments that the album "sets a thematic direction for Hancock to express how black people have been imprisoned for a long time."[13] It opens with "I Have a Dream," titled after Martin Luther King Jr.'s famous speech at the 1963 March on Washington. It is a lyrical ballad buoyed by a bossa nova beat. The title tune, "The Prisoner," is a wild, intense romp, offering a soloistic vehicle for Henderson, as he turns bits and pieces of melodic figures around and about, trying them out in multiple refractions, supported by intense drumming. The solo continues after a brief, unusual horn refrain, with flute floating far above the rest. Hancock's comping is at times spare and always highly responsive to Henderson, reminiscent of some of Hancock's playing behind Wayne Shorter and Miles Davis with the Davis Quintet. Piano and trumpet solos then follow.

Buster Williams's "Firewater," its theme played with a full, colorful horn section reminiscent of Gil Evans, is another showcase for Joe Henderson's saxophone. Wong notes: "The title indicates the social duality of the oppressor and the oppressed. The fire and water idea symbolizes, for Hancock, the feeling of fire in violence and in power play and the feeling of water in Dr. King."[14] "Firewater" became part of the Sextet's repertoire for the next three years. The piano solos on "He Who Lives in Fear" and "Promise of the Sun," both tunes with titles relating to the theme of freedom from oppression, are among the most expansive and open on the recording. Quartal harmony allusions are found in "Firewater" and "He Who Lives in Fear," displaying some of what Hancock gleaned from McCoy Tyner. "Promise of the Sun" makes use once again of the six horns to offer a dense harmonization of the melody, calling to mind some of the arrangements on Miles Davis's *Birth of the Cool* sessions.[15]

Joe Henderson and the Configuration of the Sextet

The Sextet joining Hancock on tour throughout the United States and Europe in 1969 and 1970 included most of the players on Hancock's 1968 Village Vanguard gig: trumpeter Johnny Coles, trombonist Garnett Brown, Herbie Hancock, plus bassist Buster Williams. By the band's third appearance at the Village Vanguard in December 1969, Joe Henderson had replaced Clifford Jordan and Albert "Tootie" Heath had become the drummer.[16] *The Prisoner* rhythm section of Williams and Hancock turned out to represent the only members of the Sextet to stay for the entire life of the band, continuing during its Mwandishi period.

Hancock's horn configuration for his Sextet mirrored the lineup in Art Blakey's Jazz Messengers during the early 1960s. The grouping could be viewed as a microcosm of a big band or as an expanded bebop trumpet and saxophone front line. The mix of instruments offered a broad pallet of sonorities and coloristic possibilities, even with only half the horns used on *The Prisoner*. While Hancock describes the Sextet as having "a much softer, more gentle kind of sound," their music integrated Hancock's lyrical melodies with the driving solos of hard bop. The repertoire of the Sextet consisted of Hancock's recent compositions, including "Toys," "Speak Like a Child," and "I Have a Dream," from the pianist's most recent recordings *Speak Like a Child* and *The Prisoner*; earlier compositions such as "Maiden Voyage" and "Eye of the Hurricane"; and later, material from the rhythm and blues–infused *Fat Albert Rotunda* (1969). The set lists also included bassist Buster Williams's tune "Firewater" from *The Prisoner*, which continued to be played during the Mwandishi phase of the band. The *New York Times* review of a Carnegie Recital Hall performance a year later likely accurately describes what was already happening in 1969: "The group had a tremendously spirited attack in which solo lines and ensembles slid into place, coalesced and erupted in a constant and colorful flow of development."[17]

Joe Henderson's intensity and his crafting of sounds as he explores the ins and outs of phrases and musical figures influenced the musical direction the Sextet would take. Three years older than Hancock, Henderson was also raised in the Midwest and arrived in New York in the early 1960s, to become part of the stable of musicians who recorded on the Blue Note label.[18] While Hancock's avant-garde experience was with Eric Dolphy, Henderson had played with pianist Andrew Hill. In 1967, Henderson briefly joined Miles Davis's touring band. His 1969 *Power to the People*, which included Hancock on electric and acoustic piano, mixed elements of hard bop and free jazz with, on some tunes, the fresh sound of electric bass and Fender Rhodes electric piano.

Since there are no available recordings of Herbie Hancock's Sextet period during 1969, *Power to the People* also offers an unusual glimpse into the kind of ensemble playing Hancock was engaged in with a core member of his Sextet, albeit under Henderson's leadership. It was recorded in two May 1969 studio sessions,[19] a month after the sessions for Hancock's *The Prisoner* and during a period when the Sextet was actively touring. The rhythm session joined Hancock with fellow Miles Davis Quintet alumnus and bassist Ron Carter, along with the drummer in Davis's contemporaneous quintet, Chicago-born Jack DeJohnette. Trumpeter Mike Lawrence filled out the front line in the first session, a date that featured electric bass and, notably, Hancock playing electric piano on "Afro-Centric" and "Power to the People." The quartet that played on the second session was acoustic, except on the ballad "Black Narcissus," with Hancock sitting out the final tune.[20]

"Afro-Centric" displays an angular hard bop melody, but one with a difference. It is twenty-six measures in length. The combination of a four–eighth note pickup plus bar-crossing sustained notes throws the rhythmic feel off kilter. The tied notes that extend the melody across bar lines are contrasted with a funky rhythmic electric bass line. A related rhythmic pattern, which appears in the bass, is echoed a few bars later by the horns. Hancock's comping emphasizes the syncopated interplay between the melody and the bass and horn lines.

Henderson's saxophone solo begins just before the one-minute mark, constructed from a long series of brief, three- and four-note fragment call-and-response. The opening section concludes with a longer phrase, while Hancock punctuates and pushes against the pulse with insistent, repeated chord patterns. Henderson extends this construction by interspersing lines that move at greater speed, while Hancock plays a repeated, ascending series of sustained chords. The effect of his comping is metrically in synch yet in rhythmic tension with the saxophonist.

A half-minute into the solo, the saxophonist pauses for two seconds, backed by Hancock's longer sustained rhythmic chords, and he then continues with a series of pulsating two-note figures. Henderson continues to follow this pattern of a pause followed by variants of his previous figures, ending in trills or entering into more expansive phrases.

Hancock next comps by playing a rapid chromatic ascending series of parallel lines, and then rhythmically punctuates the solo lines using Latin-tinged short attacks. Henderson rises into the altissimo range and, following a low note, pauses yet again, eliciting from Hancock repeated and more insistent chords, which heighten the tension. Tension is released by Hancock's slowly ascending arpeggio before Henderson concludes his thought with a descending four-note phrase, with a penultimate blue note.

The release lasts but a moment, as Henderson kicks up the intensity of his solo, concluding the phrase several seconds after the two-minute mark, while Hancock twice plays an ascending chordal phrase. As Henderson takes a breath, Hancock plays a repeated chord, using a sharp attack. The next section of the solo is accompanied by a brief spurt of Hancock's atonal pointillism, followed by rhythmically accented chords, periodically alternating between ones with a short attack and others with longer sustain, until the end of the solo, just before the three-minute mark. The exchange between Henderson and Hancock is part cat-and-mouse and part intimate support and encouragement. The underlying level of complexity within the context of a palpable pulse characterizes their interplay both on this recording and in the live Sextet performance I witnessed a year later. Henderson's angular solo runs on "Afro-Centric" are keenly set up by Hancock's alternation of sharp attack, percussive chords, and more deeply sustained sounds.

Afterward, Hancock accompanies the trumpet solo with countermelodies constructed from broken chords and sequences of chord ostinati that follow the harmonic changes. As the solo builds in intensity, Hancock's ostinati increasingly punctuate the trumpet lines, ultimately allowing his rhythmic sequences to rise chromatically and bridge into his own solo.

Hancock's piano solo opens with rapidly stuttering repeated chords, followed by rapidly ascending parallel lines and then, repeated abstract, descending arpeggiated chords. The sequences of musical events that follow, as the five-minute mark approaches, include a relatively (for bop tradition) idiomatic angular phrase, repeated figures built from tone clusters, and then more recognizable, repeated broken chord figures. These rise chromatically, flowing into an extended serpentine phrase. Hancock returns us to the head over a forty-second period, beginning with an idiomatic, blues-inflected passage that shifts into brief, rhythmically stuttering two-note figures. At first, these rise, and then rapidly descend, concluding with a trill and brief coda.

Despite its cascading electric piano figure intro, "Power to the People" follows a similar pattern of intense extended solos, accompanied by a steady driving pulse in the bass and drums. Hancock closely follows the soloist's every move and changing mood. His electric piano constantly, and at times relentlessly, presses at the soloist's heels, using rhythmically driven figures as if he were a second drummer. Hancock's comping punctuates the solo lines with ostinati chord patterns, serving to counter the sense of motion in the solo. Hancock, in this manner, alternates between exerting pressure and creating the allusion of backing off. His patterns seem to create an environment of stop action, ironically resulting in the feeling that the soloist is soaring above the fray. The possibility that these dynamics represent the interplay between soloists and the rhythm section in Herbie Hancock's own Sextet offers an otherwise unavailable window on the evolution of the band since the emotionally engaging yet somewhat less intense recording *The Prisoner*.

Touring the Coasts

Only a few days after the recording sessions, the Sextet began a West Coast tour, beginning in the San Francisco area, moving to Los Angeles, and then to San Diego.[21] The Sextet's tour swung to the East Coast at the end of June.

Highlights included shows in Virginia at the Hampton Institute Jazz Festival[22] and an appearance in Rhode Island at the controversial 1969 Newport Jazz Festival on the first Sunday evening in July.[23] The controversy was unrelated to Herbie Hancock but concerned the programming mix of jazz, rock, and pop music and the response by festival officials and critics to the contrasting crowds sharing the same event.[24] The Herbie Hancock Sextet, largely acoustic, fit within the Festival's jazz programming and played Sunday evening, following a show-stopping afternoon performance by James Brown. Brown offered his mixture of bottom-heavy grooves, cathartically emotional songs, and political calls to action. The evening closed with British rock phenoms Led Zeppelin. The act that caused the most ripples the evening before was Sly and the Family Stone. It is unlikely that members of the Sextet witnessed Sly or James Brown, although festival producer George Wein recalls seeing Miles Davis listening closely and noticing the sizable and engaged audiences that the programming attracted.[25] The Newport Jazz Festival took place notably one month before the recording of *Bitches Brew*, and the influence of Brown's vamps would appear distinctly on the spring 1970 sessions for *A Tribute to Jack Johnson*, on which Hancock played.

The integration of jazz and rock influences was already in the air, thanks to Tony Williams Lifetime, the trio led by former Miles Davis Quintet drummer and featuring guitarist John McLaughlin and bassist Jack Bruce. Their premiere recording, *Emergency*, was recorded in May, around the time of *In a Silent Way* and six months prior to *Bitches Brew*. Other early bands were also moving in a related direction.[26]

During this period, the Herbie Hancock Sextet's musical approach was changing, albeit in ways quite different from the emergent jazz-rock. Philip Elwood wrote in the *San Francisco Examiner* that some of Hancock's tunes were "derivative of earlier sounds but often only casually similar to such of his earlier well known works as Maiden Voyage or Empyrean Isle."[27] Sets now consisted of tunes that could last forty-five minutes to more than an hour, but, as Elwood observed, "what a three-quarters of an hour!" Hancock was conscious of the musical changes, as he responded to Elwood's question, "Is all this jazz?" "Oh, yes," laughed Hancock to Elwood, "it's jazz—or at least it's as much jazz as, say, Stockhausen and Berg are 'classical.'"[28] Leonard Feather perceptively described Hancock as "an adventurous writer, concerned with overall sounds and a broad spectrum of colors rather than with definite, easily identifiable chords. Some of the pieces have no clear tonal center, but all are moody, ethereal mirrors of the writer's inquisitive and limitless imagination."[29]

Feather and Elwood raved about the band's performances.[30] The *San Francisco Examiner* described the Sextet as "the sort of band that has something happening all the time, yet it doesn't over blow or resort to trick-stuff in order to hold attention. Just good, intellectual music."[31] *Down Beat* described the April 26 afternoon concert in Berkeley as a buoyant love fest with the fans: "The audience was quick to show its gratitude when Maiden Voyage began floating up, around and beyond the amphitheater in the Berkeley hills. Heath was beaming, and the group exuded joy and friendliness. All the people on hand suddenly melded into one grooving mass. . . . Hancock's Sextet must have made a sizable recruitment of fans."[32] Johnny Coles's trumpet sound was described as "brisk, smoky," and Buster Williams offered "huge, languid tone, fast fingers, and beautiful ideas." Joe Henderson "flew masterfully around his horn, projecting his unique hard-warm tone." Garnett Brown offered "enthralling staccato" and "dramatic circular breathing," Tootie Heath was "all drums, including mammoth eardrums . . . a spellbindingly perfect fit," and "Hancock, of course, has everything going for him."[33]

I have not found documentation of additional Sextet road gigs during the latter part of 1969. During this period, Hancock remained actively engaged in studio work. In August and into fall 1969, he participated in a handful of Atlantic Record sessions, on a recording by Ron Carter, and on several CTI sessions.

Fat Albert Rotunda

I had just read an interview in *Playboy* of Bill Cosby, and in the introduction to the interview it mentioned that he had a management company. He's a friend of mine from 1963, so I called Bill. He said, "Good thing you called. I'm doin' an animated thing for television. It's from one of my concerts, called Fat Albert." I knew that show was about black kids from Philadelphia. They weren't into jazz, they were into rhythm and blues. But I did like that kind of James Brown beat. Bill wasn't on Warner Bros. Records anymore, but he was still good friends with [label president] Joe Smith and he played the tape for Joe and Joe loved it. He called me in New York and I wound up moving from Blue Note to Warners because of Bill Cosby.[34]

HERBIE HANCOCK

The recordings for *Fat Albert Rotunda* were Herbie Hancock's next sessions as a leader and first under contract with Warner Brothers. They took place between October 8 and November 28, 1969, at Rudy Van Gelder's studio in Englewood Cliffs, New Jersey. This period places it within a time frame when Hancock was engaged in a fascinating and diverse mix of recordings, beginning with Miroslav Vitous's *Infinite Search*, continuing with the final session for *Fat Albert Rotunda* and his final 1969 session with Miles, and concluding in early December with *Kawaida* (1970). On October 17, he also performed at a fundraiser for the Harlem Jazz Music Center, the first of three he would play for the community workshop being built at Lenox Avenue and 111th Street.[35]

Fat Albert Rotunda is really three recordings in one. The first is an upbeat and exuberant rhythm and blues tableau, offering opportunities for solos over rhythmic vamps; the second focuses more on the vamps themselves; and the third consists of two lushly arranged ballads. As Garnett Brown comments, "We stayed pretty close to the sensibility of the music of James Brown; it referenced that stuff, particularly 'Wiggle-Waggle.' Many musicians were recording similar material during that period, including with James Brown's own productions. This was really bread and butter for those New York musicians who were known for their specialties in rhythm and blues and pop." Hancock's arrangements are orchestrated with depth and attention to detail.

The band on the tunes "Wiggle-Waggle" and "Lil' Brother" is supplemented by additional horns and by a crack rhythm and blues rhythm section. The Sextet's regular rhythm section absolutely excels not only in the ballads, but also equally on the other R&B-inflected tunes, holding a tight groove and providing a rock-solid underpinning for Hancock's jamming.

Of the straight-up vamp tunes, "Fat Mama" is foot-tapping groove music, well suited to the Cosby kids-on-the-block theme. "Oh! Oh! Here He Comes" lives somewhere between the deep pocket grooves of "Fat Mama" and the syncopation and interplay between funky electric piano and band on "Wiggle-Waggle" (which is discussed further in chapter 4). The title track "Fat Albert Rotunda" offers Henderson and Hancock more space to solo, but even there, the focus is on creating a groove and exploiting the rhythmic interplay between his chordal patterns and the rhythm section of Williams and Heath and, at times, the horns. We will hear this kind of rhythmic interplay a few years later to great effect, in "Sleeping Giant" on the second Mwandishi recording, *Crossings* (1972). "Lil' Brother," which also includes some solo time, closes with a vibrant horn and rhythm section vamp, under which Hancock comps with funky syncopated chord patterns.

Fat Albert Rotunda is not entirely the rhythm and blues recording it is often made out to be. Two of the tunes reflect the lyricism first heard during Hancock's early days with Donald Byrd and continuing through his own tunes like "Maiden Voyage" and "Dolphin Dance," through the ballads in the repertoire of the Miles Davis Quintet. ("Tell Me a Bedtime Story" is discussed in chapter 4.) "Jessica," named after the pianist's newborn daughter, is the only piece on the recording where Hancock plays acoustic piano. The opening piano figures are arpeggiated, upon which the tune is introduced on flugelhorn, with an alto flute countermelody. On the repetition, the fuller horn section joins. The use of acoustic rather than electric piano adds a light, delicate quality to the music and sustains a fragile horn arrangement that is really a through-composed work in itself. Hancock's own solo is understated, direct, and, like the best of his work with the Miles Davis Quintet, delicately held together by a thin textural thread.

Hancock explained to Bob Blumenthal in 1971: "I chose to record *Fat Albert Rotunda* as my first album for the label—which gave me the freedom to do *Mwandishi* next."[36] The album did surprisingly well commercially. Warner Brothers took out a display ad in *Billboard* magazine that read: "Best Seller Herbie Hancock *Fat Albert Rotunda* wins him a big pop following."[37] While it took twenty-three weeks on *Billboard* magazine's "Best Selling Jazz LP's" charts to reach number one, *Fat Albert Rotunda* steadily rose following its release. During its second week, Miles Davis's *Bitches Brew* premiered at number two, with *The Isaac Hayes Movement* on top.

The critical response in *Down Beat* was hostile and condescending. Writer Jim Szantor expressed the hope "that this LP is just a minor derailment" and termed *Fat Albert Rotunda* "esthetic regression . . . in the soul-rock-r&b pop-corn and onions vein . . . somewhat akin to a distinguished actor spurning a long-sought Shakespearean role in favor of a TV soap opera."[38] The article's main complaint is the lack of improvisational space for Hancock and the horn players except on the ballads. While this is the case for tunes intentionally constructed to build a groove, other tunes do include substantial improvisation. Nor are Szantor or other reviews interested in "jazz pianist" Hancock's skill at funky rhythmic phrasing, where he crafts a multilayered interplay between the horns and rhythm section. Hancock responded: "I'm not trying to make jazz become popular music. It may not be in its nature to become popular music because it stays ahead of the public. But young people . . . are not aware of jazz. We have young kids coming into clubs where we play and they're overwhelmed. They haven't heard anything like it."[39]

Hancock's desire to lead rather than follow would guide his agenda as the Herbie Hancock Sextet began to shift in personnel and musical direction. Hancock's conception of the sonic possibilities of the electric piano were about to expand dramatically, far exceeding its musical function on *Fat Albert Rotunda*. For Hancock, the Fender Rhodes would become a sound design vehicle, presaging his interest in synthesizers. That story is the focus of chapter 4.

4

New Musical Directions

Electric Piano and a New Sound

The integration of the Fender Rhodes electric piano was integral to the tone colors of Herbie Hancock's music during the latter days of his Sextet and continuing into the Mwandishi period. As we shall soon see, Hancock had been open to new sounds since the 1950s and early 1960s. By the late 1960s, he sensed the timbral as well as percussive possibilities of the Rhodes. It also provided a vehicle for Hancock's hybrid, genre-crossing stylistic approach. The combination of its ringing tone and sustain with its percussive attack was as well suited to music with a rhythmic drive as it was to melodic lyricism. The sustain pedal and later electronic treatments like the Echoplex created blurred sounds suited to abstraction: Harmonic function could be rendered indistinct, and notes, phrases, chords, or clusters could be shaped with attention given their pure, malleable sonic qualities. Between 1968 and

1970, Hancock explored how to develop each of these elements using the electric piano and, as we shall see, their integration.

Hancock's first time playing an electric piano was an unanticipated surprise for him, opening unexpected vistas:

> When I walked into the recording studio to record with Miles one day, I didn't see an acoustic piano. So I asked Miles: "What do you want me to play?" And he pointed at the corner of the room and said: "Play that!" And it was a Fender Rhodes electric piano. In my head, I was thinking: "He wants me to play that toy over there?" I had heard about the Fender Rhodes electric piano from some other musicians, piano players, and they were saying: "It's not an acoustic piano." So I went in with that kind of skepticism, which was kind of negative. But I had never heard it. So I said: "OK." I turned it on and played a chord and much to my surprise, I liked the sound.

In an interview with Paul Tingen, Hancock remembered it as "this big, mellow sound coming out"—"it sounded beautiful, with a really warm, bell-like sound."[1]

The shift from an acoustic to an electric instrument is actually quite substantial, aesthetically, conceptually and in performance technique. Hancock remembers that at first, while he appreciated its warm, broad sound, the touch didn't seem comfortable.[2] His subsequent observations about that experience were self-reflective: "I learned a big lesson, too: don't come to a conclusion about something based on someone else's opinion. Form your own, unless it's something dangerous."

Hancock's first Fender Rhodes session, in mid-May 1968,[3] was the third and final day of recording for Miles Davis's transitional *Miles in the Sky*. The instrument, soon to become the electric keyboard of choice in jazz, was first marketed only three years earlier, in 1965. Hancock's playing on the tune "Stuff" draws on core capabilities of the Rhodes, its ability to sustain rich sounding chords with a ringing sound and slow decay, and its short attack. Hancock's use of parallel fourths, beginning with the first statement of the tune, helped define his future funk playing.

The tune opens with a snare pickup played by Tony Williams, joined by Ron Carter's bass line. Hancock enters playing a perfect fourth (B-E, forming a 7th and #9 over a Db ground), with a funky sounding mordant (a slow single trill down one note and back up) on the E. He lands on the fourth two measures later, again on the downbeat. After the horns in unison play the theme,

Hancock continues to comp in perfect fourth patterns, at one point conclud-ing with a sustained chord on B-flat. At various points in the melody, Hancock plays a chord with a sharp attack, followed by another long sustained chord with a long decay, which brings out the richness of his voicing. This was the beginning of Hancock's ongoing practice of using the Rhodes sustain pedal to blur chromatically ascending chords, creating a moderate level of abstraction, obscuring harmonic function to contrast with more harmonically grounded chord changes.

Later in the repetitions of the melody, Hancock comps by playing a step-wise countermelody in half-note durations, which morph into slowly arpeg-giated figures. As the melody becomes more assertive, Hancock's individual chords land right on each beat, contributing to the building drama, abetted by Tony Williams's increasingly insistent drumming. At the end of one state-ment of the tune, he plays a single, quiet sustained chord to emphasize the low F-natural, drawing on another device he would come to use periodically, the volume knob on the Rhodes, which he uses to fade the sound in and out. Hancock's alternation of short rhythmic attack and long, rich sustained chords continues during Wayne Shorter's solo. Qualities of attack and decay, volume increases and fades are becoming not simply devices to heighten harmonic function, but as sound design elements in themselves.

This session with the Fender Rhodes turns out to have not been Hancock's absolutely first experience playing an electric piano. That was a Wurlitzer elec-tric piano on Davis's "Water on the Pond," recorded six months earlier, in late December 1967.[4] While the Wurlitzer offered a far less resonant or deep sound than the Rhodes, its distinct timbral qualities mesh well here within a musi-cal texture that includes orchestra bells, electric guitar, electric harpsichord, and drums. The tune has an experimental feel, suggesting Davis's awareness of psychedelic rock and electronic music.[5] Comparing Hancock's use of the Wurlitzer with his Fender Rhodes playing on "Stuff," side by side, it is clear that some magic happened with the Rhodes, making this both his instrument and as the moment he remembers as his "first." This was the moment that sparked how Hancock imagined the instrument becoming his own.

Backdrop: The Electric Piano Is Introduced to Jazz

Miles Davis, among others, became aware of the electric piano, a Wurlitzer in 1966, when Josef Zawinul played with the Cannonball Adderley Quintet. The instrument's ringing, reedy sounds have more sustain than an acoustic piano, adding an extra emotional resonance to the gospel feel of a tune like his "Mercy, Mercy, Mercy." Zawinul was likely influenced in his choice of the Wurlitzer by Ray Charles,[6] who had begun to play the instrument in 1954 on "I Got a Woman" and first recorded with it on *What'd I Say* in early 1959. The tune was the fruit of a development in Charles's music from rhythm and blues toward a fusing of blues forms, gospel, and secular, even sexual, imagery and themes. The longer sustain and percussive attack supported the emotional intensity and rhythmic life of the new music, which controversially appropriated a religious format, with its call-and-response structure, into secular song.[7] The Wurlitzer's sound was young, vibrant, soulful, and ringing, and it afforded a predictability of quality and tuning impossible to guarantee in pianos on the road.

It was Sun Ra, the remarkably creative but underappreciated bandleader and a pioneer of electronic instruments, who first brought the Wurlitzer to jazz, also in 1954. Sun Ra subsequently became an early adopter of the Clavioline, a monophonic electric keyboard instrument invented in 1947 and marketed by Selmer and Gibson in the 1950s, and the Mini-Moog synthesizer, when the latter came out in 1970.[8] Sun Ra's interest in these instruments was an expression of his search for unusual timbres to orchestrate his widely ranging musical works.

The sound of the Wurlitzer, however, lacked the fullness and richness of the Fender Rhodes, which became Zawinul's instrument of choice when it became available. Davis must have liked what he heard during the mid-May 1968 session for "Stuff"[9] because, beginning with *In a Silent Way* and *Bitches Brew*, both recorded in 1969, the Fender Rhodes became the keyboard featured on his recordings and concerts through 1975.[10] The explanation Davis himself offers for his interest in the Fender Rhodes is this:

> I'm crazy about the way Gil Evans voices his music, so I wanted to get me a Gil Evans sound in a small band. That required an instrument like the synthesizer which can get all those different instrumental sounds. . . . It didn't have nothing to do with me just wanting to go electric. . . . I just wanted that kind of voicing a Fender Rhodes could give me that a regular piano couldn't.[11]

Maybe Miles liked its electric sound, which provided an alternative to the electric guitar, an instrument central to rhythm and blues and rock and roll.

Or maybe its rich, bass-heavy sound provided a more solid bottom than was possible with an acoustic piano.

The first Fender Rhodes electric pianos were relatively simple instruments, not only lacking the well-known electronic additions that came later, but, as Hancock explains, "It didn't even have output jacks on the side, [just an] internal speaker. There was an RCA cable that connected the keyboard to the electronics on top. That's all there was. It had a chorus kind of thing, like a speaker sweep panning thing, but it wasn't electronic." As the Rhodes developed, it continued to be the main instrument for Davis's pianists Herbie Hancock and Chick Corea for some time to come. Hancock recorded a handful of studio sessions on electric piano between May ("Stuff") and the November 1969 dates[12] when *Fat Albert Rotunda* was recorded. "Tout De Suite," one of three songs included on *Filles de Kilimanjaro*, particularly stands out in Hancock's evolution on electric piano.[13] During the opening half minute, we hear blues-derived figures, almost the embodiment of Ray Charles, yet played with Hancock's light and nuanced touch. Beginning at 2:30, Hancock adds sparse, rhythmic, three-note riffs, down a half step and back, which dance around the beat and become the bedding for Davis's solo.

These same figures become the starting point for Hancock's own solo, shortly before 9:00. He soon begins to play longer runs, echoing his previous acoustic piano playing with Davis, yet with an edge added by the tone color of the Fender Rhodes. His use of the sustain pedal adds tension to the chromaticism if not dissonance by blurring some of the chords and chord fragments. The alternation between dissonance and consonance brings them into a dynamic tension that would later be a cornerstone of Hancock's playing with the Mwandishi band. This interplay differs from a more conventional tension-release pattern by creating an uneasy stasis that keeps listeners on edge, ever rising and falling, even while kept moving in their seats by the rhythmic drive.

Additional notable Fender Rhodes sessions with Davis include his multi-keyboard recordings in mid-November 1968.[14] These sessions join Hancock's gospel feel and signature oscillating octaves with Corea's percussiveness, short attack, and dissonant tone clusters. Two weeks later, with Zawinul added to the mix,[15] the swirling overlay of contrasting keyboard textures on Zawinul's "Ascent" hint at the coming February 1969 sessions for *In a Silent Way*.[16] The latter recordings mark an early stage in the development of another aspect of the aesthetic that would combine to define the Mwandishi band: floating textures, placid on the surface, beneath which activity is often percolating.

Influence of the Miles Davis *Bitches Brew* Period Sessions

One of the more suggestive summer events for the next stage of the Sextet may have been the appearance of future Mwandishi band saxophonist Bennie Maupin on a crucial mid-August 1969 session for Miles Davis's *Bitches Brew*.[17] Maupin's angular, serpentine bass clarinet lines and countermelodies help establish the mysterious emotional tone, particularly in "Pharaoh's Dance." Maupin had built a reputation the previous year playing with Horace Silver. Hancock himself didn't play on the sessions released as *Bitches Brew*, but, joined by Maupin, he returned to the studio with Davis two months later[18] as part of an electric piano duo with Chick Corea. The tunes include "Yaphet," which reaches back to *In a Silent Way* in its drone-like qualities, enhanced here by the addition of sitar and tabla. It is juxtaposed in places with a pulse, played on this occasion by drummer Billy Cobham, echoing Tony Williams's approach to "It's About That Time."

Hancock's comping on "Yaphet" centers on repeated sequences of rhythmic, melodically rising chords, sometimes broken. The tune, which is relatively static, breaks down into further abstraction later on, particularly within the context of Corea's playing. "Great Expectations," which opens Davis's 1974 release *Big Fun*, has a similar aesthetic with its stop-start structure. The Josef Zawinul tune "Orange Lady" is even more spacious and glacial in its pace during its first half, reaching back to the tune "In a Silent Way"; the meter and level of activity picks up for a few minutes around 7:30, after which it returns to the opening ambience.

The closing tune on the first *In a Silent Way* session,[19] "Corrado," is closer to *Bitches Brew* in its level of abstraction, the use of echo in postproduction, and the prominence of Maupin's sinuous bass clarinet. The role of the electric pianos is integral to the sense of a boiling stew in constant motion, but it lacks simple clarity. The most definable solos are by Davis and, toward the end, guitarist John McLaughlin. One can find hints of the first Mwandishi band recording *Mwandishi* (1971) in how "Corrado" combines a state of constant flux and engagement and in how "Orange Lady" gradually unfolds.[20] Hancock does not appear on Davis's *Brew*, although other related sessions were part of the mix of his activities during that period. The Mwandishi band, as it unfolded in late 1970, shared certain qualities with *Bitches Brew*—rhythmic dynamism and multiterraced, yet improvised interplay between musicians—yet *Mwandishi* and Hancock's recordings that follow it assume a more collective flavor, less centered on its leader. Other contrasts with *Bitches Brew* are discussed in chapter 7.

Power to the People and *Infinite Search*

Other important sessions during this period featuring Hancock on electric piano include Joe Henderson's *Power to the People*, recorded in May 1969 with Hancock on both acoustic and electric piano,[21] and Miroslav Vitous's *Infinite Search* (also released as *Mountain in the Clouds*), recorded in early October 1969, a month before Hancock's *Far Albert Rotunda* sessions.[22] While two of the tunes on *Power to the People* are discussed in chapter 3, it is appropriate to comment here that on the ballad "Black Narcissus," Hancock's bell-like chords, the shimmering sounds at times accentuated by a rapid tremolo and reverb, add a lustrous quality to the rising melody that climaxes and falls. This is but one example of the way the sounds Hancock produces throughout these recordings are radically different from what would be possible on the acoustic piano and contribute to the distinct sound that marks his work during that era.

Infinite Search[23] features as lead soloists bassist Vitous and, secondarily, saxophonist Joe Henderson. Hancock's electric piano and John McLaughlin's electric guitar work in tandem to create an intense rhythmic drive. Hancock's solo on the opening tune, "Freedom Jazz Dance," is particularly percussive and is followed by a flowing solo by McLaughlin, his lines periodically set off by repetitive figures and Hancock's heavy chords and ostinati. In contrast, Henderson's more linear solo seems almost calming, despite its periodic spinning figures that create caesura restraining his forward motion.

The rhythmic accompaniment continues unabated, albeit a bit quieter than during the previous solos, until the climax of Hancock's solo after eight minutes into the tune, where his playing takes on an almost ritualistic quality, and the drums swirl and spin with greater intensity. Hancock plays a more background role in most of the other tunes, adding an intense, linear solo to "I Will Tell Him On You," which culminates in strongly attacked tone clusters. "Epilogue," which closes the version of the recording released as "Infinite Search" includes a sprawling, exploratory Hancock solo, drawing on the Fender Rhodes' tremolo feature to blur and thus abstract its sounds.

While *Infinite Search* may shed less light on the work of Hancock's Sextet than does Henderson's *Power to the People*, recorded six months earlier, it offers another window on Hancock's state of mind during this period. The Vitous recording, particularly when heard in light of *Power to the People*, points to Hancock's rhythmic drive in his role as accompanist, particularly as he learned to master the sharp attack of the Fender Rhodes electric piano. The swirling atmospheric qualities *of Infinite Search* owe much to the long sustain of the Rhodes and the blurred sounds created when Hancock holds down the sustain pedal, as do his mastery of its ringing qualities, particularly in Vitous's version of Eddie Harris's "Freedom Jazz Dance."

The Rhodes and R&B on *Fat Albert Rotunda*

The opening tune on *Fat Albert Rotunda*, "Wiggle-Waggle," is an up-tempo tune with the most solo space on the recording. It begins in a manner unexpected for an R&B romp. The sounds we hear first may be strummed dulcimer or banjo, resting on a bed of saxophone and trombone long tones. Floating further above is an Echoplexed trumpet figure. Around twenty seconds in, a spicy guitar lick is joined by drummer Bernard Purdie's backbeat and Jerry Jermott's electric bass. Just before 1:00, Herbie begins to comp on electric piano, drawing on the instrument's combination of percussiveness and sustain. Before we know it, Joe Henderson is off and running with a solo that shows marks of R&B—rapidly repeated riffs, reaching up for an altissimo held note—all refracted through Henderson's sound and his knowledge of post-bop. The R&B feel is supported by the funky sounds of the Fender Rhodes. A more scalar, melodic trumpet solo follows, highlighting Joe Newman's shimmering tone as he blows over the big band long sounds. The solo winds down when Hancock's comping creates a suspended chord holding pattern. There is a pause like a sigh.

After a five-second upwardly rising electric piano riff, Hancock is off and running on his own solo, which he prefaces with a single repeated note and then a middle register repeated chord. A five-note pentatonic melodic fragment repeats above it, forming a bridge to the upward-moving arpeggiated figure that launches the solo, which bears many of the marks of the funky style to appear next on Freddie Hubbard's *Red Clay* (1970); on "Ostinato: Suite for Angela," which opens *Mwandishi* (1971); and again later on *Head Hunters* (1974). These include short call-and-response phrases, trades between solo lines and repeated left-hand chords, momentary thick chordal phrases, tension built as he moves up the electric keyboard and resolved with an octave tremolo. Hancock crafts endless variations on simple melodic fragments, and he lands right in the pocket when he wishes. A few of Hancock's brief repeated figures conclude with a blue grace note, which resolves to the tonic. There is a proliferation of pentatonic melodies, perfect fourths, and increasing intensity of rhythm. Hancock uses the Fender Rhodes to suggest a multipitched drum, sonically reminiscent of a balafon, a West African marimba. Hancock's characteristic octave oscillation heightens this referencing. This is a sound that Hancock will use on Hubbard's *Red Clay* and continue to cultivate on the recording *Mwandishi*.

The ballad "Tell Me a Bedtime Story," simultaneously melodious and rhythmically catchy, includes a lush horn arrangement, contrasted with brief moments when the ringing timbre of the electric piano is used to great effect. Hancock's electric piano solo is brief, simple, and to the point, playfully considering variants of the tune. The entry of the horns toward the end of his solo adds to the emotional richness and is followed by a full repetition of the tune and brief coda. The smooth, rich sound of Hancock's rich chords resound, forming a solid backdrop for the band. He draws on the ringing sounds to great effect during his electric piano solo.

Red Clay

Freddie Hubbard's landmark second CTI album, *Red Clay*, again joins Hancock with Joe Henderson. The sessions were recorded in late January 1970.[24] The title track shows Hancock's further evolution as a rhythmic electric pianist, building on his playing on "Wiggle-Waggle" and on the title track from *Fat Albert Rotunda*. "Red Clay" begins with a minute-long free blowing opening section, reminiscent of John Coltrane's use of the *alap* form drawn from Indian raga form, where the musicians lay out the modal and harmonic material to be drawn on later.[25] During this section, Hancock uses the sustain pedal to blur the runs he plays on the Rhodes. He draws on the newly added tremolo feature to suggest a tanpura, the drone instrument in North (Hindustani) and South (Karnatic) Indian music. Hancock had to previously create a tremolo manually by rapidly turning the volume knob up and down. He uses this device to create and shape the colors and thereby shape the mood of the opening section.

The tune itself opens with six chords, two descending and four ascending. These become the basic riff on which the entire tune is built. The two horns play the melody over the continuing riff, on which Hancock contrasts short, ascending chords, paralleling the movement of the melody, with a long sustained chord at the cap of the ascent. The final chord is accentuated by holding down the Rhodes sustain pedal. Hancock's percussive comping throughout "Red Clay," playing the Rhodes as if it were a balafon or marimba furthers the style seen in the *Fat Albert Rotunda* sessions. This is particularly apparent during his two-minute-long electric piano solo, which begins at 4:30. Hancock alternates melodic passages, at times pentatonic, with sharply attacked chords or gentle, rich sonorities. Hancock's drumming-like playing remains a dominant feature of his approach to the title tune to Hubbard's next recording, *Straight Life*, in mid-November 1970[26] and then, six weeks later, on "Ostinato: Suite for Angela," the first recording by a newly configured Herbie Hancock Sextet.

The percussive yet lyrical approach Hancock developed to playing the electric piano proved to be highly influential among pianists of his own and younger generations. But it was also just the beginning of a long odyssey, as he began to realize the sonic possibilities the instrument might offer when expanded with newly emerging electronics, some becoming popular with electric guitarists and, subsequently, synthesizers, which were just then becoming commercially available.

The listener in search of an explanation of how Hancock reconciles the melodic/funky/abstract elements of his playing can find their integration emerge as he developed his approach to the Fender Rhodes. These perceived polarities become creatively integrated and reconciled in much of Hancock's music beginning with *Fat Albert Rotunda* and continuing through the Mwandishi period. Hybridism was built into Hancock's playing from his beginnings in Chicago, rooted in his playing hard bop, an essentially eclectic, hybrid movement in which rhythmic elements from gospel and popular music played an important role. The sum of the musical qualities found in *Fat Albert Rotunda*, *Infinite Search*, *Power to the People*, and *Red Clay* point to Hancock's rhythmic intensity and drive, angularity, and use of call-and-response and rhythmic chordal sound gestures to build solos. They are heightened through his command of the Fender Rhodes electric piano, from which his unique touch elicits warm, ringing tones as well as forceful rhythmic emphases. All of these features coalesce in the creation of his next recording, *Mwandishi*.

Electric Piano as a Sound Design Instrument

In a very real sense, the Fender Rhodes represented for Hancock a new way to shape sound. What began for him as an exploration of the timbral possibilities of this new instrument began to broaden in scope thanks to the availability of electronic devices that could alter its sound. Soon after commercial production of the Rhodes began, Fender and another instrument company, Vox, began to offer a range of electronic expansions to the Rhodes, introducing tremolo in 1967. These additions appealed to Hancock, whose pregnant imagination was piqued, most strongly exemplified in his August 1970 dual electric piano session (with Josef Zawinul on the recording *Zawinul*), in which the instruments' bell-like sounds are treated with Echoplex to create a swirling texture, a dramatic soup of Fender Rhodes timbres. This suggested all sorts of new sonic possibilities, pointing to how the keyboard's sounds could be expanded beyond the simple, albeit beautiful sound it made *as is*. Teo Macero had used the Echoplex to treat Miles Davis's trumpet on the postproduction of *Bitches Brew*. This device was supplemented by the wah-wah pedal, available in 1969 and popular among rock and funk guitarists, and also the fuzz box and ring modulator, the latter invented around 1960 and first used in jazz by Chick Corea in 1970 while playing with Miles Davis.

Hancock saw the electronically expanded Rhodes as being "like the precursor to synthesizers":

> [Later] I thought of synthesizers as instrument makers. You program a
> certain way and you get a sound. You can't do that with an acoustic piano.
> An acoustic piano basically has one sound and that's it. Whereas these other
> instruments, because you can tweak them in different ways and make other
> sounds out of them, they were like sound design devices. The Rhodes was a
> preview of that in a way.

Sonic distortion was already a mainstay in mid-1960s psychedelic rock and roll, and the tonal toggling that wah-wah provided had become an element within funk. The master tightrope walker of live sound design was guitarist Jimi Hendrix, who was also on Davis's radar by 1968. Hendrix calibrated new techniques integrating his guitar with both amplifier feedback and electronic circuitry including fuzz boxes and other distortion pedals, to allow him to artfully shape noise elements within his guitar sounds while performing. His well-known performance of "The Star Spangled Banner" at the 1969 Woodstock Festival shows Hendrix crafting cascading sounds of bursting bombs and whirling rockets. Portamenti of distorted sounds and guitar tones that waver between tone and noise characterize his performance of "Sgt. Pepper's Lonely Hearts Club Band" at the 1970 Isle of Wight Festival.[27]

The availability of electric instruments and electronic processors did not easily translate into the development of a technique that affords their most musical use. Pat Metheny observes:

> Herbie's Rhodes and then Clavinet playing had an identity to them that was directly tied to his piano touch, which I think we would all agree is exceptional, and totally funky. [The way he used it with electronics] was all happening at the moment where the thing with the Echoplex and moving the tape head around, and then the Maestro ring-modulator were all the rage. And again, in Herbie's hands, it was all really, totally, super hip! I would even say hipper than the synths that came after [so it] couldn't be for tech reasons. The early instruments that were around during that time were crude, with no dynamics. Herbie went on to be just about the only one of that generation besides Zawinul who really seemed to understand how to use them to get a personal sound.

Hancock was one of a handful of pianists who recognized that the sonic possibilities of the electric piano, and then synthesizers, could open new doors. While his practice of incorporating electronics didn't begin until the late 1960s and early 1970s, the *idea* had occurred to Hancock as early as his first year with Miles Davis. In the 1964 interview with John Mehegan, the twenty-four-year-old Hancock credits this interest to teenage drummer Tony Williams:

> I first heard electronic music about a year ago and now I am beginning to "hear" or relate to it in some sense. Tony Williams and I are going to buy an oscilloscope and tape apparatus and start fooling around with it.... [Y]ou don't even need human beings in order to create music. Have you ever heard the beauty of sound passing through trees? That's the beauty of nature.[28]

Once Hancock began to use the Fender Rhodes, first alone and then with its growing set of electronic expansions, he not only more fully integrated his hybrid musical approach, but he found a way to use electronics to design and shape sound, features that would become a mainstay of the Mwandishi band. Rare among musicians, Hancock intuitively realized that expressive electronic musicianship required adaptive performance techniques. The Mwandishi band was his vehicle for perfecting his new composite electric-electronic instrument and placing it at the center of a musical ensemble.

Hancock so quickly cultivated an appreciation for the sonic potential of the Rhodes for multiple reasons. Certainly he was constitutionally an aficionado of electronics and devices (his first major in college was electrical engineering). But on a deeper level, he was fascinated by sound, as evidenced by his 1964 interview with John Mehegan. Hancock's evolution began when he first came to appreciate the intricacies of harmony, which as skilled orchestrators know, is intimately connected to tone color. Over time, he listened to music that heightened the relationship between the two and, tellingly, suggested their interchangeability.

Hancock became aware of the subtleties and complexities of harmony as a teenager. He listened closely to the chord voicings of popular 1950s singing groups like the Hi Los and Four Freshmen. What he learned found expression years later in the enriched harmonies on *Speak Like a Child* (1968) and *The Prisoner* (1969): "I really got that from Clare Fischer's arrangements for the Hi-Lo's. [Arranger] Clare Fischer was a major influence on my harmonic concepts."[29] Hancock also listened to orchestral arrangements, particularly "mood music orchestras . . . like Robert Farnon's orchestra from England,"[30] and deepened his understanding by exploring the harmonic conceptions of Miles Davis arranger Gil Evans, French impressionist composer Maurice Ravel, and pianist Bill Evans.[31] Hancock's lush arrangements in his late 1960s recordings combine carefully crafted chordal voicing with a careful sensitivity to timbre. His choice of an unusual combination of wind instruments— alto flute, flugelhorn, and bass trombone—offered a broad timbral palette. Hancock built on the aesthetics of French impressionist composers Claude Debussy and Ravel who built musical phrases using texture and tone color. Hancock was keenly aware of how John Coltrane and, through personal experience, Miles Davis in the mid-1960s made use of sense impressions, textures, and emotional sensations as musical organizing principles. Tony Williams helped him conceptualize these ideas, intellectually and in practice.

Hancock also listened to the music of Edgard Varèse while in college. Varèse was one of the first Euro-American composers to think of music in terms of shaping sound as if it were sculpture, broadening his conception beyond the organization of pitches. Joel Chadabe describes Varèse's *Integrales* (1926) in this way: "The pitches that the instruments play, their loudnesses, their spacings in orchestral chords, their crescendos, attacks, and durations, were important because of the way they contributed to a composite timbre."[32] Varèse's concept pointed toward the development of electronic music. Hancock was also exposed to the music of John Cage and Karlheinz Stockhausen as early as 1963, thanks to Williams.[33] As Hancock expressed it at the time: "I've been listening to [Stockhausen's] *The Song of Children* [*Gesang dur Jünglinge*]. I don't know if the sound is that of human voices or whether it is electronically produced, but it is fascinating. I haven't as yet been able to absorb it into my emotional makeup. I've been affected by it."[34] In the early 1970s, Stockhausen became important to Miles.[35]

These new sonic conceptions place Hancock's fragmentation of chords and a greater textual and coloristic emphasis into a broader perspective. Sound itself became a strong personal interest, as witnessed by his confiding to John Mehegan:

> I have been fooling around with the wires, the sounding board and the
> pedals on the piano and I have been listening to the sounds, not only
> of the instrument, but the entire physical components of the piano. For
> instance, my telephone bell can be made to vibrate on my piano by striking
> the pedals. . . . I would like to emphasize that any sound can be used in music
> because any sound can become part of an organized composition.[36]

We hear Hancock's sonic sensibilities growing on *Kawaida* (1970), *Zawinul* (1970), and other recordings that point directly to the Mwandishi band. The use of a wide variety of little percussion instruments on *Kawaida*, a practice continuing with the Mwandishi band, derived from the Association for the Advancement of Creative Musicians (AACM).[37] This feature added to a growing timbral emphasis that increased its weight as a core value as the textures of Hancock's Fender Rhodes electric piano grew increasingly electronic when paired with electronic devices like the Echoplex. The addition of Bennie Maupin, who had explored texture and timbre while playing with Marion Brown, heightened the sonic focus.

Later in the band's history, Patrick Gleeson's synthesizers would shift the balance even further toward an aesthetic that privileged sonic qualities. Hancock recounts how wide his ears remained open to new sounds during the Mwandishi era: "[Before playing a show] I sometimes put on a series of different records. . . . I usually put on a series of contemporary things just to open my head up: John Coltrane's *Live in Seattle* . . . then some Stockhausen . . . maybe Debussy." Gleeson recalls that Ravel's highly textural *Daphnis et Cloe* suite was often the music of choice in Hancock's hotel room.[38]

Clearly, the Fender Rhodes electric piano was not just an instrument of convenience for Hancock. Rather, it reflected a larger conception of sound, one that he could treat as a sound design engine. It was also an instrument that invited his unique touch, enabling him to craft his unique sound. This was a sound that could have abstract elements, yet due to its rhythmic attack and ringing sustained tone invoke popular black music with its resonances of gospel, rhythm and blues, and funk.

People will say "I don't understand your music," or "I don't understand Coltrane," and I'll tell them neither do I really. The important thing is to leave yourself open so you can experience the thing without any knowledge whatsoever. If you can do that, you'll be in better shape than the musician who can name all the changes you can play and hasn't heard anything.

HERBIE HANCOCK, 1972

5

Moving toward Mwandishi

Herbie Hancock Sextet bookings were sparse in early 1970. The band spent February on the West Coast.[1] In early March,[2] the Sextet appeared in New York City at Carnegie Recital Hall. The *New York Times* appreciated the band for its "constant and colorful flow of development." John Wilson bemoaned that the arrangements rarely made use of the full horn section, playing mostly a series of trios and quartets, with only a "few sparse bits of ensemble color," but appreciated the rhythm section as "a formidable trio, built around Mr. Williams's strong bass lines, which provided a core for the somewhat exotic sound—muffled, tinny, but filled with warm, tinkling bells—of Mr. Hancock's electric piano."[3]

The next documented Sextet show took place in mid-April[4] at the Jazz Workshop in Boston, with Miroslav Vitous subbing for Buster Williams. The set list continued the mix of older Hancock tunes, "Eye of Hurricane" and "Maiden Voyage," with tunes from *Fat Albert Rotunda* (1970): the R&B-inflected "Wiggle-Waggle," the ballad "Jessica," and Buster Williams's "Firewater." Bob Blumenthal observed: "The music had become far more open. Hancock spent almost all his time on electric piano while [Joe] Henderson even played a bit of flute, and there was now loads of solo space on extended performances."[5] The next week, the Sextet played a fundraiser at the Mary McLeod Bethune School on West 134th Street in Harlem, as part of a four-day music festival sponsored by the Harlem Jazz Music Center.[6]

Pete Yellin, a band mate of Henderson's, recalls having subbed for the saxophonist during this period, "somewhere way upstate New York . . . we drove for 4 or 5 hours. It was a Black history month celebration." He notes: "It was hard for me to jump in because the tunes were played much differently than they were written and I wasn't comfortable on tenor. . . . I'm an alto player and I borrowed one for the gig. They doubled and tripled up tempos. I was scuffling. They were helpful and encouraging and knew it was a tough scene to jump in on since they were smoking." Henderson had begun to cancel on Sextet engagements in favor of other projects of his own, in part because of his own aspirations and in part because Sextet engagements were limited.

In mid-June, a prerecorded performance by the Herbie Hancock Sextet on noted producer Ellis Haizlip's show *Soul!* was the first of several televised broadcasts. It had been videotaped at New York's PBS television station Channel 13 WNET.[7] The program included a reading by poet Felipe Luciano and a performance by The Last Poets. "Ostinato" appears on the set list, suggesting that it had entered the band's repertoire. Here it was wedged between "Wiggle-Waggle" and "Maiden Voyage." Plans had also been entertained for a June six-concert tour joining Hancock with members of the Indianapolis Symphony, but this never materialized.[8]

Back in the Studio for Influential Sessions with Miles Davis

Although the Sextet seems to have played a limited number of gigs in early 1970, Herbie Hancock was not idle. His return to the studio with Miles Davis in April and May marked what might be described as a parallel musical life to that of the increasingly musically expansive Sextet that still maintained its bebop lineage. These were unplanned appearances, as Billy Cobham recalls: "Herbie walked in with a bag of groceries. . . . [H]e just dropped by the studio to hand Miles a copy of his latest release on Warner Brothers called *Fat Albert Rotunda*." Hancock found himself seated at an unfamiliar instrument, the Farfisa electric organ, in a situation reminiscent of Hancock's earlier experience with Davis and the Fender Rhodes. Davis reportedly pointed to the organ and ordered him to play. Hancock demurred, but after Davis continued to insist, Hancock sat down at the organ, Cobham continues, and "he and Stanley Tonkel, the engineer, are trying to figure out how to get the thing to work until finally you hear this one long chord cluster of notes: 'Waaah!' That's Herbie trying to figure out how the blasted thing turns on.... He played the solo, he gave Miles the record and he split."[9]

Instead of betraying signs of technical struggle, the recording of core elements of Davis's *A Tribute to Jack Johnson* (1971) displays substantial organ playing.[10] On "Yesternow," which draws on a James Brown bass riff from "Say It Loud, I'm Black and I'm Proud," Hancock contributes a funky edge to this hard-driving jam. On the edited composite of multiple "Right Off" takes released on the recording,[11] Hancock punctuates the proceedings with an insistent rhythmic chordal riff on which Cobham locks into a groove. Hancock's continues into a rollicking blues-inflected solo featuring downward glissandi and various rhythmic devices he would pursue a few years later on the Hohner Clavinet. A long sustained chord (Cobham's "Waaah"?) appears just after 3:00. Hancock's repeated rising three-chord riff, reminiscent of Horace Silver, heightens a wonderful groove, into which Davis steps with a solo.[12] The recording of "Honky Tonk"[13] showcases Hancock's rhythmic Clavinet-like repeated note organ riffs in a funky triumvirate with Keith Jarrett's wah-wah electric piano and John McLaughlin's guitar jabs. Recordings during the following two weeks included the beautiful ballad "Nem Um Talvez" plus "Selim" and "Little Church," which appear on *Live/Evil* (1971), all graced by Hancock's organ washes. Two takes of the rock romp "Little High People" are built on a Sly-style riff taken to a more abstract plane by the ring-modulated electric piano and Airto Moreira's vocal-sounding drum sounds. Hancock is back as part of a dual electric piano team with Jarrett, joined on organ by Chick Corea.[14]

What is striking about Herbie Hancock's participation in these sessions is the ease with which he settles into a funky groove, without relying on the comfort zone we hear on *Fat Albert Rotunda*. This rock-oriented and funk setting is less familiar territory, and Hancock exults in the luscious new sounds of the organ, allowing them to swell and at other moments articulating rhythms that point toward his future funky, percussive Hohner Clavinet playing we will hear on *Sextant*. Hancock has again used an unanticipated encounter to whet his appetite for the next creative leap.

Another piece of the puzzle fell into place during the 1970 recording of *Zawinul*, which continued Hancock's experience of the static, floating qualities of Davis's 1969 *In a Silent Way*. Following the 1969 Davis model of the duo electric piano sessions for Davis's "Great Expectations" and "Orange Lady" (Hancock and Corea), the recording of *Zawinul* similarly paired Hancock with session leader Josef Zawinul.[15] The core idea was that improvised music could unfold at a slow and gradual pace, without losing its dynamism, continuity, or rhythmic drive. The interplay between the two electric pianists is heightened by their two Echoplex machines facilitating the motion of the music through subtly changing textures, ebbs and flows, climaxes, cascades, and returns to rest. Hancock would soon become a master at using these devices, which became an integral extension of his Rhodes. We hear Hancock unleashed in the cat-and-mouse chase of "Double Image," urged on by two drummers, one of them new Sextet member Billy Hart. The static pace and unfolding textures of both *In a Silent Way* and *Zawinul* anticipate aspects of the *Mwandishi* recording, particularly Julian Priester's "Wandering Spirit Song" and Hancock's band's subsequent fragile collectively improvised textures.

A Band in Transition, Seeking a New Audience

There had been little work booked for the Herbie Hancock Sextet during summer 1970, leading some members to seek other sources of income. Garnett Brown recalls: "I don't remember traveling a lot with Herbie's band." Various musicians began to sub for trumpeter Johnny Coles, particularly Woody Shaw, who would be a part of the *Zawinul* sessions. Drummer Albert "Tootie" Heath, who had a family to support, left to join Yusef Lateef's band. His replacement, beginning on July 31, was Billy Hart. Pete Yellin had been but one of several subs for Joe Henderson, and clearly it was time to find a permanent replacement. Buster Williams suggested Bennie Maupin, most recently a member of Lee Morgan's band.[16] Maupin joined the Sextet on Sunday, August 2, for an afternoon show at the Embassy Room in Baltimore. This was part of a new Gentlemen of Jazz series, set up to complement the not-for-profit Left Bank Society series where both Hancock and Maupin had previously appeared, separately.[17] Maupin drove to Baltimore with Hancock and rehearsed in the car, Maupin memorizing the music along the way. The band was in flux, but a remarkable stability was on the horizon. And for one final hot and sunny midsummer evening, July 31, 1970, Joe Henderson remained as saxophonist.

I was a fascinated teenager sitting in the audience for that show, which took place at the Wollman Skating Rink in New York City's Central Park.[18] My Uncle Milt brought my cousin Wendy, my brother, and me to see the main act,

Iron Butterfly, a popular California rock band. From my perspective, this was to be one of my first rock concerts. It had been a month since my final piano lesson after seven years as a young conservatory student. Only a few months prior, my musical life had been turned upside down when I first heard Jimi Hendrix. I had grown bored and disaffected after years of musical exposure limited to classical music. What captivated me about Hendrix was the tight-rope walk I felt he took with every note, wavering between pitch and noise. The new musical sounds shocked and surprised me. Discovering Hendrix guided me in search of new sounds. And so here I was, in no small part thanks to my uncle's eagerness to explore something new, in Central Park.

Frankly, Iron Butterfly's performance didn't interest me, but Herbie Hancock's Sextet piqued my curiosity and attention. I couldn't think fast enough to process what was taking place. My memories of the evening soon folded within an array of shows I attended in Central Park and, in the coming year, at the Fillmore East. They faded until, while researching this book, I read Hancock reviews from the period and then stumbled on a flyer for the concert. I took a double take as I viewed the names on the bill, looked back at some of the contemporaneous reviews of the band I had recently read, shook my head, and went "oh, yeah."

The programming at the Schaefer Music Festival fit within the pattern of an increasing number of bills that paired rock and jazz bands. Only a few weeks earlier, on July 6, Davis had appeared opposite Buddy Miles in this same venue. The Herbie Hancock–Iron Butterfly double bill came about because the two bands shared a manager, as Hancock recounts: "Lee Weisel, a former classmate of mine from Grinnell College, had become a lawyer, then a manager. Lee called me one day and asked if he could manage me, I didn't have one at the time. He admitted that he had a tin ear and knew nothing about music but he liked what I stood for. Lee managed me for about a year."[19] In fact, though, Hancock had already been in discussions with Iron Butterfly about recording an album together, after hearing them in a studio.[20] Needless to say, this collaboration never took place, although the two bands performed on the same bill on several occasions.

And so, on July 31, after a first set by Iron Butterfly, and with just a brief announcement—"The Schaefer Musical Festival welcomes the Herbie Hancock Sextet"—a group of intensely focused black musicians took the stage. It was in front of a largely white audience in their teens and early twenties. The audience was thin, with people milling in (and out) as the band played. This crowd had come to hear the headline band, Iron Butterfly, eagerly anticipating the band's signature drum solo on the hit tune "In-A-Gadda-Da-Vida." The Sextet opened like a whirlwind. Hancock's own recollections are that "we must have sounded awfully weird to that audience. There was polite applause but no one booed." Indeed, the audience showed little interest in the unusual display that was taking place at this moment. The air was thick with pungent smoke, the audience talking loudly as they ignored the performers on stage, making it difficult to focus on the music at hand. But the music was emotionally intense and intricate. Saxophonist Joe Henderson etched lengthy surging and jagged melodic lines. The rhythm section of Billy Hart and bass player Buster Williams were right on his heels, nudging him ever forward. The ballad "Maiden Voyage" slowed down the pace, allowing the two brass players to stretch out, joining Henderson with long tones, seemingly well in keeping with this lazy summer night. Onaje Allan Gumbs, five years old than I was at the time, describes his impressions:

> People walked out as soon as Herbie's band came on stage for their set. During that set, my friend and I were jumping up and down, but everybody else was still. When they played "Fat Albert Rotunda," it was the funkiest version, much slower than on the recording, but people weren't feeling it. The audience reminded me of an old Van Heusen shirt ad, where two guys in their Van Heusen shirts were alive and everyone else was made of clay or plastic. The audience was pretty hostile. Herbie tried to explain his music to the audience and he became a bit defensive, saying that there seemed to be a lot of speakers on the stage and with that can come feedback. Clearly, he was upset. In retrospect, I realize that the audience wasn't coming to hear jazz or to hear Herbie. They were coming to see Iron Butterfly. I went backstage to talk to Herbie and introduced myself. In my eyes he might as well been Duke Ellington. Buster was upset about what had happened on stage, but couldn't be bothered. Joe Henderson was philosophical, just trying to figure it out. I don't remember how Woody Shaw or Billy Hart felt. Later, on different occasions, I would hang out at Herbie's house and we talked more.[21]

Ironically, that afternoon, drummer Billy Hart had experienced his own personal first, as he walked through Central Park, checking out its paths and byways, anticipating his first gig with the Herbie Hancock Sextet.

The August 2 Baltimore show with Bennie Maupin was hailed by the *Sun* as "brilliant, interesting, intense, experimental, absorbing."[22] The Sextet played an August 3 show at the Hartford Festival of Jazz[23] and then at Shea Stadium, in Queens, New York. Summer Festival for Peace, an antiwar fundraising concert organized by Peter Yarrow, was held on August 6, 1970, to mark the twenty-fifth anniversary of the atomic bombing of Hiroshima, Japan.[24]

A configuration of the band in transition—Bennie Maupin, Woody Shaw, Garnett Brown, Buster Williams, Herbie Hancock, but no permanent drummer—next traveled to California, again playing on two bills with rock groups. The first took place on Saturday night, August 22, at the Inglewood Forum, on a bill with Iron Butterfly and Canned Heat.[25] Ndugu Leon Chancler, then a teenager "fresh out of high school where I had started playing professionally" became drummer for that gig:

Herbie had heard about me through pianist Walter Bishop, Jr. and also because he had come to my high school to give a talk in 1969, and I was asked to play a few tunes with him and a bassist from the high school. One of those was "Maiden Voyage." Herbie maybe have also talked to Shelley Manne, and just took a chance on me. Bennie Maupin and I talk about it today; the standing joke was "take a chance on Chancler.

All my high school friends were into the original Sextet and we would go hear them when they were in town. We'd all go to see all the bands that came to Shelley's Manne-Hole and the Lighthouse. Seeing Joe Henderson was an incredible thing, particularly seeing him and Herbie together. Johnny Coles and Joe didn't get to the West Coast that much during that time, except with Herbie. I first saw Miles at Chick Corea's first gig, late in 1968. It was all-acoustic then, playing "Miles in the Sky" and that kind of thing.

Before the Inglewood Forum gig, I picked Herbie up at the airport and I looked at some of the charts while I was driving. He laid out the program right there in the car. We never rehearsed. A lot of that music had a lot of freedom to it anyway. I remember looking over the chart of "Eye of the Hurricane" in the car. Herbie had gotten a lot of stuff intellectually from Tony Williams, including writing triplets in four beat measures, written across the bar lines. The gig went extremely well. It was smoking . . . we were opening for Iron Butterfly. That was a new way they were booking in the late 60s. The audience was responding. There were some Herbie fans there, and some people were into both bands.

Billy Hart was in the drum chair for the next shows at the Fillmore West in San Francisco, August 24, 25, and 26, from which point he would remain with the band. They were playing opposite British blues singer John Mayall and headliner, blues-rock guitarist Elvin Bishop.[26] Backing Bishop was singer Jo Baker and a group that would reappear on the same bill during the final days of the Sextet, the Pointer Sisters. Critic Philip Elwood enthused about the Sextet:

> The subtle jazzman Herbie Hancock was utterly, all the way together. Never compromising, never over-reacting or grand-standing, Hancock created his own delicate mood, that shifting, floating rhythmic base of "Maiden Voyage" and others, and let the huge Fillmore crowd adapt to his emotional pitch. . . . Hancock mixes into the rock scene from jazz because he plays honestly and well. His music, which has in some "jazz" circles been dismissed as too far-out, found an enthusiastic reception last night.[27]

The Fillmore West was one of the premiere rock concert halls in the world, and home to the famous psychedelic bands of San Francisco. It was owned by rock producer Bill Graham,[28] a man who had a strong interest in black music, including jazz, as did his future partner and soon-to-be Herbie Hancock producer David Rubinson. His programming periodically mixed and matched jazz and rock acts, with pairings as unusual as Cecil Taylor and The Yardbirds, Sun Ra and Ten Years After, Miles Davis and Leon Russell, Thelonious Monk and Dr. John the Night Tripper. Young white baby boomers seemed to Graham to be the next potential audience for new and old forms of jazz.[29]

Hancock, recently turned thirty, was eager to play before larger and younger audiences, so the opportunity to play venues other than jazz clubs had strong appeal. He was also seeking a way to move beyond the confines of the jazz business and its paternalistic approach to recording sessions, where musicians have little or no say over sound engineering or production, and clubs, where bands play multiple shows per evening. Donald Byrd, Hancock's former employer and mentor, tutored him to assume control over his own business affairs. Despite his serendipitous choice of Lee Weisel as manager, conscious of it or not, Hancock was looking ahead, aware that times were changing. Hancock's future producer and manager David Rubinson witnessed that: "He was getting some negative audience reaction when they'd play a jazz club, some of the new stuff. But when he played some of the rock clubs, that's what they loved. There was that kind of positive feedback." Rubinson adds that the band was also playing "in college towns where younger people came to listen and, often, to dance."[30]

As we will later see, playing in rock settings proved less interesting, if not problematic, for Hancock's band members. As early as the first Fillmore East show, even as part of an all-jazz series, trombonist Garnett Brown was not particularly enthused: "I had never played a rock club before the Fillmore gig. Never. I didn't think of it as anything really special. It was a little perplexing to me that we'd be there. We just played the gig and went home. Since playing the Fillmore was important to Miles, it might have been important to Herbie. For me, it was minimally memorable."

All Things Coming Together; Preparing for the London House

Even before the personnel of the band changed, the Herbie Hancock Sextet was steadily continuing to stretch out musically. Tunes continued to expand in length, with the interplay between instruments taking on a more central role. Hancock had brought his experiences with loosely structured improvisations to bear on the band's approach. These included his work with the Miles Davis Quintet, on *Zawinul* (1970) and parts of *Kawaida* (1970), as well as the recent floating sessions with Davis. Hancock's playing took on an increasingly intuitive quality, and now he had found musical peers who shared this sensibility. While continuing to thrive on vamps, and lyricism, the band was moving away from more conventional melodies, chords, and even modes, toward an intuitive, more emotive and textural approach. It often did so while simultaneously deepening its rhythmic concept and intensity. The decision to choose both texture and rhythm reaches back to Hancock and his band mates' roots in hard bop and R&B, and is an affirmation of their shared interest in African traditions and, most generally, black music.

In fall 1970, two personnel changes finalized the core of the Mwandishi band. Trombonist Julian Priester temporarily filled in for Garnett Brown at an engagement in Vancouver at the club Old Cellar, September 28 to October 3.[31] This was a setting where Hancock had played with Davis and whose bookings spanned hard boppers and Ornette Coleman. Brown was busy composing a score, but never returned; Priester stayed on. This was followed by a show the next evening in Seattle, at a festival run by the Seattle Jazz Society,[32] followed by two nights at the Club Ebonee, through October 9 and 10.[33] Eddie Henderson filled in on trumpet during a weeklong engagement at the Both/And in San Francisco. Johnny Coles had left to play with Ray Charles, and his temporary replacement, Woody Shaw, was unavailable, having teamed up with Sextet member Joe Henderson. Shaw recommended Eddie Henderson, who had never played on the road or at a recording session, as a sub. The kidding by his band mates was sometimes relentless, loving but tough. He was nicknamed "Rookie of the Year." But he was the right choice, and the chemistry began to do its work right away. Rubinson recalls: "[The Both/And] was extraordinary since it was such a mixture of music. Bennie had a new tune and Herbie had a song he had written for an Eastern Airlines commercial, "You'll Know When You Get There." And then they just jammed. The shape of the music kind of accumulated as they played and as the week went on, it went more and more out."

In 1970, the personnel needed for the unfolding of the Mwandishi band in its next stage was now in place, with an unusual chemistry. Bennie Maupin remembers:

> The first night we played together I knew something magical was happening. . . . We had no time to rehearse. Herbie had given the horn players the music, so the three of us we looked through the music. We were in the hotel and started playing through the part. The sound from that very moment was just the most gorgeous sound. We just blended. There was nothing about it that was ever out of kilter. We got to a point where we breathed at the same time; we'd phrase the same way. It was three of us, but it was like one mind. The blend would be so incredible, I wouldn't know if I was playing, if Eddie was playing. We went to the club, and Billy and Buster and Herbie were there. We played the first set; we must've played an hour and a half, two hours. After it was over, people just went completely crazy. We went in the dressing room and we couldn't even talk to each other. It left everybody speechless.[34]

Accompanied by a uniquely creative and both musically and personally bonded group of musicians, a new phase of Herbie Hancock's musical development was beginning to unfold.

In mid-October,[35] the fully constituted band played a weeklong gig at the Cellar Door in Washington, D.C., in a double bill with comedian Richard Pryor. The review in the *Washington Post* was stellar: On "Wiggle-Waggle," described as a tune with "an infectious jerky rhythm," "[Bennie] Maupin played a volcanic solo full of noise fragments and disjointed melodies. It had raw emotional power, but he never lost his sense of construction. [Julian] Priester's solo on 'Maiden Voyage' was one of the most arresting individual jazz performances I have heard in several months. He was superb in his use of stop-time elements and odd-placed rhythmic accents."[36] *Down Beat* writer Brooks Johnson added: "The group really let it all hang out on *Fat Albert Rotunda*."[37] As the band gelled, it was ready for its month-long stand at London House, in Chicago.

6

Mwandishi
The Recording

Closing Out 1970

The pivotal year of 1970 now entered its final quarter. That fall in mid-November,[1] Herbie Hancock continued his activities as a studio musician. Recording in the midst of the month-long stand at the London House, he joined Joe Henderson and drummer Jack De Johnette on Freddie Hubbard's *Straight Life* (1971), the trumpeter's third CTI date. During the same period, Hancock also appeared on John Murtaugh's *Blues Current* (Polydor, 1970), a Moog synth album that includes drummer Bernard Purdie and electric bassist Jerry Jemmott, who both played on *Fat Albert Rotunda* (1970). The *New York Times* review hails the use of synthesizer on this "fascinating group of compositions that reveal a striking variety of Moog-induced colors and textures, in a jazz context, ranging from what might be urgent harmonica riffs behind Hancock's rollicking piano to a haunting horn-like figure that floats through 'Blues for Dreaming.' Throughout, Herbie Hancock's piano 'jumps and drives and rocks.'"[2]

The Sextet's final appearance of 1970 may have been the late November taping of a second show for the WNET *Soul!* series, which had gone into syndication. It was viewed in the New York metropolitan area on WNET, Newark, New Jersey, nearly a year later.[3]

David Rubinson Introduces Hancock to Rock Production Techniques

With 1970 coming to a close, it was time for the band to enter the studio to record *Mwandishi*. Hancock continued to be under contract with Warner Brothers to follow up on the rhythm and blues–inflected *Fat Albert Rotunda*. The label's expectation for what would follow was for Hancock to produce more recordings in a similarly popular vein. Toward this end, Warner Brothers decided that Hancock needed a producer who had demonstrated commercial success before and so assigned David Rubinson, who had worked well with another band on the company's label, Malo.

Rubinson had built a reputation as a visionary rock producer. At the age of twenty-one, he landed a staff job at Columbia Records, having found some success as an off-Broadway theatrical producer in New York City with *The Cradle Will Rock*, the 1964 revival of Marc Blitzstein's 1937 musical about a struggle to unionize against a corporate power. By 1966, Rubinson had signed and was working with high-profile rock bands like Moby Grape and the Chambers Brothers and, soon after, with an eclectic mix including pop songster Anita Bryant, Irish musicians the Clancy Brothers and Tommy Makem, Latin jazz star Mongo Santamaria, and blues legend Taj Mahal.

The dramatic rise of youth culture found its quintessential expression in rock music. Sensing that the future of rock was unfolding in San Francisco, Rubinson sought to steer Columbia in a direction that could engage the rising youth culture, as Rubinson's engineer Fred Catero[4] recalls:

> He came out to San Francisco and scoped out the scene and went back to Columbia and said: "You guys are wasting your time here. You ought to open up a studio in San Francisco because that's where the talent is." They said: "We can fly them in." He said: "No, you don't understand. These are not like Tony Bennett and Jerry Vale. These are *hippies*. These are flower children. These are people who hate the man, the establishment. You can't bring them here

with this corporate environment where it's 9 to 12, and expect them to create. Put up the tie-dye. Put up the lava lamps. Make them feel comfortable. Relax some of your stringent corporate ideas. Get rid of the union up there because the unions treat the creative arts like they are an assembly line. You [can] create 9–5; take a break, then three more hours. [The Columbia people] said, like corporate executives: "Well, we have to do some research, a cost analysis, whether this is just a flash in the pan, if we should set up facilities."

Columbia became more open to rock music in 1967, after hiring Clive Davis and signing artists like Janis Joplin and Santana.

Rubinson left New York and moved to San Francisco to become an independent producer and business partner of rock impresario and owner of the Fillmore West and East, Bill Graham. Rubinson sought the flexibility to meet the budding rock scene on its own new terms. Freed from exclusive contractual obligation to any particular record company, he began doing work with Atlantic and Warner Brothers and others closer to the youth music scene, while keeping his ties to Columbia. Graham and Rubinson shared a love and interest in advocating for black and Latin musicians. The two of them, along with attorney Brian Rohan, set up the Fillmore Corporation.[5]

Lee Weisel, at that point manager of the rock group Iron Butterfly, referred Rubinson to Herbie Hancock. The first time Rubinson heard Hancock's band was quite possibly the same concert I attended at the Wollman Skating Rink in New York's Central Park, at the end of July 1970.[6] Rubinson recalls: "I was approached by Warner Brothers to follow up on *Fat Albert*. I had done all different kinds of records and they wanted to move in that commercial area." Hancock adds, in an interview with Joy Williams: "So then they figured maybe if they could get me with a producer that would kind of edge me toward that funkier stuff that would sell. . . . They chose David Rubinson, who came to hear my band to see what he had to do with it."[7]

But what resulted defied the expectations of Warners Brothers. As hoped, a synergistic chemistry developed between Hancock and Rubinson, but it wasn't the kind that the company had in mind. According to Hancock, "The band not only had gotten away from doing the funkier *Fat Albert* stuff, it was much more avant-garde."[8] And Rubinson saw his goal as helping a recording artist realize a creative goal, whatever that might be: "I was the guy to say 'OK, where do you want to go? What do you want it to sound like? Where do you want it to lead?' Herbie and I would listen to James Brown and we were together listening to all the contemporary electronic music. And so when we walked into Warner Brothers to play them *Mwandishi*, they were blown away, they had no idea." The results were creative, but not conventionally commercial. Warner Brothers hadn't realized that they had paired a musician ready to embark on his most experimental work with a producer with knowledge and sympathy for that approach. As a result, explains Hancock, "instead of him pulling us over to what Warner Bros. wanted us to do, he became like the spokesman for our side, to try to figure how to keep the music as it was but put it in a form that was palatable enough to sneak it through Warner Bros."[9]

Recording began in the beginning of January. The date has often been listed as New Year's Eve, but Rubinson believes that it took place over several days following the turn of the year.[10] Rubinson remembers Hancock visiting his house in San Mateo, California, sometime before the sessions, in late 1970 or after the first of the year 1971.

Mwandishi—The Sessions and the Music

The recording sessions took place at Wally Heider's studio in San Francisco, in studio C, a small upstairs room. Heider's was one of the leading California studios, the scene of notable rock recording sessions by Jefferson Airplane (*Volunteers*, 1969), Grateful Dead (*American Beauty*, 1970), Santana (*Abraxas*, 1970), and Crosby, Stills, Nash, and Young (*Déjà Vu*, 1970). Rubinson had previously worked at Pacific Recorders in San Mateo, starting in 1969, because of its sixteen-track Ampex tape recorder. Difficulties with the studio owner suggested the need to find a new location. The soundboard in studio C at Heider's was an eight-track DeMidio tape recorder,[11] but as Rubinson recalls, "we configured it to work for sixteen."[12] Mixing took place in another room.

The tune was recorded in a single take. Rubinson's production process, as he describes it, "combined old recording techniques and new ones; recording a live group performance, and then using tons of modern post-production techniques."[13] Postproduction included the addition of effects, but only very rarely, tape edits. Rubinson's goal was to maintain the integrity of the original recorded performances, often using electronics to expand tendencies that are implicit in those performances.

The band added a second drummer, Ndugu Leon Chancler, on the tune "Ostinato." Chancler notes:

> At the session, everybody was playing together, playing time. These were
> nighttime sessions. We would just get in and play and roll the tape. That was

a period when various electronic studio tools were used in post-production. Not only was the music changing, but also so was the concept of recording, studio gear, and electronics. In the *Mwandishi* session, all of this was invisible because we were all playing live. Unlike on the East coast, where you had the classic Rudy Van Gelder sound, with the sound of the studio and the sound of the engineer, people in Los Angeles were used to post-production. On the West coast, because you had film work, the concept of recording was an added tool for the music. You didn't have as many straight jazz sessions being recorded on the West coast; you had the Crusaders and a few other bands here, but by and large, most of the music being recorded on the West coast was recorded by studio guys—with and without click tracks—recording snippets of music which would be put together in post-production. Thus, the sound of the technology and of the engineer, and not just the sound of the room, made a recording what it was.

The opening tune, "Ostinato: Suite for Angela," is built on the continual repetition of an odd-metered phrase. "Ostinato" is the term used in classical music for a repeating phrase; a "riff," its parallel in jazz, the blues, R&B, and rock music, is designed to establish a steady, repeating pattern, a rhythmic leitmotif above and around which musicians can create interlocking or contrasting melodic and rhythmic phrases. In this respect, Hancock's use of ostinati references key aspects of the musical world of the African diaspora, as defined by musicologist Olly Wilson.[14] A common thread within that tradition is highly syncopated music that embraces rhythmic complexity and interplay. Rhythmic patterns overlap and clash, but find resolution. There is also an emphasis on timbre, call-and-response patterns, and in some (but not all) music of the African diaspora, improvisation. In the tune "Ostinato," solos move in and out of a single riff/ostinato played by various combinations of instruments. Hancock's solos and his comping for other soloists also repeatedly engage complex call-and-response patterns. There are moments when the density of musical events can be overwhelming in intensity.

The infusion of blues, R&B, and gospel influences into the hard bop of Hancock's early career explains his exploitation of this device, but only to some degree. The constant repetition of small cell-like structures also bears the mark of early French electronic music, based on Pierre Schaeffer's concept of the "locked groove."[15] As discussed in chapter 4, Hancock had become familiar with early electronic music in 1964.

Schaeffer's idea derived not from a rhythmic conception, but as a consequence of new recording technologies, beginning in the late 1940s. In his early experimentation and subsequent compositions, Schaeffer would record short sound clips, first on physical discs and, when it became available, on magnetic tape. The discs would be recorded in a manner that caused constant repetition. With the advent of magnetic tape, segments of tape would be cut, with the beginning and end connected using splicing tape, to create a "tape loop." Schaeffer and others used this mode of repetition as a compositional device. Early modular synthesizers designed in the mid-1960s by Robert Moog, Donald Buchla, and Donald Pearlman (such as the Arp 2600 used by Patrick Gleeson) incorporated an electronic and more mechanized tool ("sequencers") to repeat note and sound phrases, one that could be altered on the fly.

The Mwandishi band used the ostinato as a device to suit a range of musical goals. One function was to serve as a vamp, a steady riff on which soloists could improvise. A related function occurred when ostinati gradually shifted in time and by adding and subtracting melody notes, which created a sense of motion. Bassist Buster Williams was, as he continues to be, a master of invention when it comes to shifting ostinati, sometimes causing a gradual evolution and sometimes a sudden shift in mood or level of activity. Hancock at times added and subtracted repeats of an ostinato to cause subtle shifts in the musical texture or sense of time.

Another way that the Mwandishi band made use of ostinati was to freeze time by repeating short phrases multiple times, thereby creating a lack of motion. This could create tension between musical objects in motion and others in a holding pattern. Hancock often used this locked groove approach to effect musical stasis, sometimes momentarily, which could result in either a timeless quality or the building of tension, which could then be released by the dissolution of the ostinato. Hancock's use of ostinati was a key mode by which he playfully directed musical direction and the level and style of interplay between his band mates.

In "Ostinato," the repeating riff is only sometimes used as a constant vamp. During improvisational sections, it is also used to momentarily freeze time and create patterns of tension and release. These dynamics were intentionally built into the rhythmic structure of the ostinato theme. Hancock recalls:

> I wanted to write a tune with an underlying rock beat, but using it in a more open way than usual. I finally achieved it by making the number of beats uneven—it's in 15/8, one bar of 4/4 and one of 7/8. I started with a repeated syncopated bass line in 4/4, a regular thing. The way I chose the notes in

Example 4. The ostinato theme of "Ostinato: Suite for Angela"

the riff was that I figured most of the rock bass lines telegraph their chord so distinctly that there's no escaping it. I wrote something that could imply many chords . . . some fourths even, like Trane and McCoy . . . a kind of pentatonic scale, but starting on a different degree of that scale.

But then I thought "Why should I keep that all the way through?" so I changed it slightly and shortened every second phrase by half a beat. Now if, instead of two 4/4 bars, I had a 4/4 and a 7/8, it meant I had to change the notes to make them sound natural. Having done that, I had to decide what to put on top, and what it is, is different degrees of tension and release. Music and life flow because of those qualities, as do all the senses. It's contrast: to know what cold water is, you have to know what hot water is. Music's like that; it has to flow, and if there's no tension and release it will be totally bland, with no vitality. . . . Having 15 beats in a bar automatically sets up a little tension, because just when you think you've got it figured out, it eludes you. At the end of each bar we all hit a phrase together, and that's a release. That's also true of harmony. Very little of the music is consonant, but the dissonance varies so greatly that it's a matter of some of it being less dissonant and thus becoming consonant by comparison.[16]

The perception of shifting in and out of synch during collective improvisation serves to heighten this effect. There is much rhythmic interplay with Hancock using the steady pulse as a bouncing board to present ever-changing, syncopated chordal patterns. Despite the complex meter, Buster Williams "laid down the 'Ostinato' rock solid for the entire duration of the tune."[17] The steady pulse against which the improvisation pivots was reinforced by the addition of Ndugu Leon Chancler as a second drummer. Percussionist José Chepitó Areas, on congas and timbales, alternately reinforces and pushes against the beat.

Chancler, whose Swahili name means "brother, sister, or friend," recalls how he became involved with this project:

After I played the Inglewood Forum with the band, Herbie invited me to join the band. I didn't do it since I had a scholarship to college. So Herbie said that since you bailed us out, why don't you join us on our upcoming recording. Before the session, we never talked conceptually about what two drummers would do. We just started playing. Billy Hart and I just kind of blended for what it was and intervened in between each other. A lot of these guys were used to playing in four and we were doing this thing in fifteen. That was a different twist in itself! For me, I had been dabbling with Don Ellis,[18] who was local; I had played on a few rehearsals and was a fan of his band, so I was familiar with odd times. While I had not yet done a recording session with two drummers before, since I had played avant-garde music during that period, playing with two drummers or percussionists was a familiar idea. We had been playing in a Coltranish kind of vein, but not with Herbie. When two drummers get together, both roles are suppressed a little; James Brown was already doing it; I was coming out of that first. All of it was in conjunction with the groove. The groove was first and foremost. It was just a matter of us getting a swing out of it. It wasn't that hard. All the guys were there. They had a feel for it; they just took it and ran with it. Man, it was a great experience. I heard the *Mwandishi* recording when it first came out and I bought it. I dug it. It was mixed extremely well for the number of instruments that were there. There was a lot going on.

Rubinson also recalls the recording sessions: "I remember Ronnie Montrose playing [guitar], and me on my knees working the wah-wah pedal with my hands."

"Ostinato: Suite for Angela" opens with a textural introduction constructed from Echoplexed electric piano figures and angular saxophone lines. Following two seconds of silence, the ostinato itself begins at the half-minute mark. It is initially announced by a tag-team, first by the bass clarinet, then bass, and after that, by the two together, with the addition of congas and flanged drums. Around one minute, Hancock adds Echoplexed electric piano lines, which add another layer of rhythmic complexity. The Echoplex is a tape delay device first sold in the early 1960s. The addition of a moving tape head allowed a performer to shift the length of the delay in real time. Hancock developed a technique that allowed him to use the delay time for its rhythmic possibilities, used to great effect on this tune. At times during "Ostinato," Hancock complements the delays with electronic pitch shifts. Pitch shifting is a technique we now take for granted on synthesizers, introducing a glide between notes that is impossible on an acoustical keyboard instrument (since there are no notes between the piano keys). But here, the effect is not a simple slide between notes, but a wobbling of the pitches, one part distortion and one part glide.

The ostinato continues steadily with each of the musicians adding and subtracting elements into the musical mix. For instance, at a minute and a half, Eddie Henderson plays three-note figures on trumpet, with Julian Priester adding a countermelody on trombone. Soon, the bass clarinet shifts from the ostinato to an oscillating countermelody. Closing in on two minutes, Hancock adds a rising figure on Echoplexed electric piano, which he manipulates live in real time. The overall effect of the countermelodies and counterrhythms is akin to a collective jam that sounds simultaneously free yet, due to the close attention to the ostinato and its variations, discernably structured.

The improvisations that follow feature call-and-response (between Hancock and trumpeter Henderson), multilayered drumming, and Hancock's periodically generated several-chord ostinati, playing against the bass line or drumming. At various points, the drumming increases in intensity and complexity, heightened in Hart's case by flanging[19] in postproduction (Chancler's kit remains unprocessed). Various members of the band periodically join in the ostinato, strengthening its gravitational pull.

Hancock's solo reflects a masterful integration of rhythmic playing and the use of ostinati and tone clusters, heightened by his use of the Echoplex. A detailed description offers a sense of the flavor of this solo. Hancock begins with short phrases played in call-and-response patterns, variously repeated, followed by increases in the Echoplex delay time and insistent repetition of a chordal figure. Between seven and eight minutes the level of intensity builds by Hancock's use of repeated tone clusters, chords rising up the keyboard, and chordal ostinati, while he explores changes in the repeat time of the Echoplex. After more call-and-response chord patterns, as we approach eight and a half minutes, Hancock plays a distinctive melodic figure.[20] This figure ascends, with increased Echoplex, followed by a new pattern, a chord played low in the electric piano's register, repeated three times an octave up, and concludes

Example 5. "Ostinato," 8:20–8:30, Hancock pattern one

Example 6. "Ostinato," 8:35–8:50, Hancock pattern two

Example 7. "Ostinato," 8:35–8:50, Hancock pattern three

with three quick repetitions of a chord up and down the octave. Hancock's solo winds down with syncopated multiple-chord patterns before joining in the ostinato.

Next, Bennie Maupin offers his atonal and segmented solo over Hancock's syncopated, rhythmically accented comping, with Hart's drumming picking up intensity, around eleven and half minutes. This is heightened by the addition of more flanging in postproduction. Once again, Maupin returns to the ostinato, soon joined by Hancock and the rhythm section. Hancock's solo phrases alternate with drum flourishes and some conga, as Hancock repeats patterns that expand and shift in his comping. As the ostinato continues on the bass and bass clarinet, Hancock varies the patterns of notes and chords he plays, leaving space between sets of chords. The tune ends shortly after thirteen minutes, Hancock having rejoined the ostinato ensemble. The overall effect is an exhilarating display of collective improvisation that is all at once rhythmically solid yet complex and multiterraced, abstract—and—what we'll term "funky."

As we will see in chapter 7, "funky" is not a strictly musical word, referring more broadly to a celebratory attitude toward life coupled with a joyful loosening of inhibition.[21] But most relevant to the present description of Hancock's playing, it is useful to speak in strictly musical terms. Within hard bop, "funky" refers to a syncopated music that pushes against the beat, sometimes anticipating and on other occasions following it. Horace Silver's tune "Filthy McNasty" (1961) captures both the musical and extra-musical sides of the term "funky." During the late 1960s, a new musical dance form emerged in which the groove was central. The rhythmic emphasis was on the downbeat, as opposed to the practice in rhythm and blues as well as idiomatic jazz, where accents land on the second and fourth beats. The bass plays a leading role in creating the groove, joined by other instruments, each creating its own distinct syncopated rhythm. Together these interlock, forming a rhythmically complex whole that anticipates, comments on, and prepares the arrival of the downbeat.[22] In his solos on "Ostinato," and from that point forth within the music of the Mwandishi band, Hancock comps by creating syncopated rhyth-

mic/melodic patterns (*ostinati*) that dance around and about the pulse, forming an integral element within the band's chain of interlocking beats. The more
that Hancock's figures anticipate and ornament the beat with syncopation, the
funkier his playing becomes. Borrowing a practice developed by rock, R&B,
and funk guitarists, Hancock routed his Fender Rhodes through a wah-wah
pedal that, when toggled, emphasizes different frequencies, heightening the
attack and emulating vowel sounds. This effect heightens the *funkiness* of his
playing, in part due to the referencing of similar guitar techniques increasingly utilized within the new genre. The wah-wah drew on a practice within
early jazz where vocal sounds are mimicked by placing a plunger within the
bell of trumpets and trombones. The "dirtying" of the sound suggested the
lack of timbral purity, a "nastiness" that was integral to both early jazz and,
subsequently, to funk.

The second tune on side one is Hancock's lyrical "You'll Know When
You Get There." It opens with an introduction: three repetitions of a chord
by Hancock, each time moving to a higher octave. This is followed by the
melody, played by trumpet and flute. There is an ascending A-E figure at bar
11, and then a pause. After some jingling bells, Hancock plays three high register chords in bars 13–14, thick with reverberation, to which Williams adds
some rapid filigree on bass and Maupin holds a sustained flute note, ending
with a double stop by Williams, which he slides downward. After that there is
another pause. Then, the bass line continues, joined by a countermelody on
trombone and trilling flute. Henderson continues the melody on trumpet. A

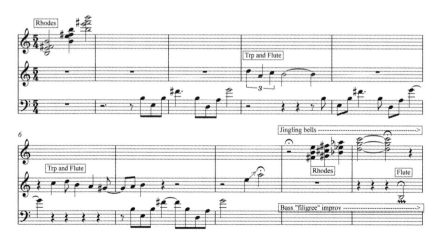

Example 8. Opening passage to "You'll Known When You Get There"

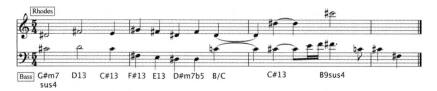

Example 9. "You'll Know When You Get There," segue harmonies, bars 29–32

broad, reedy toned soprano saxophone, overdubbed, lays in a singable countermelody a little before the one-minute mark.

A brief harmonic segue is played by bass and electric piano, followed by
a return to the melody, played in unison by trumpet and flute, the final note
echoing. This is followed by a brief pause. Close to a minute and a half, Hancock's rising chords repeated from bars 13–14 precede a flute trill and some
rapid bass filigree. Next, the trombone countermelody returns, the second
time accompanied by an extended trumpet trill.

A brief trumpet cadenza is tagged on, placed in a deeply reverberant space.
The trumpet continues to play solo approaching the two and three-quarter-
minute mark, when the bass and, very quietly, electric piano return, playing
the harmonic segue. During this solo section, one can hear very faint echoes
of what may have been other instrumental tracks. At three minutes, Hart offers a defined, yet relaxed drum pulse, as the trumpet solo continues. The
bass playing is lyrical and melodic, yet it anchors the trumpet solo. Hancock's
lightly echoed electric piano comping sets a gentle mood.

With the trumpet solo continuing, shortly before four minutes, Williams
plays a bass motif built on a B octave leap up-and-down motion and then
moves into more soloistic territory at four minutes. The rhythm section repeats the harmonic segue, extended and just after four and a half minutes, the
whole band plays the refrain.

The opening bass figure returns, but rather than returning to the melody,
a three-minute flute solo begins, starting over a melodic bass line. The lyrical
mood shifts, as Hancock introduces a fast-moving solo line of his own, the
flute rapidly fluttering, elongated by reverberation. Maupin then plays brief
notes and turns of phrase on the flute, accompanied and countered by a rhythmic bass riff, which builds on the octave figure used during the trumpet solo.
Hancock plays an echoed, rising riff that he repeats as a response to Maupin's
phrases. Hart locks the beat into a metered feel soon around five and a half
minutes, with Hancock's electric piano playing a five-note/chord riff (three

notes downward and two back up), the piano sounding like a vibraphone. At six and a half minutes, the pulse briefly takes on a swing feel, and then the harmonic segue returns, bringing Maupin's solo to a close. There is flanging on the drums during the latter portion of the tune. The band plays the refrain to close out the flute solo, followed by a return to the opening bass line, and a drum roll.

Hancock's two-minute solo begins around seven and a half minutes. The solo line is quasi-tonal, drawing on heavy echo and reverberation, and accompanied by soloistic drumming, flanged in postproduction. Hancock plays a descending melodic figure that moves all the way down the keyboard, followed by a military march figure on Hart's snare drum (with flanging continuing). We seem to enter a very different emotional space as Hancock plays a twelve-note melodic phrase. After a bass note and some drum fill, Hancock repeats the phrase, transposes it, and repeats it yet again in the original key. One minute into his solo, Hancock's harmonies suggest an expanded version of the segue section that is also used to comp for the other solos.

Bass and drums play a brief duet, joined by Hancock's harmony around the nine-minute mark, continuing the segue harmonies. A twice-repeated series of sharply attacked chords on electric piano, bass, and drums bring his solo toward a conclusion. One final series of the chords, played more delicately, lead to the refrain. This is followed by a return of the opening bass line, the melody played by trumpet, with the trombone countermelody, concluding with the upward E-A trumpet sweep; Hancock plays a reverberant upward slide. Bells precede a brief pause, a hint of the three ascending electric piano chords from bars 13–14. Then a flute trill ends the tune.

Pianist Billy Childs reflects on the version of this tune that appears on the recording:

> The album *Mwandishi* strikes me as a very impressionistic album, very influenced by things like Ravel and the French impressionists. In Herbie's playing with the Echoplex, he plays a run and the echo follows it, it's like a harp doing a glissando. It's a beautifully electronic sound but the result is like an acoustic, natural instrument. He plays the Rhodes like it's an orchestra. This is because the acoustic aspect of the sound is real salient here. The Fender Rhodes solo on "You'll Know When You Get There" has some of the most beautiful interplay between musicians that I've ever heard. Herbie plays a lyrical riff, like an elegiac lullaby, while Billy Hart is playing a rudimentary, almost military-like snare figure, and the image that comes to my mind is like fallen soldiers. And

Buster Williams' bass playing behind Eddie Henderson's trumpet solo. Billy is like the core, propelling the music in those cool environments. Billy shows such a finely tuned musical intuition, a decision making about what is appropriate for the most dramatic effect at any moment: how can the music hit you viscerally in the most effective way. He's a storyteller, like a *griot* on the drums. He uses the drums as orchestration to tell stories.

Filling the entire second side is Julian Priester's "Wandering Spirit Song," captured in an exploratory, intuitive studio performance. The tune begins with an extended pedal tone, which provides a stable harmonic grounding, over which rises a simple, long phrase, which is answered by two variations on it, the final one floating back down to earth, followed by a light jazz waltz and then a series of solos whose length allows a depth and breadth of reflective consideration rarely found on jazz recordings. The band coalesces periodically at peak moments and during more freely drawn passages, eventually coming to a conclusion that feels like settling into a resting place of deep quietude. "Wandering Spirit Song" mirrors the dynamism of the band in live performance in its changing moods, varying textures, and surprising turns of events.

The first half of the tune is reflective and placid, beginning with the opening statement of the melody and a trombone solo, followed by a restatement of the melody at nine and a half minutes. The essentially static mood is suddenly broken when the final phrase of the melody splinters apart. The horns break into a polyphony based on a three-note phrase, first heard in the trumpet. The gesture descends by a small interval and rises steeply and is echoed freely in time by each of the horns, calling to mind the opening of John Coltrane's *Ascension* (1965). The atmosphere becomes highly charged but, after a minute, begins to collapse on itself.

In keeping with the band's shifting moods and textures, even at this early stage in their development, a jagged-edged solo by Maupin emerges from the fog. The solo is comprised of short melodic fragments, sometimes just one or two notes. The sense of instability and fracture, at odds with the tune's opening repose and stasis, is heightened by the postproduction application of tape delay and reinsertion. Hancock further emphasizes the tense mood by building his comping on phrases of four, and later two, descending parallel fourths. The tension continues to build over the ensuing three minutes, when a cacophony of free improvising horns, supported by the rhythm section, charges the air.

But the mood once again shifts with the sudden return of the waltz section of the tune, restoring the initial calm. This state of calm doesn't last long, as the band briefly considers a return to free improvisation. But this strategy soon dissolves into a static texture reminiscent of the opening of the performance. The listener detects the conclusion of the tune. But instead, what follows is a lengthy coda, a spare but expressive interchange between Hancock and bassist Buster Williams. A fine line separates what constitutes a bass solo with electric piano comping, from a delicate duet, pointing to the camaraderie and empathy that had grown between the two musicians.

Despite a placid opening, "Wandering Spirit Song" has taken the listener on an emotional and often stormy ride. Rather than stasis, one experiences sharply changing moods and textures and passages of passion and intensity. Waves of building collective energy alternate with tumultuous solo playing sometimes supported and other times challenged by the collective. Moments of fragility and beauty coexist with elements of dynamism and pandemonium, all within the performance of single composition.

The Critical Response to *Mwandishi*

Neither Warner Brothers nor Hancock's manager were pleased with *Mwandishi*, as Rubinson recalls: "The manager had a fit because he expected me to make a Santana record. He thought I was going to make him [Hancock] commercial. And I did, but the people at the record company didn't get it. That record was enormously commercial. That record should have done what *Head Hunters* did. But Warners didn't get it." Still, *Mwandishi* opened at number 16 in *Billboard*'s chart of "Best Selling Jazz LP's," dropping to number 20 in its second week.[23] Warner Brothers' marketing directors did not know how to sell the new recording, as Rubinson explains: "*Mwandishi* was inscrutable. It had no obvious radio target, and Warner Brothers was basically a white company, with few resources for entry into the black college, jazz, or progressive markets, which was the clear target audience."[24] As a consequence, the Sextet completed just one more recording with Warner Brothers, *Crossings* (1972), and then signed with Columbia Records. The irony of this switch to Columbia is that it brought Rubinson full circle, back working with his original record company. The departure from Columbia had been congenial, and so it was possible for him to contract future projects of mutual interest.[25]

Mwandishi received an overwhelming affirmation in the *New York Times*: "[It] sounds like jazz, but it comes across to you with the evocative, personal directness of song. Once you are oriented, it is accessible to any kind of musical sensibility, rock, classical or jazz . . . the genius of his new jazz is that it dwells in emotion and concept, and is, therefore, a universal language in an event in which we all take part." This universality, critic James Lichtenberg aptly noted, was an extension of Miles Davis's discovery that "musicians could play directly off the patterns of emotions," thus rendering the highly specialized forms of bebop and post-bebop unnecessary. By following this path so successfully, Hancock has "thrown the doors open to everyone."[26]

Lichtenberg particularly appreciated Hancock's solo on the tune "Ostinato" "that explores rhythmic counterpoint to a degree undreamed of in classical or rock music." Lichtenberg credited Maupin's bass clarinet sound with "a subtlety and refinement of sound that is impossible on saxophone," and Henderson's trumpet and flugelhorn is played "with the delicacy and breathlessness of a flute." The tune "You'll Know When You Get There" is termed "a trembling, vulnerable lyrical experience," a "chronicle and the experience of discovery" that includes a trumpet-piano duet whose "notes hang and flow like bubbles in the air."[27]

Lester Bangs, in his *Rolling Stone* dual review of both the Blue Note *Best of Herbie Hancock* compilation and *Mwandishi*, compliments the latter as "a session of driving, firebrand improvisations that reflect the full maturation of his art's social awareness (though without getting heavy-handed about it, thank God), as well as some new and perhaps inevitable influences."[28] Bangs places the recording in the context of Davis's recently released electric albums:

Miles' recent pioneerings turn up, of course, as they have on just about every jazz record released in the past two years—the yearning, benediction—like opening of "Wandering Spirit Song" is especially reminiscent of "In a Silent Way," and Miles' pervasive new space tempi crop up, though not nearly so obviously or imitatively as usual. The emphasis on a large percussion section puts them through some changes and imbues them with an angry bite that was entirely missing from the airy labyrinths of a *Bitches Brew*.[29]

But the Bangs review expands on what he saw as a political subtext, presumably due to the title of "Suite for Angela," a reference to activist Angela Davis (initially Rubinson's idea, but quickly embraced by members of the band): "[Mwandishi displays] his latest band getting into a personal militance and searing solo attack that may not be as gorgeously complex as the best of his past work but possesses more sheer seething intensity than anything he's ever done." Bangs compares what he hears as "screams of reed rage and African polyrhythms" to pianist Andrew Hill's *Compulsion* (1965) and drummer Max

Roach's *We Insist: Freedom Now Suite* (1960). Bangs notes about the latter, "Priester was on that album, too, and his playing is, if anything, more bitterly moving now than it was then."

The review concludes, however, in a manner that appreciates how successfully the album claims a musical middle ground:

> As beautiful as Hancock's past work is, it's really gratifying to see him moving in this direction, because this is the brand of black music which will probably be most crucial in the Seventies. And while neither of these albums is . . . extremely experimental nor as "commercial" (as in the current predilection for lame, preachy vocals) as much other current jazz, they're both intensely musical, solid and uplifting from stem to stern. We should be so lucky every day.

Bangs correctly situates *Mwandishi* as a vitally creative music of black America that had the potential of appealing to a broad audience were it marketed appropriately. The *New York Times* listed the recording *Mwandishi* as one of five new jazz recordings on November 21, 1971.[30] *Billboard* offered a brief promotional review of the new record, with this closing: "A broad appeal for this set because Hancock is a respected name for the rock crowd."[31] Warner Brother's disappointment that *Mwandishi* was not a more conventional recording was, in fact, a sign that the recording represented something new and exciting. Rather than retreating, Hancock and the band chose to further their exploratory trajectory, toward the recording of *Crossings*.

I think that the idea of color spectrum is one of the key elements in this band—with the percussion instruments that we use, with the various acoustic instruments that we play, and now with the addition of the synthesizer. . . . That really adds practically a total color spectrum. Almost from the beginning of this band we've been into sounds beyond the conventional note sounds of instruments. For example, the fact that I use Echoplex and a fuzz-wah pedal, and with the horns using harmonics. It just happened today that Mwile [Bennie Maupin] was making sounds by just hitting the keys of the flute and by humming the vocal sounds that he makes. There's just a whole spectrum of things that we can call on because of the scope of the music at this time.

HERBIE HANCOCK, 1973

7

Crossings

Crossings would prove to be a revolutionary work integrating performance and postproduction. Although Eddie Henderson recalls percussion overdubs, the initial studio recording was done in mid-February[1] as if it were a live session, on which few edits would be made in postproduction. For this reason, producer David Rubinson chose Pacific Recording Studios, San Mateo, California, because it had a larger sound console than Wally Heider's, where *Mwandishi* (1971) had been recorded.

While *Crossings* replicated the live technique used on *Mwandishi*, it also both represented a return to earlier jazz practice and mirrored many rock recordings. This was different from contemporaneous practice for pop recordings, which were increasingly compiled from separate, individual instrumental studio tracks. Also, as Rubinson recalls: "What I think separates *Crossings* for example from other recordings was that it wasn't done for the first time in the studio. We were recording the band live and I mean, everybody was there at the same time. Just like when we were playing [in concert settings]." The band was supplemented by Santana's conga player Victor Pontoja; a vocal choir was added later, using singers Vitoria Domagalski, Candy Love, Sandra Stevens, Della Horne, and Scott Beach.

Crossings thus differed from the heavily edited composite approach of Teo Macero's Miles Davis recordings. It is difficult to determine the true compositional credits for the tunes on Bitches Brew (1970) because Macero used the postproduction studio as a personal compositional instrument, blurring the lines between the actual recordings and the final product. In contrast, producer David Rubinson and engineer Fred Catero were equal partners with Herbie Hancock in all phases of production, as opposed to the "engineer and producer are totally in charge" model at Blue Note, CTI, and other jazz labels.

I wonder whether it was Crossings that ultimately led Davis to invite Hancock and Billy Hart to join in the sessions for On the Corner (1972), on June 1, 6, 12, and continuing on July 7, 1972. If Hancock was always listening closely to Davis, On the Corner shows that Davis was acutely aware of what was coming back. Certainly, Davis would have been attracted by the chemistry between Hancock and Hart, who believes that Davis, having attended several performances of the Mwandishi band, actively sought to emulate their sound: "We ended up doing On the Corner because Miles was coming to hear us." Hancock was one of three keyboard players, the other two being Chick Corea and Harold Williams. Hart's drumming was complemented by Jack De Johnette, Indian tabla player Badal Roy, and percussionists James Mtume and Don Alias.[2] As compelling as are the grooves, rhythmic multiplicity, and juxtapositions of material, to my ears, the uniformity of On the Corner is quite unlike the explosive, ever-changing qualities of the Mwandishi band during this period.

Crossings includes three compositions. Spanning the entirety of side one is an extended Herbie Hancock suite, "Sleeping Giant," the title referencing the continent of Africa. Side two includes two Bennie Maupin tunes, "Quasar" and "Water Torture."

"Sleeping Giant"

"Sleeping Giant" is an expansive suite, a series of improvisational sections organized around and separated by brief through-composed passages. The work opens with an ecstatic display of collective, multilayered percussion, intermixed with electronic sounding "granules" that swell and become ever more water-like. The pulse is often maintained by a clave and cowbell, around which the dense, polyrhythmic display unfolds amid Hart's solo drumming and the call-and-response, rise-and-fall of Hancock's electronically processed electric piano. An amorphous low, rumbling sound cluster slowly grows in volume, sonic complexity, and intensity,[3] a sonic eruption from which Hancock's expansive electric piano solo emerges.

Nearly five minutes in length, Hancock's solo is a remarkable display of improvisational invention, sparse at first, building on Buster William's pedal tones. Hancock builds his solo in waves, drawing on electronics to supplement his use of clusters, movement within and outside of tonality, and rhythmic accenting, to heighten tension, create holding patterns, then to release the tension. Hancock smudges and distorts the sound of the electric piano with Echoplex, pitch shifts, and tape feedback.[4] He alternates between strong syncopated chordal figures and extended chromatic lines, followed by melodic playing, sometimes culminating in octave tremolos.

Early in his solo, Hancock plays an assertive rhythmic figure in fourths and short chordal ostinati followed by more melodic playing. A dance unfolds between Hancock's continually rotating rhythmic patterns and Williams's ever-shifting pedal tones and spontaneously changing bass riffs. Each creates holding patterns that periodically find cadential release, only to begin again in a new direction, as if traversing a complex maze. Hancock's solo concludes with descending chord clusters that are treated with tape feedback. The clusters, groupings of notes closely knit yet not organized into recognizable chords, present an element of surprise and abandon, rendering the playing rhythmic yet abstract.

Example 10. "Sleeping Giant," 2:46–3:05

Example 11. "Sleeping Giant," 3:14ff

Example 12. "Sleeping Giant" cadential theme, 7:16ff

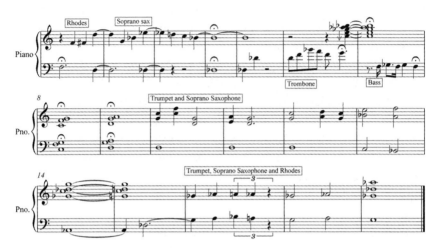

Example 13. "Sleeping Giant" lyrical melody, 7:46–9:15

Hancock segues out of this section with a cadential theme. leading into a lovely lyrical melody in the horns and electric piano, joined by bass and drums. The sections that follow include a Julian Priester trombone solo, an intense minute and a half–long funk jam built on rhythmically interlocking acoustic piano, fuzz electric bass, wah-wah electric piano, drums, and tambourine; a quiet horn chorale that returns us to the lyrical horn melody; ending with another cadential piano riff. Hancock's wah-wah heightens the call-and-response gospel feel of a brief electric piano solo, leading to a reprise of the lyrical horn choral.

Emerging from the fading final chord is Maupin's extended soprano saxophone solo, at first a duet with Williams and momentarily altered with reverberation and a slight delay. The solo grows in intensity by means of multiphonics,[5] tape delay, and stereo panning and later, an uptick in the tempo, when he is backed by funky electric piano comping, riffs, electronic effects, and wah-wah, before it is capped by the cadential melody. The suite comes to a close with a final return of the lyrical horn melody, the cadential figure, and a dissipation into abstraction, as Maupin's long tone and sparse echoed notes are joined by altissimo trumpet and trombone notes and breathy sounds floating across the horizon. The closing is the final in a long series of *Alice in Wonderland*-like in and out of the rabbit hole segues between contrasting moods and textures, and solos. The Hancock-Williams-Hart rhythm section masterfully provides the continuity needed for the lengthy work to function as a coherent whole, supporting each soloist to explore the rhythmic and melodic material as far as he wishes to take it. Electronic processing, part of Hancock's own live performance technique, and, for Hart and Maupin in postproduction, heightens the magical ride on which the band embarks.

I've always thought of the "Sleeping Giant" suite as abstract funk. I use the term "abstraction" to refer to the periodic movement between tonality and atonality, and between sounds with harmonic function and sounds used simply for their sonic qualities. (Abstraction is discussed in greater detail in chapter 2.) What remains constant is the presence of a beat as a common denominator, however complex and variable may be the rhythmic interplay. Regarding funk, as discussed in chapter 6, the ostinati, vamps, and use of wah-wah lend what we termed a "funky" feel to Hancock's piano playing. This highly syncopated, multilayered, rhythmically interlocking musical form plays off the downbeat, the *one*, unlike rhythm and blues, which emphasizes the backbeat (beats two and four). Hancock was introduced to funk by Miles Davis: "When we'd be hanging, I'd notice that Miles would have all these albums strewn about the room and lying on his bed,"[6] among them James Brown and Jimi Hendrix. Hancock "was fascinated by people like James Brown, once he did 'Papa's Got a Brand New Bag.'"[7] When producer David Rubinson began visiting Hancock's apartment on Riverside Drive in Manhattan in 1970, they, too, listened to records by Sly and the Family Stone, James Brown, and Tower of Power.

During the culturally and politically alive period of the late 1960s, funk emerged as more than just a musical form, but as an attitude, a sensibility. Rickey Vincent describes it as "an aesthetic of deliberate confusion, of uninhibited, soulful behavior that remains viable because of a faith in instinct, a joy of self, and a joy of life, particularly unassimilated black American life." "The implicit nature of The Funk, in its inherent *nastayness*, which cannot help but drive people closer to their funky soul, peels off the veneer of pretense and exposes the unpacked self for all to see."[8]

The adoption of funk elements was, for Hancock, an important part of listening to and reflecting the music and culture of the time. On "Sleeping Giant," he does so in a manner that simultaneously assimilates funk into his broader conception while reunderstanding the meaning of the whole package through the lens of this new sensibility. But a striking feature of Hancock's solos is the periodic movement between recognizable harmonic and melodic elements and abstract sounds. It is unusual to find these tendencies blended in the playing of a pianist. But here the two seem to coexist on the same plane, one used as material for the other. At times this integration is achieved with electronic processing, such as the Echoplex, introduced above, and pitch shifting. At other times, it is a function of Hancock's use of tone clusters in place of chords, blurring specific harmonic identity. In a sense, the clusters become purely rhythmic figures, while suggesting something amorphously chordal. At this stage in Hancock's development, the lines between harmony and atonality cease to matter.

A passage can show all the signs of a funk jam while its contents can be harmonically atonal. A melodic solo line can be chromatic and intuitive in its movement, yet meaningful within the context of the tune. Texture and harmony are weighted equally. Foreground and background, comping and soloing merge. Noise elements and musical tones coexist in the same space. Beauty becomes redefined as clarity of emotional expression. Musical substance takes on new meanings depending on the context. Like some of the most important music of Charles Mingus and Thelonious Monk, distinctions between avant-garde and idiomatic jazz, composition and improvisation, art music, and popular music are rendered meaningless. At its core, the music is music.

Patrick Gleeson Makes a Surprise Electronic Appearance

At this point in his musical evolution, Hancock was expanding his electric piano technique with the use of electronic pedals and devices in live performance. Tape delay and feedback and other effects were added in postproduction at Pacific Recorders studios. But following that, another round of postproduction took place at Different Fur Trading Company. This small studio in San Francisco was co-owned and operated by sound designer, producer, and synthesizer player Patrick Gleeson, with John Vierra. The results of this decision helped facilitate movement toward the greater integration of electronics in *Crossings* and for the future music of the band. The two tunes on side two of *Crossings* were complemented in postproduction by Gleeson's work.

Gleeson had been a literature professor at San Francisco State University, but found greater satisfaction and excitement composing electronic music. He developed his craft in the fertile creative environment of the San Francisco Tape Music Center, at that point housed at Mills College. Founded in 1962, this was a significant hub of creative, multimedia activity. Electronic music and multimedia composers Morton Subotnick and Pauline Oliveros, and visual artist Anthony Martin, were among the founding figures, joined by minimalist composers Terry Riley, Steve Reich, and others.[9] Gleeson composed on the Tape Music Center's Buchla Electronic Music box, an early analog synthesizer system developed by Donald Buchla, based on Morton Subotnick's conceptual ideas.

Gleeson began to compose for dancers who were members of choreographer Anna Halprin's company. They "hired me directly to write music for two different performance pieces. . . . I began experimenting with electronics, at first homemade conceptions of musique concrète." Gleeson, on track to jump with both feet into a studio career in electronic music and production, "cashed out my middle class life, went in halves on an early Moog III, and began presenting myself as a studio musician. . . . I met some art students, fell in love with one of them who introduced me to her friend John Vierra, who owned a small Moog, and some quite bad music was made over the next dozen years." This led to Gleeson and Vierra opening the Different Fur Trading Company.

David Rubinson remembers Gleeson's studio as "a tiny little place and I, knowing what I do, had bought the first bunch of hours from him, a blanket bunch of hours. I thought that I could do synthesizers over there. There was nobody in town who really knew how to do that, very few anyway." After initially working on relatively small projects, including Paul Kantner and Grace Slick of Jefferson Airplane fame,[10] Gleeson worked on a dozen recordings produced by Rubinson, mostly for rock musicians,[11] for which Rubinson purchased blocks of time in Gleeson's studio. Gleeson was making "some kind of plausible living," but his true musical loves were jazz, contemporary classical music, and funk.

The circumstances that brought Gleeson into the picture were seemingly happenstance, yet prescient. Hancock told Rubinson that he was interested in learning how to play synthesizer. Since Rubinson knew Gleeson's studio, Rubinson suggested that Hancock head over there. Gleeson recalls:

> Herbie told me that David said to him: "There's a guy I've been using for
> some little studio tasks. He's not really a musician, he's more a programmer,
> but he knows how to use the instrument. He's got a little studio in the Mis-
> sion [called Different Fur] and you can go over and see if you like anything
> he's doing. He can patch the Moog for you and you can play it." Herbie came
> over. Of course I was thrilled to death.

Neither Hancock nor Gleeson could anticipate what would ensue from this first meeting. Hancock came over with the recently made studio recordings of Maupin's "Quasar." Gleeson patched his massive Moog III synthesizer to create sounds that might be appropriate to overdub at a particular point. While Gleeson thought he was demonstrating how one might make use of the synthesizer, Hancock asked whether he was recording the results because he liked what he heard. Hancock made some suggestions and offered comments. This process continued for some time, until Hancock left Gleeson to continue working until he completed "Quasar." Gleeson remembers: "It just blew his mind. He had never heard anything like it; it was the beginning of a new era for him."

Excited about what he heard, Hancock said to Gleeson, as Gleeson recalls:

> "I'm going to get the rest of the album, and I'll be back." So he came back
> with "Water Torture." He left me alone for a while and he came back and
> that's when we added the Mellotron and the Chamberlain.[12] It was a situation
> where I wouldn't have presumed to do something chordal at that point in my
> career. I was an ignoramus [about that], I was intuitive; I mean, I had ears. He
> went upstairs to make a phone call. When he came back, I was preparing the
> Mellotron for him to do something. He said: "I like that. Do that." So I did
> that. And then he did some stuff and I recorded that. On "Quasar" there may
> have been actually times when there were three different performances on
> synths simultaneously. I think I may have bounced everything to stereo. I was
> worried about taking up too many tracks. There were only 16 tracks. It's funny
> thinking about the relative limitations of the technology of that era.

Gleeson did not overdub synthesizer on "Sleeping Giant," although "Herbie wanted me to, but they couldn't get the tapes. The studio wasn't open," so Hancock, with Gleeson present, limited his additions to the female singer overdubs.

Listening now to the two tunes on which Gleeson participated, particularly "Quasar," I am struck by the seamlessness of the additions. Gleeson approached the existing recorded music with great sensitivity. "If there was a place where the ensemble was in a group decrescendo and thinning out, I would come in there. I often came in at the ends of phrases. I would come in effectively doing a decrescendo." The recordings first heard by Gleeson included a large amount of empty space and quiet, which he believes were quite intentional and assumed the later addition of other sonic elements. Hancock "understood that David was going to do stuff and that it would be a different kind of production," which would be created within those spaces.

One finds an unusual musical symbiosis between Patrick Gleeson and Herbie Hancock. Clearly, Hancock's electronic treatment of his electric piano, and the postproduction techniques used by David Rubinson, paved the way toward a further exploration of electronic sounds. What Gleeson offered Hancock was a shared appreciation of new sounds that flowed from the extended techniques of the band's instrumentalists. Among them were Julian Priester's breathy sounds and altissimo range notes, Bennie Maupin's multiphonics, and Billy Hart's sizzling sonic palette. Only with very close listening can one clearly distinguish the instrumental sounds from the electronics. They show a deep sensitivity to sonic nuance. The completed work is as electroacoustic as it is acoustic. Gleeson's work is so deeply embedded within the texture and flow of the music that one seems to emerge from the other. There is a give and take, anticipation and response in the synthesizer parts that creates the sensation of live performance. In fact, it never occurred to me that it was not recorded live. And this is indeed where the group was ultimately headed, as Gleeson points out: "In our live performances] you really can't tell [whether a particular sound is me or one of the horn players]. And everybody sounds like a synthesizer."

Gleeson and Hancock shared a fascination with orchestral sounds, and Gleeson's electronic sounds were orchestral in scope. But Hancock was a keyboard virtuoso, and so his use of electronics reflected a pianist's sensibility and technique. Gleeson brought something quite different, the aesthetics of an orchestrator. The pairing between the two on *Crossings* is unparalleled.

"Quasar" and "Water Torture"

"Quasar" opens with stark chromatic acoustic piano chords, followed by a ghostly prefiguring of the tune's melody in long-tone altissimo horns and synthesizer, followed by wind-like synthesizer sounds. The melody is heard full

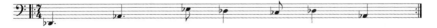

Example 14. Bass riff from "Quasar"

blown in the horns over a 7/4 bass riff. An atmospheric transitional section leads to a dramatic, angular flute solo, accompanied by walking bass and rapid, fluttering synthesizer tones and wind sounds. After a repetition of the 7/4 melody, Gleeson adds a multilayered tapestry of electronic sounds, joining Hancock's electric piano and the rhythm section, during Henderson's solo. Williams's bass line shifts several times, ultimately establishing a five-note riff (c-c-c-d-d). After a brief bass solo, "Quasar" concludes with a coda echoing the early "ghostly" passage, joining electric piano with overblown flute and, in the distance, fractured trombone multiphonics and fluttering synthesizer sounds, drifting into silence. A thin line separates what was first recorded as a spare instrumental work marked by nonconventional instrumental sounds and the completed tracks with synthesizer sounds overlaid by Gleeson. Overblown wind instruments, multiphonics, and breath sounds are matched by their electronic relations. The overall effect is one of collaboration, although the electronics were added following the conclusion of the studio recordings.

"Water Torture" begins with an intensely integrated mix of acoustic instruments and electronic sounds. The depth of the orchestration is best appreciated with a detailed description,[13] supported by a graphic score of the initial two minutes (see appendix). The piece begins with a largely electronic texture, wrapped around a spare percussion and flute improvisation. The irony, of course, is that the electronic sounds were overlaid on the recorded performance, which without the additions might have represented the core of the opening two minutes. Vocal sounds were also added as part of the composite mix, and the various elements were spatialized in postproduction using stereo panning.

After 1:00, a pulse begins; a minute later, this continued beat in the hi-hat provides the backdrop for the introduction of the main melody by bass clarinet and electric piano. The melody is repeated twice and concludes with a dramatic shattering of calm by the trumpet and trombone. The melody-repetition-horn burst pattern will reappear twice more during the performance, creating what might be a symmetrical A-B-A-C-A-D form were the interludes solos or "verses" at all predictable in shape, duration, and texture.

After the melody concludes, the band embarks on a several-minute pastiche of textures, including electronic pulses, electric piano glissandi, delayed trumpet, pointillistic playing, and sustained chords, which were added in postproduction on a Mellotron and Chamberlain. Trumpet and synthesizer gestures prepare for the reintroduction of the melody, which follows the pattern described above. A collective free improvisation at 4:30 opens the door to a trumpet solo. A brief alternate theme is played by string sounds on the Mellotron, just before 6:00, returning again to the melody, the outburst extended this time by additional instruments.

Another free improvisation takes place after 7:00, and here, Hancock again displays the "abstract funk" found in "Sleeping Giant" in his not-infrequently atonal, wah-wah electric piano playing, which is simultaneously comping and solo. Maupin adds abstract, angular melodies in his upper registers at 8:30, joined by occasional sound gestures by his compatriots. A transitional improvisational section, featuring Mellotron, synthesizer, and other instruments, leads to a coda. The coda centers around a melancholy melody on Mellotron, punctured by horn spikes, a repeated bass note, additional sustained Mellotron chords, and slow angular melodies. Various instruments move in and out of the closing texture, joined by crystalline synthesizer sounds. The timbral focus of the somber conclusion brings us full circle to the highly electronic opening.

Maupin's pair of compositions provides a fascinating contrast in works that alternate through-composed material with effective improvisational vehicles. The dramatic gestures that open "Quasar" are followed by a lilting bass riff and melody that introduce an unpredictable series of improvisational settings. Williams's bass lines play an important role in shaping their direction. In "Water Torture," the percussion and electronics prepare the way to the tune's recurrent theme, around which are wrapped improvisations that travel far afield. Gleeson's synthesizer additions to "Water Torture," following the opening two minutes, are far subtler than his interpolations on "Quasar" because the instrumental tracks for "Water Torture," recorded earlier, were more active and full. Gleeson's choice was to add color and texture to the already diverse and full panoply of collective improvisation.

David Rubinson, Electronic Sensibilities, and Studio Techniques

Herbie Hancock's adoption of the Fender Rhodes electric piano, then expanded by a series of sound- and texture-altering electronic processors, led to the Mwandishi band's gradual but increasing move toward electronics. Producer David Rubinson introduced Hancock to tape studio techniques in postproduction, beginning on the band's first recording, *Mwandishi*, and more substantially on *Crossings*. Only in retrospect can we see that the addition of synthesizer interpolations by Patrick Gleeson to music that was already highly textural would lead to Gleeson joined the touring band, and a fuller incorporation of electronics into the band's musical vocabulary. Gleeson's mark on the band became quite distinct, urging it forward in its path of sonic exploration.

By 1972, the period of *Crossings*, Hancock had traveled quite a distance in his expansion of the electric piano with electronic processing. This recording extends the techniques and sonic complexity of *Mwandishi* and then moves a giant step further toward the use of electronics to build a sonic landscape. On reflection, Gleeson realizes that something novel had taken place, but maybe not one that could be easily replicated. "There was no precedent for that production. But no one had done a rock record like that, even King Crimson. [When listening in 2008] I was really surprised at the sound of *Crossings*. It was even more revolutionary in retrospect than it seemed at the time. Of course, I always assumed this was just the beginning, that the whole thing would just get better and better." The increasingly electronic profile of the band's recordings reflected Hancock's evolving understanding of how the studio could be used as a compositional instrument and a fuller realization of his integration of timbre, harmony, and orchestration. It also reflected producer Rubinson's input and encouragement.

Rubinson had built a reputation on producing rock bands, but he had become acquainted with experimental traditions in electronic music while working at Columbia Records:

> I was really into electronic music, not just as rock and roll, but as what they call classical, contemporary American electronic music. You know, the Columbia-Princeton Electronic Music [Center] laboratories [for example, Vladimir Ussachevsky]. I became aware of it when I started working, earlier with the people who later formed the band The United States of America, through Joe Bird, but I was really eclectic, I liked a lot of different things. I had been up to [Robert Moog's factory in] Trumansburg; I had seen the original Moog synthesizer. I knew [of] Buchla on the West coast.

United States of America's 1967 song "Hard Coming Love," produced by Rubinson, is an early example of the use of the Moog synthesizer in a textural and largely nonmelodic manner. His production of the Chambers Brothers' song "Time Has Come Today," also in 1967, shows how Rubinson integrated echo and tape feedback within the context of a rock tune, a skill that would prove

significant in the production of *Mwandishi* and the two Herbie Hancock recordings that followed. For Rubinson, reflecting back on that first production
project with Hancock, recording could be "a form of expression unique unto
itself—not merely a physical-mechanical means of storing a performance—
but utilizing the tape as the substance of the performance. The recording process was an art form in itself."[14]

Although in jazz, recording was generally defined as a process of documentation, not composition, a new, very different idea was emerging in the world
of early rock music that drew on innovations that originated in 1950s European radio studios. There, pioneering electronic music composers were using the studio as the center of compositional, not documentary work. Among
these techniques were means of changing and distorting recorded sounds
by reversing the direction of a recording tape, altering its playback speed,
generating sound electronically, and modulating them with other electronic
sounds.

In the United States, the development of the multitrack recorder allowed
musicians to overdub their work, shifting the balance between performance
and nonreal-time recording. The final product could be a composite of material recorded in multiple recording sessions, expanded even further with postproduction techniques borrowed from electronic music. The idea that studio
and compositional techniques from electronic music could be translated into
rock postproduction captivated Rubinson: "In the modern way of recording,
post-production was as important. . . . The technology was there for us to use
as we see fit . . . all of this could be incorporated into my music." Musicologist
Albin Zak has traced the evolution of studio music production as an art form
during the 1950s.[15]

These types of practices had not yet entered the classical music world.
With the exception of the relatively conservative tape editing that Teo Macero had done with Miles Davis's recordings prior to a substantial shift on
In a Silent Way (1969) and *Bitches Brew* (1970), it was not part of the culture of Columbia Records. Rubinson realized that "they weren't going to
let me do any creative work in the console. The union would say 'you can't
touch the board.' Many people would say 'are you joking, that's impossible;
get out of here!'" For his work with the Mwandishi band, "mixing and post
production—studio technique—had become a key element, a performer itself. But we did long 'live' takes, so there was both a group consciousness and
a cohesiveness, shocks and surprises together with the multilayered textures

from post production. This was a very rock and roll technique, and Herbie used the mix as an instrument."[16]

Rubinson's process was quite different from Macero, who reported:

> I had carte blanche to work with the material. I could move anything around and what I would do is record everything, right from beginning to end, mix it all down and then take all those tapes back to the editing room and listen to them and say: "This is a good little piece here, this matches with that, put this here," etc. and then add in all the effects—the electronics, the delays and overlays. . . . [I would] be working it out in the studio and take it back and re-edit it—from front to back, back to front and the middle somewhere else and make it into a piece. I was a madman in the engineering room.[17]

Macero recorded almost every session like a performance, but, unlike Rubinson, later cut and paste elements of various performances to assemble a final product. Recently released "complete" studio recordings from those sessions offer a window into that process by allowing us to hear the unedited versions. Musicians who participated in the *Bitches Brew* sessions couldn't recognize their performances when they heard the recording after its release, due to Macero's use of tape editing, which determined the final shape of Davis's compositions as we have come to know them. Rubinson and Hancock's approach on *Crossings* was to largely maintain the integrity of the studio recordings and build on that, working together as musical collaborators.

Other members of the Mwandishi band were present for at least portions of postproduction, but not involved in a significant way. Rubinson recalls welcoming their input, but band members seemed generally uninterested. Eddie Henderson notes: "For all this aspect of it, I had no contact with it at all. With the editing, the mixing . . . when I finished playing the last note on the record, that was it for me." Buster Williams adds:

> Sometimes [I was aware that postproduction was taking place], but most of the time not, because Herbie was the gadget man. And he had all of this knowledge of [technological matters]; it seemed like a lot of knowledge because we didn't have it. And I wasn't interested in all that. I was just trying to play the bass. So I must say that when I would listen to things after it was all done, I was surprised what I was hearing.

In some ways this lack of involvement is unsurprising, given the historically rigid wall maintained between performers and producers/engineers, limiting artistic control to the producer, and the view of many jazz musicians that what matters is the moment of performance. It is difficult to separate these two issues.

The change Rubinson sought required a shift in the balance between musician and record company. This was an emerging idea in the rock world, but "[less so in jazz, where] the musicians were grist for the mill, and had little or no control or participation in the creative process of post-production or mixing, as little as there was of that then."[18] In working with Hancock and others, Rubinson sought to afford musicians greater control and involvement in the production of their records.

The Mwandishi band, however musically collective, was not an economically cooperative organization (a topic that is discussed in chapters 9 and 11). It was Herbie Hancock's band, and Rubinson was responding, as a producer within a more commercial world than those in which most collectives have operated:

> The structure of the record business is basically a plantation where the white guys ran the record business and the studios. When you went to record an album for Frank at Blue Note, you did it his way. And you went to Rudy van Gelder's studio, his way. And a lot of the impulse, a lot of the great creativity of a lot of musicians could never really reach their fullest expression because they were left out of half the recording process. With them, the recording session ended when they finished playing and then Rudy or somebody, one engineer or the other would say "OK, guys, we'll send you a reference [recording]" and everybody would go home and that would be it."

In response, Rubinson sought to operate in a different way, one that was closer to rock music production:

> There was no apartheid rule. There was no plantation. I mean, there were royalties working for the man, but creatively, the musicians in my life came and they went freely and they contributed to the whole process. They were there for the recording, they were there for the editing, they were there for the post-production, for the mixing, mastering, I mean it was all part of the creative process.

For Rubinson, Hancock, a musician captivated by technology and eager to embrace new sounds and new techniques, was the perfect find. And Rubinson offered Hancock a first opportunity to fully participate in the fruits of these opportunities:

> What really happened with Herbie was that his creativity was exposed to the entire creative process of making records and making music. He was insightful and he just opened up like a flower . . . and expressed himself in the whole process. . . . It increased his palette of colors and effects. And the basic, the most important thing was that he could participate in how it was going to be used, how it was done, how he could set up, the effects he has. . . . Then when we got to the post-production and we were in the mix-down and he was part of it, he just went "oh my God, there's power . . . this incredible power is available." And he exercised all and expressed himself in the whole process, not just coming in, playing his stuff, packing up his bags and leaving the mixing to the plantation owners to do with it as they will. And I think that was really the beginning of the explosion of his creativity.

Still, this was an early point in the development of music studio technology. Rubinson recalls the scene:

> We had tape loops running around the room. This was in the days before you could do sampling. You can't tell, but there's some sampling on this record, but it's done by putting an endless loop and running it around the mic poles. And, you know, cables and stuff so that it would not be as clearly repetitive, but we had . . . So what we were doing, we were trying to expand everything we could do at that time. You know, we did it with a lot of backwards stuff, just breaking ground, whatever it took.

Marketing *Crossings* and the Critical Response

Selling the new recording *Crossings* to the marketing executives at Warner Brothers was not an easy task. Rubinson recalls that he was able to persuade Warner to support the band's direction only by pointing out the recent commercial success of Miles Davis's *Bitches Brew*: "I brought in a 7 1/2″ tape of side-two of *Bitches Brew* so that the marketing executives could see that a recording in a similar vein could sell if appropriately promoted." "To my amazement, when I put on *Bitches Brew*, they thought it was the new Herbie Hancock LP! They had no idea it was Miles Davis. They expressed that the music had very limited commercial potential—and that they really didn't know what to do with it. I was then able to tell them that what they were listening to was an album that had been riding high on the *Billboard* charts!"[19]

The packaging was designed by artist Robert Springett, who had created posters for Fillmore music halls. It emphasizes an African or a Caribbean oceanic motif. White-cloaked older black men stand on two boats, one to the right in the foreground and the other in the center, named the *Dominique*. Squatting to the left on a rock is a young man. Craggy hills are in the distance, and large fish appear to be swimming in the foreground. Visual perspective and the line between representation and abstraction are blurred, offering a visual analog to the music. Abstractions of band member images taken by photographer Anne Foreman grace the inside cover, which opens into a double fold.

The electric nature of the band suggested the potential of its marketing within the world of rock music. In popular culture, electronics were associated with rock music and with the music business. This association proved problematic for band members. Emblematic of this was the marketing placement of the Mwandishi recording *Crossings* on its release in late April 1972.[20] An advertisement for the Sam Goody record store chain in the *New York Times* includes a grid of records. An image of the *Crossings* African-themed album cover sits in between Frank Sinatra's *Greatest Hits* (vol. 2) and folk singer Arlo Guthrie's *Hobo's Lullaby*. Immediately below are Randy Newman's *Sail Away*, Van Dyke Parks's *Discover America*, and Grateful Dead rhythm guitarist Bob Weir's *Ace*. Below that is depicted a new two-LP set by the Beach Boys. On top of the page is trumpeted the rubric "Great Sounds by Great Artists," but the message conveyed is that *Crossings* was a pop album, in the company of rock and pop musicians.[21]

An image of *Crossings* is included within a similar roster of new albums in a display ad for various labels in *Billboard* magazine. There, the album was described as "modern instrumental ear-openers by the most honored pianist in pop music. A must."[22] A promotional review in *Billboard* holds: "Herbie Hancock's compositions on this release are, in the purest sense of the word, a 'Crossing.' The innovative conjunction of electronic sounds and standard instruments has leaned to the dramatic with intensity unrivaled by modern jazzists. The imagery is undeniably real and the jazz all Hancock."[23] *Billboard* magazine suggested that the LP was receiving airplay on college radio stations, such as WGSU-FM at the State University of New York at Geneseo.[24] In Washington, D.C., WVVS-FM's Bill Tullis and WHUR-FM's Andre Perry reported playing "Quasar" and "Crossings."[25] Still, it became quickly and abundantly clear to Warner Brothers that the Sextet was not about to create the commercial music they sought. As a result, Rubinson relates, "They were good enough to let [Hancock] leave the label."

Some jazz critics responded harshly to the record *Crossings*, particularly its reliance on interplay between musicians. Pete Welding complained: "The chief defect of the performance is, I feel, its discontinuity, lack of any feeling of flow or inevitability; nor is there much in the way of true rapport among the players as they execute this music. And that's the real kernel here: they execute rather than spontaneously genuinely create. There is no significant degree of interaction of the sort that would bring this music alive; this is only superficially free or free-type music. The freedom is illusory."[26] Clearly not a fan of this band, Welding continues: "Hancock could learn quite a bit by studying his own records: that he hasn't is evidenced by the fact that this album suffers from the same basic conceptual defects as did its predecessor, *Mwandishi*: Too much of the wrong kind of control by Hancock." Welding also adds with a bizarre sexualized interpretation:

> Hancock's ambitious *Sleeping Giant*, occupying all of the first side, is to my ears a 25-minute exercise in disconnected foreplay. He and his fellows spend a few moments tickling one area, switch abruptly to another for titillation, fondle it for a while, then move on to a new one, and so on throughout the piece. It never coheres, near climaxes—unless one considers Hart's final drum explosion climax enough, though it's more on the order of a premature ejaculation, over before it actually starts, and then peters out to silence. The performance's best moments, brief at that, are cops from *In a Silent Way*, which will give you an idea of just how daring this work is. All tease and no action.

Welding saved his most open hostility for the electronics, what he termed the "freaky, eerie sequences of 'spacey' effects laid into a matrix of lush Les Baxter-like exotica . . . plenty of empty, overdramatic bluster—the most obnoxious kind of speciously trippy music. . . . The less said about the synthesizer effects, the better." These stereotypic descriptions of synthesizer sounds may have reflected a general negativity to electronics in jazz. Certainly, the timbral focus was new to listeners who believed that acoustic instruments were the exclusive province of jazz and that structure should follow the head-solo forms of post-bebop. I personally find it difficult to align these comments with the depth of nuance and musicality to be found within the actual recording, although a similarly negative reaction to the use of synthesizer, cited earlier, was reported by critics responding to Weather Report's second recording, *I Sing the Body Electric* (1972).

Bennie Maupin responds to these kinds of comments:

> Regardless of what people said, I said, "You can say what you want about it." Guys [in the press and other jazz players] were really harsh in their assessment of what it was. I think they were intimidated because it wasn't something they knew. They weren't close enough to it to embrace it, and a lot of guys close enough to embrace it didn't because they thought they were going to lose something. The thinking was so distorted, so convoluted.[27]

Patrick Gleeson recalls: "At first there was an unbelievable amount of nit-picking and resentment about it [reactions to the synthesizer overdubs on *Crossings*] in the 'jazz community.'" In response, Gleeson continues: "One thing that's been a long time coming is the understanding that you can actually improvise on a track that's already been recorded, i.e., (1) it's still improvising and (2) it's OK to do it. Remember that the 'Jazz Police' went nuts when they 'caught' Miles overdubbing his solos. Idiotic."

A United Press International syndicated article, "The Year 1972: Good for Discs," however, briefly notes four very diverse recordings that demonstrate "record companies didn't seem to believe jazz is dead because they produced a good crop of albums, the best among them being . . . *Crossings*."[28]

Figure 1. Herbie Hancock at the Monterey Jazz Festival, September 16, 1972.
Copyright © photo 2011 by Veryl Oakland.

Figure 2. Herbie Hancock at the Monterey Jazz Festival, September 16, 1972.
Copyright © photo 2011 by Veryl Oakland.

Figure 3. Herbie Hancock at the Monterey Jazz Festival, September 16, 1972.
Copyright © photo 2011 by Veryl Oakland.

Figure 4. Herbie Hancock at the Monterey
Jazz Festival, September 16, 1972.
Copyright © photo 2011 by Veryl Oakland.

Figure 5. Herbie Hancock with Fender Rhodes
and, on top of acoustic piano, kalimba,
small instruments, and electronic devices.
At Montmartre, in Copenhagen, Denmark,
July 24, 1971. Photograph © Jan Persson.

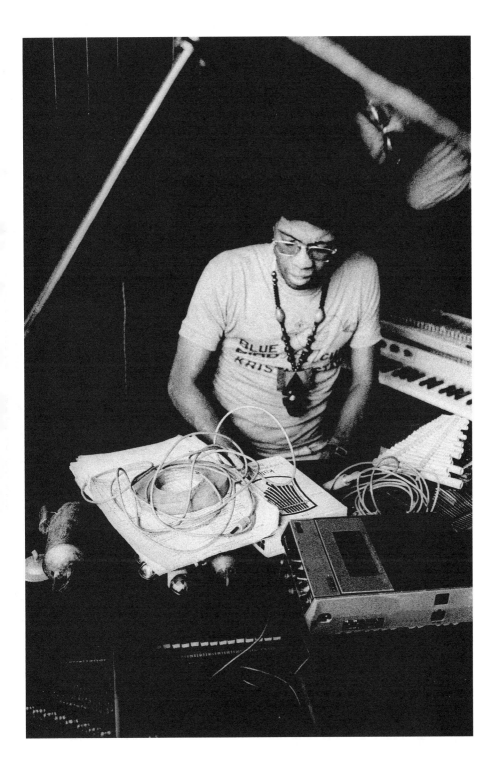

Figure 6. Performance on the PBS television program *Soul!*, October 13, 1971.
From left: Herbie Hancock, Buster Williams, Bennie Maupin, Billy Hart, Eddie Henderson, and Julian Priester. Photographer unknown. From the personal collection of Max Schleuter.

Figure 7. The band in 1973. *From left*, Billy Hart, Patrick Gleeson, Eddie Henderson, Buster Williams, Herbie Hancock, Bennie Maupin; *front row*, Julian Priester. Photograph by Don Nguyen. From the personal collection of Nashira Priester.

Figure 8. Reunion performance at the Newport Jazz Festival, Carnegie Hall, New York, June 29, 1976. Photographer: Tom Copi/Michael Ochs Archives/Getty Images.

Figure 9. Album cover, *Crossings*.

Figure 10. Album cover, *Sextant*.

Hancock's is listening music, not dance music, although anyone who has been swept up by its irresistible power cannot help but fantasize flowing figures in free-dance floating to the free-blown sounds.

PHILIP ELWOOD, 1973

8

Quadraphonic Sound System
Patrick Gleeson on Tour and Sextant

Fundi and the Quadraphonic Sound System

As the Mwandishi band's sounds grew increasingly electric and then electronic, it became clear that jazz venue sound systems were inadequate to the task. This complaint was voiced in the press by critic Vic Field, after a late May 1972 show at the Whiskey-a-Go-Go in Los Angeles.[1] It was time to take action and around this time, Herbie Hancock while in Europe purchased a raft of serious sound equipment. Billy Bonner, the band's road manager and driver, who was known by his Swahili first name Fundi, assumed the responsibilities of sound engineer. Fundi had appeared on the 1969 album *Kawaida* playing wooden flute and percussion. Hancock himself also handled some of the driving and gear handling. Hauling one's own gear from city to city and setting it up for every show was not for the faint or weary, particularly when the equipment was as sophisticated and substantial as what the band required. As pianist Victor Lewis recalls: "The band members were all schlepping their stuff themselves. They had Fundi helping, but they didn't have roadies. . . . This was certainly some early dues-paying for Herbie, who would roll up his sleeves and like the rest of the band, assemble their stuff."

Melody Maker described the $13,000 of sound equipment as "invaluable, and gave them the best sound quality and balance of any jazz or rock group I've ever heard."[2] Pat Metheny remembers hearing the effect of the Quad sound system in Kansas City, Missouri: "It was incredible then, and would be incredible now. It was so far ahead of the curve that no one has ever really done it since. It was a timeless way of doing something that just happened to be really modern." Critic Philip Elwood remarked on the obvious when he wrote:

> Identifying Hancock's ensemble as an octet is intentional, although only seven artists are on stage. An extended definition is needed since Hancock's quadrasonic sound engineer, named Fundi, is as important to the group's pro- duced sound (or perhaps more important) than the stage-dwelling traditional instrumentalists within the ensemble. Fundi controls an impressive Maezzi- built panel (from Italy) that looks like a surrealistic cigarette dispenser, and balances the sound pouring from the stage through Hancock's own four- speaker amplification system.[3]

Fundi's soundboard included quadraphonic pans and an Echoplex, which allowed him to radically change the nature of the sound mix. Fundi thus re- ally did assume a role as a member of the band. Onaje Allan Gumbs recalls that at a 1972 concert in Buffalo, Fundi "did sound effects and everything. Since there wasn't a lot of electronics happening on the bandstand [aside from Hancock; Gumbs doesn't recall Patrick Gleeson at this concert], Fundi did it from the soundboard. For instance, Eddie [Henderson] might play a note and Fundi would press a knob for echo. It was like he had ESP with the band." Billy Hart adds: "He could throw the band into echo whenever he wanted . . . a guy could take a solo and all of the sudden his whole environment would change. . . . He could actually change your whole psychological thing by doing that if you were vulnerable. We all liked it. It was like: 'wow!' It was like some movies you have today. All of the sudden, it depends upon your imagination, you were in a whole new environment." Fundi's role was quite distinct from

Gleeson's. While Fundi spatialized the sound and added electronic processing to the acoustic instruments, Gleeson was himself an instrumentalist, albeit one who played electronic instruments. Both contributed different elements to the overall sound design of the band.

Patrick Gleeson Joins the Road Band on Synthesizer

Hancock's decision to bring Patrick Gleeson into the mix was audacious. Electronics had clearly been on Hancock's mind and reflected an evolution of his sonic concept. In Hancock's hands, the electric piano had already become a malleable electronic instrument, and driver/sound technician Fundi's role was expanding into treating all the instrumentalists' sounds as malleable, all an extension of Hancock's perspective that all sounds could be part of a larger sonic tapestry.

Gleeson's involvement on *Crossings* (1972) was serendipitous, but Hancock's decision to invite the synthesizer player to join the band was even further-reaching in its implications. Hancock was clearly pleased with the results of his collaboration with Gleeson and the new direction it represented. It was an answer to something Hancock had been seeking, even as its specific manifestation came as a surprise. Gleeson's gift was the ability to neatly expand on and embed electronic sounds within the existing timbral depth and emphasis of the band. Hancock's next step on returning home from touring Europe was to invite Gleeson to go on the road as a member of the Sextet.

The newly expanded Mwandishi band, now a septet with the addition of Gleeson and further augmented by Fundi at the soundboard, played its first shows during a weeklong stand at the Village Vanguard in New York, the scene of Hancock's original Sextet premiere in November 1968. These shows most likely took place in early May 1972.[4] Gleeson recalls that Miles Davis and Davis's collaborator, composer/arranger Gil Evans, were in the audience. Evans invited Gleeson over to his apartment a few times that week to listen to recordings of the shows and discuss how they went. "One thing [Gil] said, obvious now but not to me then, was that sometimes he'd have trouble thinking of what to play, and so when that happened he'd just stop and listen, and pretty soon, listening to the guys playing, he'd find he was playing again. That was a lifesaver." Hancock also helped mentor Gleeson. Certainly, it was one thing to learn how to improvise on the synthesizer, but quite another matter improvising with such high-level musicians.

In 1972, there was no existing paradigm for Gleeson to follow in performing electronic instruments live with a jazz ensemble. He was not playing melodic lines that drew on historical acoustic instruments, as in Wendy Carlos's *Switched on Bach* (1968). His aesthetic was equally different from jazz pianist Paul Bley's "Synthesizer Show," and progressive rock musician Keith Emerson, who had pioneered his own distinct orchestral and virtuosic approach with the band Emerson, Lake, and Palmer. Nor was he playing exclusively abstract electroacoustic music, like John Eaton's works on Paul Ketoff's Synket. What Gleeson was attempting to do was create real-time sound design on an orchestral scale, often using noise elements, and doing so within an improvisatory jazz context. But how does one do that with a synthesizer that wasn't being played in the manner of a keyboard instrument?

There was no simple solution to the most obvious question: What kind of instrument could be taken on the road? Hancock describes Gleeson's reaction when first broached with the idea: "He said, 'Travel with a band?' I said, 'I know, it's never been done.' There had been no jazz groups with synthesizer players. . . . [T]his was before programmable synthesizers, so he could only do weird bleeps and squawks and a lot of white noise things. Because it wasn't programmable, how were you to move from one sound to the next while the music was still going?"[5]

Analog synthesizers of the time, such as Gleeson's Moog III, were modular, meaning the instrument was actually the sum of multiple electronic devices. These included oscillators that generated waveforms, filters that gave further coloration to the sounds, and envelope generators, which shaped how quickly the sound began, how long it was sustained, and the ramp-down of its decay. They were also designed as voltage control devices, meaning that individual modules were controlled using variable voltages, set either manually using knobs or by other modules. A low-frequency oscillator, for instance, could send silent, periodic, slowly rising and falling voltages (control voltage) to subtly influence the frequency of an oscillator. The oscillator whose sound the listener heard was being controlled, very slightly rising and falling in pitch (vibrato) in response to the control oscillator.

Interconnections between modules were usually achieved using plug-in cables called patch cords, but newer live performance instruments were coming onto the market, among them the Arp 2600 and Mini-Moog, whose connections were largely hard wired. The sum of all of the often-complex interconnections and the settings on each module's knobs and sliders were called patches. The Arp allowed additional performer flexibility by offering the option of designer patches, the ability to overwrite internal connections using patch chords. The Arp 2600 was certainly far more portable and simpler to program on the fly than the Moog III installed in the studio, and it fit into a carrying case. The physical layout of the instrument was easy to follow, modules grouped together by function. Patch chords, ubiquitous on Moog synthesizers prior to the Mini-Moog, were optional, contributing to making rapid, intuitive decisions about sound design. Sliders were easy to access.[6]

But, as Hancock pointed out, interconnections between modules could not be stored on analog devices (since they communicated using voltage rather than data, as in today's digital devices). Every time a knob was moved or a patch cord changed, the settings changed. The sonic texture of the band's music could change suddenly, and Gleeson had only two hands and two feet. He thus augmented his setup with simpler electronic processors, an Echoplex and a wah-wah pedal, similar to those used by Hancock on his Fender Rhodes. These could easily and dramatically alter the sounds of what he was playing. He occasionally used a simpler synthesizer, an Arp Pro-Soloist.

Gleeson developed his synthesizer performance technique through experimentation and steadily grew in proficiency at approximating patches on the fly. Improvisation was the order of the day, as Gleeson remembers:

> In performance I usually just tried to clear my mind, then go wherever my hands or an impulse led me. Planning was pretty much out of the question anyway, except maybe general ideas associated with the heads of tunes. When things were going well I really couldn't have told you why I plugged this patch-cord in there or what exactly the result was going to be when I then raised the slider associated with it. I did have some confidence that it was going to be within the range of acceptability, and then I just dealt with it.

Pat Metheny recalls his fascination with Gleeson's technique during a stand at the Landmark in Kansas City:

> The tech was all so crude at that point I am kind of amazed [Gleeson] got anything at all to work! I remember him spending most of the breaks setting up patches that would kind of do one thing and then there would be another fairly long setup time to get to something else. But it was all really hip and interesting to me. It was the first time I had ever even seen a synth in person.

Gleeson's Electronic Sounds Enter the Live Mix

Gleeson's sonic conception matched Hancock's ideas during this period, interrelating harmony and timbre. Gleeson developed a connection between chordal harmony and the construction of complex electronic waveforms. "Just intuitively, I related that information to analog synthesis, especially FM and AM modulation and filtering." In sum, Gleeson created complex sounds with unusually rich harmonic components,[7] as he puts it: "You get a feeling of complexity, a kind of vague allusiveness and richness that's hard to achieve any other way short of the intelligent use of a full orchestra. You sense the 'pitchness,' but there's more."[8] At times, Gleeson would use sounds with a great degree of noise to contrast with the pitched sounds played by other members of the band. His sounds complemented and were set off from Hancock's electric piano, even when the piano was electronically altered.

Gleeson's playing was incorporated into nearly every tune in the band's set list, including Hancock's acoustic jazz standards such as "Maiden Voyage," the only exception being "Toys." "[In my performances on] 'Maiden Voyage,' I was trying for [Claude Debussy's orchestral work] La Mer, to be perfectly frank, something slightly vague, delicate, amorphous but compelling." A February 1973 live recording from the Strata Gallery in Detroit shows Gleeson comping behind the horns stating the melody to Buster William's "Firewater." He then comps behind the trumpet solo, using a sculpted band of white noise. This particular sound became a Gleeson signature texture.[9]

Two 1973 performances of the tune "You'll Know When You Get There," the first at the Strata Gallery in late February and the second a month later at a show called the Jazz Workshop in Boston, provide contrasting examples of how Gleeson's electronic sonic textures were thoroughly integrated into the overall group improvisations and sound. Since these performances were never officially released on recordings, I offer detailed musical description to impart the flavor of the full integration of electronics into the band's sound.

The performance at the Strata Gallery begins with an atmospheric opening; an angular rhapsodic flute solo is placed above wind-like white noise from the synthesizer, altissimo range trombone sounds, and little percussion. The combined texture has an electronic feel, particularly when, shortly after 3:30, the trumpet and trombone add sustained sounds using extended techniques. Among these are the player blowing through the instrument to produce air sounds, breath and embouchure control to produce ultrasonic sounds, and carefully controlled intonation to locate microtonal pitches. Bowed bass adds to this quiet, spare, and static texture. The acoustic and electronic instruments join to create a unified body of sound. Around 5:30, Hancock adds delicate tinkling-sounding electric piano patterns and chords, which transition into the tune. This is followed by a trumpet solo that begins quietly, within the continued context of a spare sound environment. Synthesizer white noise returns as the trumpet solo builds, around 13:00 and soon after.

Later in the performance, shortly after 33:00, Gleeson's synthesizers appear, first with sustained pitched tones and then with portamenti, responding to Maupin. Gleeson follows this with plucked string sounds that echo the flute, and then a quiet roar that moves across the sound field. A breathy sound cloud and then, noise gestures accompany the continuing flute solo. Abstract sounds are next shaped into gestures, providing an unusual backdrop for the lyrical flute solo, which is joined by a continuing series of haunting, atonal low-register electric piano chords. The combination of Hancock's quasi-atonal chords and Gleeson's swirling sounds set a dark, suspicious mood.

As 36:30 approaches, Maupin brings the emotional tone back to earth with another cadenza-like episode that directly references the melody; a few seconds later Hancock challenges that grounding. He adds more swirls on the Echoplexed electric piano, imitated by Maupin and joined by Gleeson's abstract nonpitched noise gestures moving through space. Maupin responds by playing breathy sounds in rapid-fire phrases, on which Hancock picks up by playing strongly attacked clusters with maximal echo. The drama of this section stands in marked contrast to the prevailing calm.

The sound textures then become less electronic, as the flute solo becomes more lyrical. After a while, a somber duet with Williams ensues, with a hint of wind-like sounds by Gleeson, right before Hancock reappears shortly after 39:30. The flute solo winds down, now joined by the bass, a duet, spiced by some electronics. After the return of the refrain and melody, a brief trumpet coda closes out the piece, joined by a freely improvising horn choir and low-register, breathy electronic sounds. Gleeson's role in this performance is largely textural. He adds layers of mist and clouds to help shape an ethereal environment.

At the Jazz Workshop in Boston, the tune opens with a thirty-second free improvisation that opens with alto flute and high-pitched Theremin-like electronic sounds and altissimo horns, which lead into the playing of the melodic theme. Although brief, the spare atmospheric textures are similar in kind to those found throughout the Detroit performance. Electronic sounds reenter shortly before 6:30, adding to a dense texture behind Henderson's swirling trumpet solo. This solo picks up on the pulse right after 7:00, soon quietly joined by more electronic sounds and a hushed, rhythmic chord ostinato on electric piano. Gleeson answers one of Henderson's figures with a brief rattling sound burst, repeated four more times during the ensuing minute. Henderson plays short phrases that toy with the beat, on and off. Close to nine minutes into the performance, Gleeson offers a longer sound phrase that glissandos upward and bursts with higher-frequency sound components, taking on a slightly rhythmic feel. Then, Gleeson plays a nasal-sounding phrase that descends and re-ascends; the drumming takes on a higher level of energy and additional levels of activity. Gleeson again joins in, touching down at lower frequencies, with a greater degree of noise components, during which Henderson plays an extended phrase that winds around three or four adjacent pitches, inviting a drum roll closing in on 10:00, followed by more soloistic drumming, to which Gleeson adds all sorts of sounds and slurps.

Hancock's comping sounds soon become funkier, on top of which is layered a sustained electric organ chord mass (maybe Gleeson's Arp Pro-Soloist), which swirls and fades. Additional electronic sounds briefly appear twice during the following thirty seconds. At 11:30, the synthesizer sounds become ethereal, but melodic, rising slowly and unsteadily, with echo. Then they suddenly rise higher, filtered to emphasize the higher-frequency components for the next fifteen seconds, which Gleeson follows with additional filtered noise. The performance continues without electronics, but includes sounds with timbral qualities not dissimilar from electronics. These include Henderson's ghostly altissimo-register repeated staccato trumpet notes.

In contrast to his role in Detroit, Gleeson in this performance acts more like an instrumentalist than a textural sound designer. Gleeson shapes carefully crafted phrases that respond to the other musicians' solo phrases. From 8:00 to 12:00, Gleeson's articulations assume the form of ever-changing imaginative characters, alternately gurgling, buzzing, or zinging. In this show, his function as a band member is similar in kind to that of everyone else, except that his synthesizer is even more malleable than the acoustical instruments.

The increasingly electronic sound of the band with Gleeson would lead directly to the third Mwandishi recording and the most integrally electronic, *Sextant* (1973). On the road, a balance remained between the acoustical instruments and the electronics, but as we shall soon see, *Sextant* is more decisively electronic in timbre.

The Recording of *Sextant*

At this point in the development of the band, its sonic palette, acoustic and electric, has expanded to a range far broader than ever before. Hancock's sound resources now include piano; Fender Rhodes, expanded with his electronics; Mellotron, as was used in postproduction on *Crossings*; plus the rhythmic Hohner D-6 Clavinet, which was becoming a staple of funk since it gave keyboardists the ability to play the role of rhythm guitarist. Bennie Maupin appears with an array of wind instruments, including soprano sax, bass clarinet, piccolo, afuche,[10] and hum-a-zoo, a miniature kazoo. Julian Priester's trombones range from bass to tenor and alto. As on "Crossings," Eddie Henderson continues to move between the varying timbres of trumpet and flugelhorn, just as Buster Williams ranges between the varying feels of electric and acoustic bass. To Billy Hart's drums is added Buck Clarke's percussion. And Patrick Gleeson's work has shifted from his previous studio instrument, the Moog III, to his road gear, the Arp 2600 and Pro-Soloist. The recording, released by Columbia Records, opened at number fourteen in *Billboard* magazine's "Best Selling Jazz LP's" chart[11] but rose to number three after sixteen weeks. Ahead were only Quincy Jones's *You've Got It Bad Girl* and Weather Report's *Sweetnighter*.[12] At week twenty-nine, *Sextant* was still in the top forty jazz charts, at number twenty-six, and a week later, at number twenty-four.[13]

"Rain Dance"

Hancock soon added new tunes that were particularly suited to the synthesizer addition. Among them is "Rain Dance," recorded for the Mwandishi band's third and final recording, *Sextant*, recorded in fall 1972. This nine-minute composition fills half of the first side of the original LP. Multiple layers of synthesizer ostinati are a constant, serving as both a complex rhythm section and solo instrument. The ability to craft and shape ostinati was a compelling feature of modular analog synthesizers like the Arp 2600 and Buchla electronic music performance systems. The ostinati in "Rain Dance" draw on the sequencing module that temporarily stored and output a series of voltages that could be applied to pitch (or other musical parameters). Compositions by Morton Subotnick and others make use of such repeating figures, which can be subtly altered during performance. Gleeson's adaptation of sequencing techniques on *Sextant* is intriguing in how easily its use as a rhythmic instrument suited the context of the Mwandishi band.

Example 15. "Rain Dance," opening sequence

The core of "Rain Dance" is found in its accumulated layers of rhythmic activity. This is a reworking of the basic idea of "Ostinato" for an electronic age. Its predecessor's relatively static repeated riff played on acoustic instruments and electric piano has been updated with multiple layers of highly elastic electronic sequences, around which other electronic and instrumental sounds playfully interweave and dance.

"Rain Dance" opens with a bouncy, rhythmic sequence, which is soon given emphasis and syncopation by the addition of a sustained, rising note added at the end of each repeat. An electronic ticking pulse then joins, followed by watery sounds. Appearing next is a sharp and fluttering electronic timbre, echoed by a brief, solo, rising trumpet line that ends in altissimo range. Together, these elements form an intricate rhythmic interlocking funk-like puzzle. The fact that this is not going to be a funk tune is reinforced by a sudden pause, followed by a brief explosion of collective improvisation, leading into a trumpet solo. The drums enter, followed by an asymmetrical walking bass, accompanied by swirling semipitched electronic sounds. As Hart's drumming picks up energy, the electronic sounds develop a noise component and unfold in an improvisatory fashion as part of the overall sonic texture, as pitched phrases, ostinati, or other settings for the soloists. Watery sequences set the stage for Hancock's serpentine electric piano solo, and a quiet electronic textural backdrop becomes the setting for Williams's bass solo.

We then return to the opening ostinato, joined by the rhythmic ticking. A new layering of brief electronic ostinati, calling and responding, begins to build. The watery sounds swirl, and soon only the multiple layers of electronic sounds remain, each one bouncing off the other, each subtle, changing, and growing. A minute later, brief bursts of rising notes pan across the stereo field, rising, accelerating, some given rhythmic emphasis. Syncopated longer tones periodically pierce the multiplicity of sounds. The interplay of brief ostinati and other electronic sounds continues until fading into silence, as the tune comes to a conclusion. The level of rhythmic complexity and timbral coloration provides a fascinating exemplar of Olly Wilson's conception of black music, noted in chapter 6.

"Hidden Shadows" and "Hornets"

The two other tunes on *Sextant* are jams closer to the kind that the band played live in concert. Hart's drums and Hancock's wah-wah–treated Hohner Clavinet drive both compositions. "Hidden Shadows," logging in at just over ten minutes in duration, completes side one on the original *Sextant* LP. The tune opens with a funky riff led by Maupin's bass clarinet, punctuated by Hart's cowbell and squeaky percussive sounds. This continuous riff serves as the glue that unifies the entire track. But the appearance of sustained string sounds on Mellotron and multiple layers of electronic textures, at times juxtaposed with Hancock's funky comping on Hohner Clavinet, suggest that this is not a conventional funk tune. Muted trumpet plays variants of the riff and layers of electronic textures ebb and flow. Around the 3:30, the horns play the head of the tune, accompanied by the rhythm section and Clavinet processed by wah-wah. After the tune repeats, a highly rhythmic improvisational mix fills out the balance of the recording. The listener's experience of the intense improvisations, even with its distinctly funky cast, is as if hearing it through a fog. Swirling electronic sounds, sustained Mellotron string pads, reverberant echo, and the tremendously dense level of activity renders the overall sonic image somewhat indistinct. This phenomenon is so consistent as to be a defining aesthetic, an expansion of the "abstract funk" idea explored on *Crossings*.

"Hornets," nearly twenty minutes in length, fills the entire second side of the original LP. This is a collective improvisation driven hard by Williams's syncopated electric bass riffs and Hart's shuffles on the drum kit. The tune became a staple of the band's live performances. The improvisational approach is highly conversational; the early sections feature a bird-like chatter between Henderson's trumpet, Maupin's hum-a-zoo and later, piccolo, supported by Hancock's funky Clavinet. Gleeson's synthesizer soon joins the fray,

Example 16. Opening of "Hidden Shadows"

presaging the entrance of a dramatic melodic theme in the horns just before
3:00. It begins with a six-note phrase, the fourth note sustained. The theme
continues with rapid-fire drumming and then two final sustained notes, which
descend into chaos. Solos by the three horn players are separated by brief melodic themes and collective improvisation. Maupin's saxophone solo begins
simply at 6:00, but by 6:30 and continuing through 8:30 grows increasingly
fragmented, angular, insistent, and timbrally distorted. A melodic Hancock
solo follows more cacophonous collective improvisation, featuring Maupin's
hum-a-zoo, and a return of the melodic theme at 10:50.

Hancock's solo, starting at 11:10, initially has a distant feel due to electronic
distortion of the Fender Rhodes electric piano. Hancock draws on the full
array of available electronic processing at his disposal to create a solo that
becomes tremendously diverse in its sonic expanse. For this reason alone,
it is worthy of close attention. Following a Hohner Clavinet solo that grows
increasingly atonal and distorted, Hancock returns to the electric piano and
plays bursts of short notes that are pitch shifted and timbrally altered by the
Echoplex, wah-wah, and other electronics. The rhythm section becomes more
transparent, albeit growing steadily in intensity. Hancock then engages in call-
and-response between the Clavinet and Maupin's hum-a-zoo at 12:35, eventually dissipating into an electronic fog, returning the texture to spare call-
and-response funky rhythmic figures on pitch shifted and Echoplexed electric
piano, which join the band's rhythmic mix of drums, bass, hum-a-zoo, and
Clavinet. Gleeson's sound gestures fade in and out, and he takes a rare solo
at 17:15, which pans a single note of changing timbre across the stereo field,
followed by a brief fuzz electric bass solo by Williams. After a reprise of the
theme, Williams settles into a groove, preparing the final, dense rhythmic interplay within the band, heading toward an abrupt conclusion to this wild jam.
It is a jam as electronic as it is acoustic, an unusual admixture of funk jam and
collective free improvisation, yet another exemplar of "abstract funk." A visual
and sonic image of hornets swarming in and around their nest renders the
composition's title to be apt.

Band Members' Reactions to Electronics in Postproduction, and Gleeson's New Role

The idea of applying postproduction techniques and electronics to a recording was new and initially challenging for members of the Mwandishi band. Responding to *Mwandishi* (1971) on its completion, trombonist Julian Priester

recalls his first reaction: "I remember the contrasts [between] the sounds of the music [recorded] while I was in the studio compared to the sounds of the music when the actual product was finished, after all the editing and mixing. It was drastically different . . . and I was offended." Priester correctly identifies a core part of the conflict, differing expectations about the nature of the recording process: "Up to that point, I regarded recordings as documentation of a live performance done in the studio, a documentation of something that [actually] happened."

Trumpeter Eddie Henderson's reaction to the first recording was far more positive:

> We were going to a gig after we did the session, I think in Philadelphia. And I went by Herbie's house, because I was going to drive him to Philadelphia. He said: "Oh, man, come in, quick, quick." He was living in New York, then. He went into his music room and he had the tape, you know, and he put on "You'll Know When You Get There" and I said "Wo-o-o-o-o!" That was the first time I ever heard it, before the record came out. [I was so impressed] because of the way he mixed it, like the beginning of my solo, the sounds seem to come out of nowhere.

Henderson credits studio engineer Fred Catero's skills for aspects of the successful studio work on the recording: "He's a great engineer. He knows what he's doing. And he's such a scientist."

A period of adjustment led the band members to a more positive perspective. Priester himself subsequently reassessed the situation: "Now this new technology brought in another era and another way of doing things. And so the end product no longer represented a performance. It represented the technology, the recording technique, what happened electronically. . . . I knew that it's an advanced way of making recordings. [My new thinking about] it happened later, after I got over the initial shock." Billy Hart immediately found the postproduction on *Crossings* to be "fascinating. What Herbie does on the drum solo that I take on 'Sleeping Giant' . . . is incredible. Again, it was like a drum concerto, like you had a symphony orchestra behind you. My God, there's so much going on, even before you realize you've even started."

Sextant represented a more dramatic shift, the full integration of Gleeson's electronics into the band's sonic and rhythmic textures. And it was a mark of how far the band had come in accepting Gleeson's membership since initial resistance from members. Gleeson recalls that aside from Herbie Hancock, only

Buster Williams showed up at his first rehearsal with the band, stayed only briefly, and questioned whether the synthesizer was a musical instrument.[14] David Rubinson observes: "I just don't think they realized how far we were going to go with it."

Hart came to accept the live electronics more quickly than some of the others:

It was amazing, when Patrick joined the band. It's like *The Witch, the Lion, and the Wardrobe* [a fantasy novel by C. S. Lewis]: You walk in the closet, the next minute you're outside, and then you're in an airplane. When you're that young, the shock was fascinating. I remember Buster saying, sometimes, he would lean over to me and say: "Instruments weren't supposed to be played like this!" But I always had that kind of imagination.

Williams recalls: "I liked it. I liked it. I thought that it added a new dimension. On some things I thought that it wasn't needed." Trombonist Priester came to an equally positive conclusion: "By that time I had completely accepted the change, the progress, the progression of technology, that I viewed [Patrick's synthesizer] as an extension of what we were doing acoustically, so it fit." Despite his initial positive response to postproduction on *Mwandishi*, Henderson remembers this more dramatic shift with a more critical eye: "I think that by that point [when Patrick joined the touring band], we'd grown accustomed of the sounds. . . . Everybody was so possessive of the music we were playing. And, somebody comes in doing all these other sounds; it just felt funny. It was kind of bizarre."

For Maupin, the electronics broadened the sonic palette available to him as an improviser:

When I met Patrick Gleeson, I thought, "Damn, where is he from?" He had all the wires, modules. He had this machine, the Arp 2600; I'd never seen anything like that. He'd sit down with me sometimes and show me the difference between a saw wave, and sine wave, and it just opened up my head to what sound was all about. That was the beginning of a whole other education for me. Prior to that I'd always been concerned with the notes, chords, and scales. It didn't occur to me there are infinitely more sounds than there are notes. Once I saw that, I realized you could create music in a completely different way using sounds. It can be non-pitched sounds, or sounds no one's ever heard before. . . . As good as it sounds when you put an acoustic element on top of it, I fell completely in love with it.[15]

However unplanned, the addition of Gleeson and Fundi's work in the sound booth represented a coming together of Hancock's sonic imagination. Electronic sounds and electronically processed instruments were well integrated with the acoustic instruments to create a finely stitched tapestry of sound. The next question was going to be: Where would the band, and Hancock's restless imagination, go from there?

9

Musical Collectivity and Open Forms

Collective Musical Experience

The sensation of playing music with a small group of other people, guided by intuition, is an experience most jazz and chamber musicians know. As Mithen suggests, collective music making requires, or maybe generates, a sense of group consciousness that transcends the individual. There is actually a degree of personal transcendence inherent to any music making, even solo performance. To some degree, a musician loses a sense of personal identity and is swept up in the ethereal quality of the music. My own experience of playing both chamber music and jazz, idiomatic and free, suggests more of a delicate and often unstable balance between individual awareness and group consciousness than Mithen suggests. When the music is really cooking, both aspects of consciousness, individual and collective, are present. Sometimes one way of being momentarily shifts to the other. What

Mithen points to is particularly relevant to forms of music making that privilege spontaneity. Examples include the free jazz of the 1960s,[1] which sought to balance individual and collective expression, and maybe the earliest forms that arose decades ago in New Orleans. Oftentimes, this experience of group musical consciousness was clearly manifest within the Mwandishi band. As pianist Billy Childs observes:

> The Mwandishi band was . . . highly dependent upon what each guy does. You couldn't call in other players [as subs] to do what each of those guy does as part of the chemistry. Also, the music was way abstract; the form seems to be a constantly evolving thing in the moment. They functioned almost like a chamber group, entirely dependent upon each other, but free from each other. They were free to do whatever, but what one person did affected the whole organism. It was like a living, breathing organism, like a representation of real life.

Free Jazz, Creative Music, and Evolving Forms of Collective Musical Engagement

Around the end of the 1950s and into the 1960s, two streams of musicians, post-bop jazz players, at times eschewing the term "jazz," and innovative inheritors of Euro-American Art music, began to create forms of music that highly valued the sensibility suggested by Mithen. These groups placed far greater emphasis on intuition over the previous modes of engagement. Ornette Coleman, John Coltrane, and others extended the bebop notion that the purpose of a tune is to instigate improvisation. These younger players used precomposed tunes as a starting point for spontaneous music making. As they felt greater permission to explore new pathways, Coleman, Coltrane, and others sympathetic to their musical values made careful listening and response the focus of musical organization rather than a means of adding new life to preexisting contents. Their emphasis steadily shifted from realizing new versions of conventionally structured works to crafting innovative flights of the imagination.

Among the most important foundational recordings of the budding free jazz movement, which would soon be joined in Chicago by the Art Ensemble of Chicago and other members of the Association for the Advancement of Creative Musicians (AACM), were Coleman's *Free Jazz* (1960), Coltrane's

Ascension (1965), and Cecil Taylor's *Jazz Advance* (1956) and *Looking Ahead* (1958). The former two included Herbie Hancock's musical associate, trumpeter Freddie Hubbard, as does Hancock's early employer, saxophonist and bass clarinetist Eric Dolphy. During this era of the civil rights and black power movements, many of these musicians interlaced the political with the musical. Reflecting an assertion of personal and collective autonomy, they discovered modes of form and function outside the harmonic conventions inherited from European music.

Some, among them AACM members Leroy Jenkins and Anthony Braxton, referred to the free jazz movement as "creative music"[2] or, in the case of the Art Ensemble of Chicago, "Great Black Music." The AACM was part of an informal black arts movement network across the United States, which also included Black Artists Group in St. Louis, Collective Black Artists in New York, Underground Musicians Association in Los Angeles, and the Jazz Composers Orchestra (JCO), part of a short-lived Jazz Composers Guild in New York.[3] Billy Hart observes: "We all knew about each other. It was like a dance craze going across; you don't know, but you just hear [on the streets]."

Throughout these groups, collective music making was combined with explorations of black identity and an attempt to assert freedom from the established music business, its concert venues and means of production. These tended to exploit black musicians and marginalize their autonomy and self-determination. A priority was thus placed on organizational self-reliance, the development of new concert venues and means of production. George Lewis notes: "The collective developed strategies for individual and collective self-production and promotion that both reframed the artist/business relationship and challenged racialized limitations on venues and infrastructure."[4]

The 1960s' spirit of free and collective music making was also manifest among European and US white musicians. Notable among such groups was Music Elettronica Viva (MEV), founded in Rome in 1966 by a group of academically trained yet musically free-spirited US musicians including Alvin Curran, Richard Teitelbaum, and Frederick Rzewski[5]; members of the JCO in New York; in London, the AAM, the Scratch Orchestra, Spontaneous Music Ensemble, and Dave Holland, who became a member of Miles Davis's Quintet in 1968. Noted jazz saxophonist Steve Lacy joined MEV in 1969; its numerous collaborators in Europe included the Art Ensemble of Chicago and the AAM. During a 1970 tour of the United States, MEV was joined by several new collaborators, among them Braxton.

Among the values that unite these groups is a process of collective music making that might be described as "individual within the collective." Musicologist Samuel Floyd places this perspective within the context of black music:

> Collective, the process is truly *communal and cooperative*, as is evident in Ornette Coleman's "Free Jazz" (1960) and other works of the contemporary jazz movement, as players react to and "play off of" one another's melodic and rhythmic relations and elaborations. . . . Improvisation seldom yields a distilled and carefully honed product since the process is a kind of "thinking aloud."[6]

This process combines individual autonomy with a group sound. The individual is given wide latitude to spontaneously create while at the same time giving up some degree of individuality to participate in what Floyd terms the "aggregate." It is this dual consciousness that increasingly informed the second Miles Davis Quintet and, subsequently, the Herbie Hancock Sextet, culminating in the Mwandishi band.

Expanding on Intuitive Forms Developed within the Miles Davis Quintet

In its 1969 incarnation, the Herbie Hancock Sextet was at first an idiomatic jazz band. Its music was organized by conventions of the "head" followed by solos, which were tied to the chord changes. But even during that first year and certainly in the first half of 1970, marked shifts could be detected within the band's mode of playing. Sextet saxophonist Joe Henderson's *Power to the People* (1969) shows evidence of increased reliance on interaction between players beyond the chord changes. This was certainly true of the Sextet formation that I heard perform in late July 1970. As the band's personnel changed, its final constellation falling into place, it was possible for Hancock to revisit the spirit of the Miles Davis Quintet and move it forward in an even more distinctly free direction. The shift took place almost immediately in fall 1970, during the first performances with the front line of Bennie Maupin, Julian Priester, and, finally, Eddie Henderson. The Herbie Hancock, Buster Williams, and Billy Hart rhythm section had already solidified as an integral, yet highly flexible unit. The new group's first gigs in Vancouver, Seattle (at the Ebonee Lounge),[7] San Francisco (at the Both/And), and Chicago demonstrated the necessary musical symbiosis.

As the band's configuration solidified, the performance approach of the Sextet expanded on the open, intuitive approach to playing that characterized Hancock's final three years with Davis's second Quintet. The influence of Coleman and Coltrane, each of whom Davis had watched closely, decisively entered Miles Davis's Quintet beginning in 1965. Hancock played an important role in Davis's "New Directions in Music," which became the moniker on Davis's Quintet recordings. It was at this point when Hancock began to actively integrate aesthetics and techniques he had discovered earlier in his career while playing with Eric Dolphy and Donald Byrd. These included fractured and fragmented chords, and comping defined more by mood, density and texture than by harmony. The concerts documented on *Live at the Plugged Nickel* (1982) comprise one of many sources offering clear evidence of this evolution.

Hancock tags the initial stirrings of the shift in Davis's approach to a much earlier point in time. After the release of *Seven Steps to Heaven* (1963), beginning with a performance in Detroit, the band accompanied Davis's solos as they ordinarily would, in a conventional manner, but, explains Hancock,

> when it was time for George Coleman or me to take a solo, we didn't hesitate to play our thing. This state of affairs lasted six or seven months: we became increasingly bold backing George and during my solos . . . sometimes the entire rhythm section took a solo at the same time! When Miles came back in, we would fall carefully back into line and played in a more orthodox style. One fine day, Miles turned to us to say: "how come you don't play like that behind me too?" We never went back![8]

In 1966, Davis began to follow more intuitive forms, evidenced by the aptly named recordings *E.S.P.* (1965) and *Miles in the Sky* (1968). Hancock describes the musical processes in Davis's Quintet as "controlled freedom," meaning a more heavily mediated and bounded interpretation of free jazz. Hancock recalls that Davis

> rarely told any of us how to play. Also, when anyone brought in music, he'd take it down to its skeleton, just bare bones. When we played it, all of the flesh and tendons were improvised. That meant we could create a whole new being out of that song every night. Miles always said, "Never resolve anything." . . . He'd take the inherent structure and leave us room to breathe and create something fresh every night. There were the basic elements of the song, but not used exactly as they were in the composition.

Wayne Shorter points to the nature of the musical process within Davis's band, describing the recording of the tune "Dolores" from *Miles Smiles* (1967) in this way:

> Everyone who played, after the melody and all of that stuff, took a portion of a certain characteristic of the song, and—you can stay there. And then you do eight measures of it, and then you make your own harmonic road or avenue within a certain eight measures. But not counting out the eight measures, it's like whatever you fancied. But you keep the flavor. It was keeping the flavor of "Dolores" without—in other words, now as I look back—we were actually tampering with something called DNA in music in a song. Each song has its DNA. So you just do the DNA and not the whole song.[9]

What Shorter describes is an intuitive process in which each individual uncovers an essential underlying element or quality within a tune—and then runs with it. This can be a melodic shape or a rhythmic pattern, which is then varied, extended, or imitated. Sometimes it is abstracted, taking the basic shape, such as the pattern formed by the upward or downward direction from one note to the next, and changing the exact notes. It is the pattern, but not the details that remain.

Applying New Models to the Mwandishi Band

James Lichtenberg alludes to one of the intuitive means used by the Davis Quintet in his *New York Times* review of the album *Mwandishi* (1971). Lichtenberg compares the improvisatory process used by both bands, drawing on Miles Davis's discovery that

> musicians could play directly off the patterns of emotions. . . . What, then, determines the patterns of emotions? The intricate and complex environment in which we are living and to which we are all contributing. For example, Hancock describes being alive abstractly as a multilevel web of tensions and releases whose source is the energy in the environment. The way his music works is as a carrier of these tensions and releases, in much the same way as an electric cable carries telephone conversations.

What Lichtenberg describes is something far more subtle and amorphous than the reordering of preexisting musical materials, such as a melodic theme.

Rather, it is an emotional core, a moment of psychic knowing, and an intuition that transcends any simple description. It is a translation of somatic, emotional, and other human experience into music. These form the building blocks for communication between musicians, as Lichtenberg continues: "Hancock and his band form an incredibly sensitive receiver-transmitter. All you need to pick up their beautiful signals is an openness of mind that will permit you to accept the same range of sonic experiences in music that you unquestioningly accept every day in life."[10] It is this quality of interconnection that Steve Mithen refers to when he says: "Those who make music together will mould their own minds and bodies into a shared emotional state."[11]

In fall 1970, the music of the Mwandishi band became increasingly organic, spontaneous, and ever evolving. As the lifeblood of the band increasingly became collective improvisation, the results, being of the moment, could be striking in their innovation and unpredictability. Maupin observes: "Our whole idea was to create something that was multi-textural, with multiple nuances so that it was like a moving tapestry of some sort." Priester elaborates further: "There were no restrictions . . . everyone was listening to each other, leaving our egos out of the process, just responding to what the overall group invents." Williams adds: "We all got on the bandstand every night with the willingness to be transcended and to be directed by the music itself. Which is why you'd hear us play nothing that resembled anything for an hour, before we even played the melody of the song."

What became the driving force for band members was a collective intuition about where one's fellows were headed musically. Together they would find their way through unexplored musical territory. Priester continues:

> Everyone in the band was pretty much of the same mind; even when we went in opposite directions, it was all right. I'm talking about musically, artistically. Everybody had [permission] to be as expressive as they wanted to be. And because everyone was of the same mind, everything worked. We had this group concept where what we are performing is really based on what everyone else is performing. Everyone is contributing to this unique sound. . . . The sound that comes from the band is a result of each person, each person contributing to the whole. And that whole is unified.

However seemingly by chance, Hancock's choice of musicians, all of whom had free jazz sensibilities, clearly made this possible. Hart had been heavily influenced by Coltrane's music. He had attended AACM concerts when he visited Chicago while playing with Pharaoh Sanders's band. Priester had been a member of an early incarnation of Sun Ra's band and had played with innovative polyrhythmic drummer Max Roach. Maupin had played with Marion Brown. As Hancock observed in a 1971 *Down Beat* interview, the time seemed right to experiment: "The sound is not totally unfamiliar to the musician anymore, so that certain things have been established, even in the avant-garde."[12] Hancock told me: "This whole avant-garde movement was having a bigger and bigger influence on people who were considered the mainstream, like Miles and Trane. The records were starting to reflect it, and with me too. So the band I had was getting further and further out."

Form and Process in the Mwandishi Band

The Mwandishi band's choice of musical structures initially took the notion of conventional head-solo arrangements, but stood these on their head, making use of vamps, riffs, choruses, and other devices as both formal compositional structures and spontaneous occurrences that emerged within improvisations. Herbie Hancock and bassist Buster Williams were often the instigators of these real-time usages. A typical performance would include tunes like "You'll Know When You Get There," which typically followed a consistent format, albeit varying in duration; and others like "Ostinato," which tended to change form from one performance to another; and others yet, like "Sleeping Giant," which used modular structures with precomposed sections that provided segues between freely improvised passages. Even "mistakes" could become part of the collective tapestry about which Maupin speaks, as Eddie Henderson remembers: "Sometimes I felt like I played horrible, the wrong notes or whatever, you know. And Herbie said: 'Oh no, oh no. We just played that, the band just played that entity in the universe.'"[13]

The Mwandishi band was known to improvise for an extended period of time and only eventually display elements, or the literal head, of a tune. In an interview with *Down Beat* magazine near the end of the Mwandishi band, Hancock commented: "I think of structure in a different sense now—structure as being only an element to stimulate rather than one to form. . . . A lot of times, in sections of tunes, we may want to take one basic sound, one basic cluster or chord or scale, and use that as a fulcrum."[14] On that fulcrum, the band would place layers of sometimes suddenly changing textures.

One finds parallel kinds of structures in other contemporaneous bands. One of these was Davis's post-Hancock "Lost Quintet"[15] with Chick Corea, which Bobby McFerrin remembers hearing in February 1971 at Shelly's Manne-Hole in Los Angeles: "They would get into this groove. Miles had just come out with some simple structure, like the head of a tune and he said just blow, and he'd go off the stage. As long as it was happening, he would let the playing go on, until he thought it was done. The tune was over when he'd come back on stage and play some blips and blops. The music was even freer than Herbie's band, if that is possible." What was happening often was free improvisation, particularly by Chick Corea, Dave Holland, and Jack DeJohnette, which continued in Corea and Holland's successor band, Circle.[16] Recordings of Weather Report from 1971–73 reflect a similar exploratory sensibility.[17] All groups, be they musical, political, or social, develop a vocabulary of dynamics through which their own means of interaction are expressed. One of the musical devices used by the Mwandishi band is the use of repeating phrases, ostinati, a feature shared with the Miles Davis "Lost" Quintet and Weather Report, but not Circle. A second device used by all three is the collective building and release of tension.

Form and Process in Live Mwandishi Performances: The Use of Ostinati

The nature and function of ostinati (colloquially called "riffs") is discussed in detail in chapter 6. As noted, the use of ostinati was a particular favorite of Herbie Hancock and Buster Williams, whom many members of the band viewed as the group's sparkplug. We have the advantage of several live performance recordings that informally circulate on the Internet, some from radio broadcasts. Comparing multiple performances allows us to detect shared traits, as well as detect differences and changes that emerge over time. Due to the lack of availability of unreleased live recordings, I will describe these in some detail.

An August 4, 1971, performance of "You'll Know When You Get There" at Jazzhaus in Hamburg was radio broadcast on Germany public radio.[18] In that performance, a trombone solo begins around 7:00, initially supported by very spare accompaniment. Two minutes later, the electric piano plays a series of rapidly repeating rising and falling runs, each of which ends in an extended trill. These patterns, however varied, take on some of the characteristics of an ostinato due to the repetition. The bass joins with its own slightly varying ostinato, steadily repeating a single note, periodically alternating with a lone lower tone. This ends in a bass and electric piano trill around 10:00, joined by the other horns and then drum cymbals. Later, around 11:00, the electric piano begins a long series of ostinati in three- to five-note patterns, often using atonal or altered chords (11:30) or repeated rapid runs (11:55). The trombone solo continues following a similar pattern, with minimal accompaniment, punctuated by Hancock's periodic ostinati, such as after 13:00, which ends with a wah-wah electric piano chord. Hancock follows this with a ten-note ostinato, which is layered over a bass riff for forty-five seconds. He adds a series of very short repeated riffs starting at 15:00, and two more times sequentially a minute later (the latter followed by five rising chords).

Back at 15:30, Williams plays a six-note descending riff on bass, which continues for several minutes. He introduces a new three-note waltz-like bass riff, over which Hancock plays a single electric piano chord at each down beat, and then a five-chord series and variants. Right after 16:30, Hancock plays four- and five-chord rhythmic patterns. Hancock's spontaneously crafted, brief ostinato patterns, whether right on the beat or countering it, serve to reinforce the main pulse by adding layers that accent particular beats.

This example provides an instance where the Mwandishi band used the ostinato as a device to suit a range of musical goals. The main function is to serve as a steady riff on which soloists can improvise. But, as discussed in chapter 6, gradually shifting ostinati can instead create a sense of unmoored motion or, in other cases, stasis. Bassist Williams was, as he continues to be, a master of invention when it comes to shifting ostinati, sometimes causing a gradual evolution and sometimes a sudden shift in mood or level of activity. Hancock at times adds and subtracts repeats of an ostinato, variously in or out of synch with the pulse of the tune to cause subtle shifts in the musical texture or sense of time.

Another way that the Mwandishi band made use of ostinati was to freeze time, to create a lack of motion, which at times can establish a sense of tension between musical objects in motion and others in a holding pattern. Hancock often used this "locked groove" device from Pierre Schaeffer and other early electronic music composers to create a sense of stasis, sometimes momentarily. The result is either a timeless quality or the building of tension, which could then be released with the dissolution of the ostinato. Hancock's use of ostinati was among the key ways he playfully directed musical direction and the level and style of interplay between his band mates.

The most obvious use of ostinati is on the tune "Ostinato," which appears on the album *Mwandishi*. But here, even when the core theme of the composition was an ostinato, it was only sometimes used as a constant vamp. To briefly recap the description in chapter 6, the recorded version of "Ostinato" from January 1971 begins with a brief atmospheric introduction, a wash of electric piano etched by Maupin's saxophone. This provides an introduction to the characteristic ostinato on which various solos are constructed during the duration of the tune. At times, the horns provide countermelodies. Hancock's comping makes broad use of wah-wah and Echoplex, allowing him to move between—and combine—highly rhythmic funky playing and abstract electronic textures. The main dynamic of this performance is the rhythmic juxtapositions, counterrhythms, and syncopations that result from soloists and accompanists playing off the repeated ostinato, particularly due to its unusual pattern.

I have access to just the opening fifteen minutes of a recording from Festival Juan Les Pins in Nice, France, July 21, 1971. Like the recorded version from six months prior, the opening is atmospheric. Here, a passage of drones leads to a horn choir. But rather than moving directly to the ostinato of the tune's title, the music suddenly shifts into free improvisation, and then to a hand percussion segment that includes bass glissandi and bird-like flute lines. Cacophony self-organizes into a distinctly definable rhythm and with it, a Maupin bass clarinet solo. These finally bring us to the ostinato, at around 10:00, on which a free improvisation has built. A trumpet solo follows at 14:00, built on a heavy drumbeat and Hancock's electric piano comping closely following the soloist. Information is lacking about what follows.

A second performance during this European tour is from the August 4, 1971, NDR radio broadcast from Hamburg. This fifty-minute performance lacks the spatial opening of the two previous versions. Instead, it begins with a percussion jam, more spare and fragile than in Nice. It features kalimba, shakers, claves, and Hancock's Echoplex-augmented electric piano. Again, a discernible pulse develops only slowly. During this process, a musette[19] blasts foghorn-like long tones for an extended period. Around 8:00, Maupin begins to play a four-minute-long fragmented bass clarinet solo. Three minutes into the solo, the rhythm section becomes suddenly intense and densely textured. Hancock's repeated electric piano patterns, ostinati, help spark the growing frenzy of Maupin's solo. Now, nearly twelve minutes into the performance, the activity suddenly quiets down as Maupin introduces fragments of the "Ostinato" riff, to which others join. Hancock and the rhythm section continue the riff, which quickly dissipates, coalescing into a charging pulse with cacophonous multilayered comping, providing a container of sorts for another Maupin bass clarinet solo.

Henderson's trumpet solo follows shortly after 15:30. It sets a calmer tone than what has proceeded, supported by Hancock's funky comping, drawing on wah-wah effects. Hart keeps a steady rhythmic pulse. Four and a half minutes into the solo, Hancock comps using a quietly repeated two-chord sequence for a while (another ostinato), then returns to more active comping. Hancock alternates between directly responding to the trumpet and challenging Henderson with intensely rhythmic figurations. This alternation between moods and levels of intensity, a characteristic of the chemistry between Hancock and his band mates, pervades the rest of this trumpet solo and the bass clarinet solo that begins at around 27:00. Separating the two solos is a raucous collective improvisation wrapped around bass clarinet variants on the ostinato. The variations on the ostinato treat it less as an ostinato in its technical sense than as material to be abstracted. All at once, for nearly two minutes the players each solo independently in the same sound space.

This is followed by an extended electric piano solo, between 36:40 and 45:45. Initially spare, Hancock separates his phrases and runs with silences, as the solo begins to build. The Echoplex is used alternately for rhythmic effects or to abstract the sounds, generating distortion and noise. Then, Hancock's runs up and down the keyboard lead into a highly percussive section in which he increases the intensity of the solo by fragmenting note patterns, alternating between gradually shifting, highly rhythmic two- to four-chord patterns. These patterns may be termed ostinati, although they bear little relationship to the theme riff. After taking a more scalar and lyrical direction, Hancock gives way to a three-minute trombone solo over constant rhythmic activity. The bass clarinet and electric piano join together with a variant of the ostinato; Maupin takes over the original ostinato pattern, as Hancock continues to juxtapose over it a variant. After a brief abstract bass clarinet solo, everyone joins together in the ostinato at 50:00 and concludes the performance by holding a single sustained note.

These three performances, quite distinct from one another, share in common the ostinato riff and various kinds of rhythmic interplay that ensue between soloists and band mates. The studio recording and Nice performance open with an atmospheric texture. But unlike the recording, where the core element is the ostinato, in Nice this figure doesn't appear until 9:00. Most of what precedes is free improvisation, an approach that also appears in the Hamburg performance. There, fragments of the ostinato are introduced around 12:00, during Maupin's solo. Others soon join the full-blown ostinato, which quickly dissipates, only to reappear intact at 50:00. Hancock's use of ostinati

is most often ad hoc, not necessarily related to the riff that bears the composition's title. "Ostinato" provides a forum for Hancock to explore the *concept* of
ostinati. The tune offers a vehicle for the band to enjoy free-wheeling rhythmic
interchange in the context of performances that follow intuitive structures,
textures that ebb and flow, and cohere only at times by virtue of the ostinato,
but more often by virtue of interpersonal chemistry.

Form and Process in Live Mwandishi Performances: "You'll Know When You Get There"

A second device used by the band as a formal vehicle is the collective building and release of tension. Instances of this dynamic can be keenly captured
by comparisons between multiple performances of a single tune. Fortunately,
several recordings of "You'll Know When You Get There" are available, spanning from 1971 to 1973.

In a performance recorded at Vejlby-Risskovhallen, Arhus, Demark, in late
April 1971, useful examples of form and process abound during Henderson's
trumpet solo. After a brief increase in activity, the textures thin down and
briefly simmer at 3:30. A single staccato note on trumpet is answered by rapidly swirling electric piano arpeggios. There is increasing activity in the drums
and electric piano. A second, and this time sustained, trumpet note is joined
by rapid drum sequences, each ending in a cymbal hit, and then moving into a
roll, as the trumpet reaches for a high long tone and the electric piano gestures
intensify, anchored by a rapidly repeating bass note, all of which is followed
by a sustained drum roll. The tension is released by a series of electric piano
chords, a bass line that at times walks, and rapid trumpet runs, starting near
4:00. The tension then ebbs and flows as the trumpet solo continues at a rapid
pace and the drumming rises and falls in intensity, leveling off with a regular
pulse on the ride cymbal and chordal comping in the electric piano, joined a
few seconds later by bass notes with longer sustain.

At the August 4, 1971, Hamburg performance, the trumpet solo begins
at 2:30, accompanied primarily by percussion, bass, and, soon after, electric
piano. The trumpet and electric piano play cat and mouse, imitating back and
forth. Shortly after 4:00, the trumpet speeds up its pace of repeated short gestures. In tandem, drum and electric piano figures steadily increase in intensity,
mimicking the trumpet gesture. A crashing electric piano chord and drum
roll arrive just before 4:30, followed by a rapidly repeated trumpet figure and
a pause followed by another crash. A rising trumpet note is followed by the

trumpet and electric piano playing an interlocking ostinato: The trumpet repeats a single pitch, joined on the second note by two rapidly repeated electric piano notes. This "locked groove" breaks into fluid trumpet runs backed by the rhythm section at 4:45, and the tension decreases. The passages draw on brief segments of the previous trumpet patterns. Hancock's comping returns to the rapid two-note (now chords) ostinato. The drum shifts into a steady pulse, the tension rising and falling based on the intensity of the drumming. From 5:40 to 6:00, Hancock plays a repeated chord ostinato, creating another holding pattern, despite the continued trumpet lines. Similar patterns of change continue for the duration of the solo, around 6:50.

At the July 21, 1971, performance in Nice, shortly before 4:00, Hart's drums suddenly instigate an eruption of collective activity, joined by Hancock's electric piano and Williams's bass, during what has been a slow, lyrical trumpet solo. Henderson plays rapid trumpet runs, and the drumming becomes increasingly soloistic in nature. Shortly after 4:00, the drums herald a release of tension with a series of tom-tom hits, followed by an electric piano chord right on the down beat, and the trumpet continues a fast-paced solo over a new bass riff and steadily paced drum beat. Periodically, the stew is stirred by more erupting drumming and percussive electric piano chords, but settles down to a spare yet elegant bass pattern.

The manner in which the band built tension during moments of collective improvisation or in support of a soloist at a climactic moment is related to what saxophonist Archie Shepp termed "energy-sound."[20] Musicologist Paul Steinbeck describes this as "methods of music production typified by high levels of physical energy and timbral complexity."[21] As just described, the Mwandishi band's improvisations would ebb and flow, often reaching fever pitched "intensity" moments.[22] Ostinati play a role in stalling forward motion, helping set up bursts of energy that sometimes follow. Henderson comments: "[At times, multiple layers of stuff] are all going at the same time and happen spontaneously, organically. Not pre-planned or anything like that. Sometimes it would get too congested . . . like traffic, like an accident. There was no blueprint of when to back away or when to keep going, you know. Herbie left it up to everybody's intuition and musical judgment." Maupin notes that sometimes the intensity could become too much, the music becoming too dense: "We just listened and listened and listened to each other. I mean, you had to really listen . . . sometimes it would be so dense with sound; there would be no room for anything. All the space was full. But then we would just thin out all the textures. Thin out everything."[23] This reflects a quality of openness and curiosity that is not limited by preconceptions and judgments.

Keeping It Fresh, New Music as Spiritual Practice

Making music collectively by listening and responding is neither simple nor obvious. Imitation and repetition, conventionally used devices within idiomatic formats, quickly become stale in a freer setting. Intuitive music requires listening for nuance and fleeting phenomena, rather than for the obvious like an interesting phrase. It requires what electronic music pioneer Pauline Oliveros calls "Deep Listening," which "cultivates appreciation of sounds on a heightened level, expanding the potential for connection and interaction with one's environment, technology and performance with others in music and related arts."[24] Certainly this is a skill that Hancock developed throughout his early career, as we have discussed. In the Mwandishi band, working within a more loosely structured ensemble required a heightened sensitivity to moments of opportunity: a texture taking shape that awaited one more voice, a soloistic passage that called for restraint on the part of others, the drive of a rhythmic pulse, or a collectively gathering change of direction.

What helped the music of the Sextet avoid becoming routine was its increasingly conscious adoption of spiritual language and tools. At first, this was more a growing awareness than a conscious decision on the part of band members. Williams notes: "The interesting thing with the band is that we had become quite spiritual. Not that we in the band had accepted any particular religion. But the music itself was very spiritual in that it left, it transcended, the plane, our bodies, the plane of laity."

Williams's use of religious language to describe music making is telling. Religions tend to make use of shared ritual texts, objects, and experiences within a particular tradition to help people gain a sense of a reality beyond their daily, physical realities. But musicians have similar perceptions during the act of playing. These experiences often happen unexpectedly, during moments of self-transcendence. In those instances, words, actions, and perceptions seem to arise without self-consciousness, pretense, or the usual editing that musicians engage in often when engaging in their daily activities or with other people. For some, this feels like an expression from their innermost being, expressing the fullness of who they are. For others, it is like experiencing something larger than they are. It can be as if the physical instrument and its player are part of one larger instrument through which the music is playing itself.

The chemistry between players became a distinguishing feature of the emerging Mwandishi band. Longevity and consistency supported this trend once the personnel became set; it became rare for outsiders to sit in.[25] But some members of the band also adopted a formal expression of the band's spirituality, a Japanese form of Buddhism that had been discovered first by Williams, as related and discussed in chapter 1. The practice, called Gongyo ("assiduous practice"), centers on the chanting of the title of the Lotus Sutra, a Buddhist scripture, "Nam Myoho Renge Kyo." Hancock told Michelle Mercer: "We were always searching for ways to make the music all that it could be with an amount of freedom. . . . And we were searching for a religion that would help solidify our spiritual foundation."[26]

Groups and families have their own inside stories, jokes, and coded language that both help the units cohere and act as symbols of their bond. The Mwandishi band was no exception. Quite unrelated to Buddhism, the group gave themselves a private nickname based on their astrological commonalities and shared birthdays. The name was "Quasar 4 Aires 29." It was an open secret. Hancock explains:

> There was this guy, Jerry, that discovered it, that uncovered it. We used to hang out with this guy during the day, sometimes, and always after the gig. He would tell us different things that he read. He was always into things that make you go "Wow." Four of the guys in the band had birthdays on the same day in four different months. And each of those outlined the four elements: earth, air, fire, and water. And there were four of them. But then the other three guys, we had to figure this out, how's it going to fit in. There's a four of the number 29 that's significant, because of the four elements. And it turns out that Eddie Henderson was a Scorpio and Buster and I were Aires. And there are two planets that Scorpio has. Aires is Mars. Scorpio is something else and Mars. So Mars happens to be the fourth planet from the sun—and so the number four comes up again. Although we had different birthdays, the number four connected Buster, myself, and, Eddie Henderson, to the other four guys. By the way, I'm naming seven people because one of the 29s was Fundi. He was considered one of the members of the band. It wasn't like he's the crew and we're the band. He's the band. Because he was part of that whole spiritual kind of feeling that we had, kind of a brotherhood.

Hart adds: "On the speakers that we carried, we had the number twenty-nine written on them. When they saw that we all figured out that we had this number twenty-nine in common. So then they put up twenty-nine signs all around the studio." If you look on the original inside cover of *Crossings* (1972), you'll see the band's symbol for Quasar 4 Aires 29 on the bottom left. It also appears on the cover of *Sextant* (1973) and on Hart's bass drum.

A Musical Collective, Yet Herbie Hancock's Band

The Mwandishi band may have functioned as a musical collective, but in crucial ways, it was always Herbie Hancock's band. We begin to explore how the band was and was not a collective enterprise by discussing Hancock's style as a musical leader. Hart describes the band's musical process as not simply collective music making, but the result of directed leadership by Hancock, what Hart calls a "kind of clairvoyance": "He could influence your mind just from what he did on the piano, and not from you listening to him. . . . You would be leading the process, you'd be driving the car, but he'd be the engine. I mean he could get into your mind." Trumpeter Wallace Roney expresses it this way:

> Herbie was the master composer and his band members were his instruments. Like Duke Ellington, Herbie was such an orchestral genius. He was almost like Bud Powell and Gil Evans to me, but using electric and acoustic instruments. I thought Herbie was playing the band. Everything they did he was composing, using them as his instruments. Even their solos, while they were playing from their heart, he almost willed it. They were his colors. For instance, Herbie seemed to be thinking: "I want a little bass clarinet." And Bennie seemed to feel that, and maybe the others felt it too, and it would happen!

Although the musicians may have felt that Hancock was really directing what unfolded, as a bandleader, his overt leadership style was open, flexible, and collaborative. Like his former employer Miles Davis, Hancock didn't tell his band members what to play, as he once told interviewer Brooks Johnson:

> With Miles' band we were all allowed to play what we wanted to play and shaped the music according to the group effort and not to the dictates of Miles, because he really never dictated what he wanted. I try to do the same

thing with my group. I think it serves this function that I just mentioned—that everybody feels that they're part of the product, you know, and not just contributing something to somebody else's music. They may be my tunes, but the music belongs to the guys in the band. They make the music—it's not just my thing.[27]

Hancock's mode of leadership was even looser than Davis's, as Hart recalls: "He let us do whatever we wanted to do. He didn't tell us what to do," adding ironically, "I would have wanted him to tell me what to do."

Hancock welcomed band member initiative. Williams was the first to step forward. Henderson remembers, "Buster was kind of the spark. . . . [He] would change bass lines and just open up a new door. You know, and it wasn't written down! It was just spontaneous . . . and the band and Herbie would follow along." Williams's bass lines began to leap off the page, sparkling with spontaneous invention:

> I would come up with one of these lines and everyone would jump on it. And to this day I get impatient doing anything too long. These rhythms, these lines, these motifs would morph into something else. Sometimes it would happen because I mistakenly played it wrong. You know, I always remembered what Monk and Art Blakey told me: "If you make a mistake, play it again and it ain't a mistake." What's important is whether or not it worked.

The reality that Mwandishi was Herbie Hancock's band was musically rewarding, particularly due to his open style of leadership, but it became problematic when the collectivist approach on the bandstand became in conflict with the fiscal reality that the band was not a business collective. The band's ultimate lack of financial sustainability is a topic we examine in chapter 11, when we discuss the dissolution of the band. We turn first to the extended unfolding of the band's life together on the road, a period of constant touring, memorable shows, conflicts about venue choices, and music reviewers' responses to the band, alternately passionate and critical.

The music is right and you can feel it in your bones, no matter how it may vary from the norm. This has to do with the technical skill of the musicians, which is considerable; their facility at listening to each other and the intelligence of Hancock himself. It is music from emotions below the surface.

JOHN WASSERMAN, 1972

10

Life on the Road, 1971–73, and the Critical Response

On the Road in 1971 *Mwandishi*

With the *Mwandishi* (1971) recording completed, it was time to take the music back on the road, beginning in Los Angeles and then in the San Francisco area, which had come to be their home audience base.[1] This would launch two and a half years of steady touring with few subs. "Ostinato" and "You'll Know When You Get There" were now on the set lists.[2] Ndugu Leon Chancler joined the band for the opening show of the tour:

> After playing on the *Mwandishi* recording, I would see that
> band play whenever they were in LA. I was a good friend with
> everybody in the band, and so sometimes I would play with
> them. Soon after the record came out, I joined them as a second
> drummer with a full kit for a week at the Light House. The band
> was smoking. It was smoking. I was starting to get a name for

myself, and the audience was into seeing Billy and me together. Other times, I would just sit in with a bass drum or snare drum, but not the full kit. Man, it was on fire.[3]

Leonard Feather described the music during a mid-February stand at the Both/And as "free, abstract pieces that rarely make use of confining harmony, structures or rhythms" and "impressionism, emotionalism."[4]

In early May, *Billboard* described the Sextet as being "in the midst of a nationwide tour," but there is little documentation of this period.[5] Eliot Tiegel reported on an April 6 show at Shelly's Manne-Hole: "Hancock's style is in the current Miles Davis open force style, yet retains a thread of discipline which keeps all the parts within the same musical structure. Nobody is out reaching for the moon by himself."[6] Bassist Reggie Willis, who was one of two subs for Buster Williams during a spring week in Minneapolis,[7] recalls: "Walking into a situation like this was a little bit unnerving. There were pieces with different meters. It was pretty original in terms of melodic content and we didn't have time to rehearse. I don't recall ever doing anything that resembled standards, it was all original music." Back east, some of the band's shows were in Washington, D.C.,[8] and Montreal,[9] which *Coda* called one of the "exceptional performances."[10] An appearance at the Bitter End in New York City impressed the *New York Times*: "The band demonstrated . . . to an audience composed mainly of entranced rock enthusiasts, time dissolves in the energy of their music. An hour-long set felt like fifteen minutes."[11] The Sextet next began its first full-fledged European tour in mid-July.[12] The performance in Nice, France, shows further electronic expansions of Hancock's electric piano and, on an extensive version of "You'll Know When You Get There," horn solos unfolding at a relaxed rate.

During this period, the length of tunes was growing. During a California tour from August through September, the *Oakland Tribune* noted with some concern that during a two-week stand at the Both/And, a single tune, "Ostinato," comprised the full set, fifty-two minutes in duration. Given more time to play each tune, the band was playing what Hancock described that night as "high-energy music." *Tribune* writer Russ Wilson credits this as being as good a term "as any for this strongly percussive, rarely melodic, often chaotic, tremendously loud pattern of sounds."[13] A year later, an October 8 show at Baker's Keyboard Lounge in Detroit, recorded on tape, was comprised of a nearly hour-long performance of "Sleeping Giant."

During a mid-October stand at the Smiling Dog Saloon in Cleveland,[14] part of a Midwest swing,[15] house band drummer Skip Hadden recalls that each tune, largely from *Crossings* (1972),

> could take up to 1–1 1/2 hours, the entire set. Each soloist would play until he was finished and then the next soloist would take it up after a free open section usually with percussion by everyone and then a resetting of a new groove, direction and feel. I recall that on each solo they would build and build and shift gears and take the energy higher each time. With Herbie's solos it would really build and shift gears and this would happen with continued building of energy three or more times. It would just BURN![16]

Saxophonist Ernie Krivda,[17] house bandleader, also remembers the warmth of the musicians:

> The group would chant before each set and it did seem to serve their focus. Herbie was always, in my experience a fine human being as well as a great musician. I was asked to sit in on occasion and one time there was a bassist also sitting in who was really not ready to do so. Playing "Maiden Voyage," of all things, this guy was hurting us badly, but Herbie remained calm through the tune and, in fact, at the end we were no worse for the wear. The chanting had done its work. The bassist was encouraged, having sat in with Herbie Hancock. The audience seemed not to notice.[18]

The band was attracting a following of aspiring musicians on whom the shows were having significant impact. A young Pat Metheny attended several nights of a week's stand at the Landmark Restaurant in Kansas City, Missouri, which might have come during this particular tour.[19] Pianist Mike Ning found one of the Kansas City shows

> transcending and adventurous to say the least, sounds and voicings not heard before, percussively driven, use of Fender Rhodes piano with modulators and wah-wahs. Hearing it inspired me to try the same, but only in special venues. . . . [O]n listening to *Mwandishi* again after all these years, I still find it fresh and innovative as ever, in all the areas involved, the instruments played, the playing itself, the cohesiveness of the group, solo passages building into something whether it be tonal or percussive patterns.[20]

Guitarist Gregory Applegate Edwards, then a student at the Berklee School of Music, recalls a fall appearance at the Boston Jazz Workshop:

> It was a beautiful night. . . . [T]hey started the first set off as an acoustic trio: Herbie, Buster and Billy. Hart was using brushes, Buster was walking a line of fire and Herbie was playing his ass off on what I remember must have been a standard [and,] I believe, added Bennie for one tune, then on to their electric *Mwandishi* material, with the usual crew, Priester, and Henderson, who really sounded terrific. They were especially energized and did very long versions of things that were on the *Mwandishi* album including, I think, "You'll Know When You Get There." I remember being amazed that Herbie could keep that music going and then turn around and play some amazingly complex and spacey psychedelic jazz-rock with an entirely different sensibility. Herbie was almost apologetic when he started off the first set with the acoustic trio. He said something like, "I know you probably aren't expecting this, but we still like to play some of the earlier things when we can." The crowd really dug them that night. I remember a cat who worked at the hippest record store downtown was there and he was thrilled. "Herbie is taking it out, at last!"[21]

The band's year closed with an early November show at the Beacon Theater in New York City[22] and a late December benefit in Baltimore for the Sickle Cell Anemia Fund.[23] Several members played studio sessions themselves, particularly in November.[24]

Critical Response to the 1971 Band

Trying to draw conclusions from concert reviews by critics during this stage in the band is a little like a Rorschach test, sometimes within the same review. In March 1971, Leonard Feather appreciated that "the sextet gives unsparingly of itself, and demands as much of the audience. This is music for involvement, never for casual listening." He also sounds relieved to find, in contrast with *Fat Albert Rotunda* (1970), "rewarding evidence that the leader has not pursued the rock-jazz direction with which he toyed around in an album and concerts last year."[25] Feather also enthused about a performance of "You'll Know When You Get There" at a show at the Both/And in San Francisco, calling it "a dazzling mixture of impressionism, emotionalism and savage attacks on the senses" built on Buster Williams's electric bass riff. The unusual combination of horns "lent the sextet a timbre so distinctive that it was almost like listening to a miniature Gil Evans ensemble." Feather concludes that two years after playing with Miles Davis, Hancock "has changed as drastically as Miles himself. His image today reflects more fully than ever his own special marriage of instinct and intellect. This is, in short, one of the handful of completely absorbing combos in jazz today."[26] Reviewer Don Heckman commented about the November show at the Beacon Theater in New York that "the group does everything one could ask—inventive improvising, crisp, well-integrated ensemble playing, and a surging rhythmic momentum."[27]

Coda magazine described shows at Ronnie Scott's in London, July 26 to August 3, 1971, including "some startling non-stop sets."[28] Richard Williams, writing in *Melody Maker*, adds: "It was a priceless opportunity to see and hear at length six master musicians at work, men who've paid their dues and who are completely on top of their craft. I heard several sets during the week, and although the same basic shape and form were apparent, the variety of emotion and feeling expression in the music never failed to astound me."[29]

Taking a more critical perspective, Feather offered comments that preshadowed some of the criticism that the group would face in the future, holding that "fortified by a new and stronger personnel, the group now devotes most of its time to free, abstract pieces that rarely make use of confining harmony, structures or rhythms." He added that Hancock, "using an echo-plex [*sic*], . . . extracted all kinds of weird sounds from the electric keyboard."[30] Russ Wilson added, speaking about the show at the Both/And in September: "There were times it seemed almost as if Miles, [Tony] Williams, and Archie Shepp's groups were vying for the ear-splitter title."[31]

One of the more surprising reviews appeared in *Time* magazine, during the first week in January 1972, when it declared the recording *Mwandishi* to be among the year's best albums. "Miles Davis Protégé Herbie Hancock shows what jazz might have sounded like if it had come up the river from Darmstadt, that European mecca of the avant-garde, instead of New Orleans."[32] This exclamation of approval was also an acknowledgment that some critics and listeners weren't sure what to make of the band's sound.

Darmstadt refers to Internationale Ferienkurse für Neue Musik, the International Courses of New Music in Darmstadt, Germany. Darmstadt represented the intellectual musical avant-garde of its time, beginning in the early 1950s, with summer courses offered by Karlheinz Stockhausen, Pierre Boulez, Bruno Maderna, Luciano Berio, Luigi Nono, and others. The *Time* writers were no doubt searching for an avant-garde context for the music of the Mwandishi band. Ironically, Hancock was familiar with music from Darmstadt, but no more or less than music from numerous other sources. One could have just as easily looked to African American musicians like Ornette Coleman, John Coltrane, and members of the Association for the Advancement of Creative Musicians to provide a sufficiently useful reference point.[33]

Critical Response to the 1972–73 Touring Band

Touring continued in early January 1972 with stands in Montreal, Philadelphia, and New York (at the Village Vanguard).[34] These dates were the lead-up to recording sessions for *Crossings*, in the San Francisco Bay area, which we have discussed in depth. Immediately after the sessions, the band remained in California for a month of performances.[35] Except for Hancock's electronically expanding Fender Rhodes, the electronic interpolations and postproduction of *Crossings* had not yet entered the band's live arena. The band was received enthusiastically, as *San Francisco Examiner* critic Philip Elwood observed at the Both/And:

> Hancock can claim the creation of a new concept in modern American music. . . . Hancock's is mind-music. There is an intensity of involvement about it. Exhausting and complex but never obscure nor boring. Immensely entertaining as long as one is willing to listen, and be swept up in the collective creative experience. . . . [T]he crowd was clapping and flipping, totally involved wholly caught up in the artistic intensity [with the solos on "Firewater"]. . . . [Hancock's acoustic piano was] particularly impressive—neat, rich, highly provocative for his colleagues' solos. . . . Maupin carves out towering sax solos. Hart (as always) is crisp and spare, never superfluous nor expansive.[36]

A second European tour, two weeks in March, included stops in Switzerland,[37] Italy, Denmark, Sweden, the Netherlands, and two cities in France. A Paris studio show was filmed for French television.[38] David Rubinson recalls that the European tour was not easy:

> It was bedlam—very bad reviews, lots of booing and yelling. Audiences expected "Maiden Voyage" and "Speak Like a Child," even though *Mwandishi* had come out. Warners had been poor about promoting it and there were lots of fights with the European record companies. There was lots of resistance on the European tour. I don't know if fruit was thrown!

However, existing recordings seem to reflect appreciative audiences. *Coda's* Boland Baggenaes called the Copenhagen appearance "the most intriguing jazz to be heard over here so far this year."[39]

A review by Michel Savy of the final Paris concert was absolutely stellar:

[Herbie Hancock is a] surprising alchemist, he mixes tradition and modernism with a rather subtle rigor. In this kaleidoscope of many memories we see perfect musicians whose imagination has never been lacking. An arranger influenced by some of his colleagues of occidental classical music, he brings out with the same expertise the inexhaustible source of rhythm 'n blues. His writing, with a remarkable ability, make the instruments (flutes, saxes, trumpet, flugelhorn, diverse trombones) sound sumptuous, thanks to a precise knowledge of their timbres and the possibilities of their juxtaposition. America, Europe, therefore, but also Africa (and sometimes even South America) with the permanent use of varied percussive instruments, of rhythms whose responsibility relies on each musician of the sextet. The pianist was equally exceptional. . . . A few measures of introduction to an unforgettable *Maiden Voyage* have summed up all the European piano from Fauré to Stockhausen without forgetting Debussy, Ravel and Bartok. It is not a display of erudition. But one must remember once again, that the jazz of today (the live music of today) must be open to what is "other" past or present. . . . Music is sound, one likes to remember sometimes: the one that this formation gives us is the most beautiful that one can discover in our present time.[40]

It was at this point that Patrick Gleeson joined the band with a weeklong stand, most likely in late April 1972, at the Village Vanguard in New York, from which they traveled to Boston[41] and off to the West Coast. Critic Vic Field described a show at the Whiskey-a-Go-Go in Los Angeles[42] as "a stage cluttered with an array of instruments ranging from a synthesizer to gourd maracas set the mood for elaborate liberal jazz themes. Herbie went on to perform a well-received act with little difficulty." As noted in chapter 8, an inadequate sound system in this and other clubs led Hancock to purchase and tour with his own gear.[43] A poorly documented East Coast tour by the expanded Mwandishi band began in New York[44] and included an appearance at the Newport Jazz Festival at Carnegie Hall, in New York.[45] Summer and early fall shows on the West Coast[46] included the San Francisco folk-rock club the Boarding House in August, netting kudus for all, including Gleeson: "The group is technically impressive, with reeds, brass, and percussion . . . plus Pat Gleeson's electronic synthesizer, and Hancock's keyboards. . . . Julian Priester's trombone, Buster Williams' bass and Benny Maupin's reeds were outstanding."[47]

The constant touring[48] included shows attended by pianist Onaje Allan Gumbs during a weeklong stand at the Revilot Lounge in Buffalo,[49] a club "like Buffalo's version of the Village Vanguard. . . . The band itself seemed to have ESP. Hollie I. West described shows at the Cellar Door in Washington, D.C., as "charged with turbulent energy and lyrical outpourings." West observed of Hancock: "He can be both a miniaturist working in water colors or landscapist using oils. His shifting harmonies are delicate and euphonious and the resulting colors evoke images of wind, rain, fog, playground scenes, sailboats."[50] From a seemingly chaotic collective improvisation, the band would end a song on a simple chord all in the same key." The band was growing musically, witnessed by John S. Wilson's review of an early December show in New York's Beacon Theater: "Their hour on stage was mainly divided between a look ahead to the potentials of electronic jazz, built around a mood synthesizer played by Pat Gleeson and Mr. Hancock's electric piano and reflections of the African roots of the music in a percussion section that, at times, included everyone in the group."[51] The band closed out the year back in Boulder, Colorado, and in the San Francisco area.[52]

In December, Hancock moved his family to Los Angeles and went back on the road with the band for the last time starting in February. A wide range of the band's music was on display at a concert recorded late in February 1973 at Strata Art Gallery in Detroit. The set list included a nearly forty-three-minute version of "Hidden Shadows" from the forthcoming *Sextant* (1973); "Firewater" from *The Prisoner* (1969); just under a half-hour version of a tune they never recorded, Hancock's "Revelation"; and then "You'll Know When You Get There" from *Mwandishi*. Touring continued in late March[53] with a show at the Boston Jazz Workshop, at the Berklee College of Music,[54] which was broadcast live on the radio and recorded. Their intense and expansive version of "Hornets" from *Sextant* shows the playfulness and full engagement of the band with Gleeson as a full participant. Also part of the set was "You'll Know When You Get There," a solo piano version of "Watermelon Man," and then the full band on "Maiden Voyage" and "Ostinato: Suite for Angela."[55]

Several memorable weeklong stands also took place in the Midwest.[56] Drummer Skip Hadden[57] remembers shows at the Smiling Dog in Cleveland:

They played the material from *Sextant*. The band was the same as on the recordings, including Dr. Patrick Gleeson on computers to generate the synth sounds. We often hung with them on the breaks and at the ends of gigs. . . . I recall speaking with Herbie about "Hornets" from *Sextant* and the odd time signatures (19/4) that he was exploring. Herbie explained about playing with the energy that people projected in their music and this was very intriguing.[58]

Mark Edelman wrote about one of the late shows in Kansas City, which were also attended by Pat Metheny:

People sat quietly and wondered. Control—motive and form amidst the anarchy—is the first word to fit. From way back of the band Hancock guides not only his piano, but the whole huge bank of sound, silently, without touching but forever in touch. Moog, horns, bass and percussion—all fall into precarious position as if by divine accident, either one stop late or a quarter beat early but always right on time. The music moves its shapes at thoughtful random through one lush moonscape, a Klee or Miro turned to masses of high-energy wail and slow-breathing moan. The synthesizer further textures the product, here pummeling, there caressing until the long distance legacies of Satchmo and the cotton fields back home seem bended, folded and muti-lated out of existence. But listen again. The roots, the old keyboard lines, the hard driving—it's all still gloriously intact.[59]

The Mwandishi band was musically flourishing during this period, per-forming exciting and unpredictable shows. Audiences were enthusiastic, and the band was gaining the admiration of musicians. The mix of acoustic and electronic instruments was something truly new and, as Edelman testifies, musically engaging and successful. The critical reaction, however, was mixed.

Mixed Responses in the Jazz Press

Like Edelman and Elwood raved about performances of the Mwandishi band, Elliot Meadow observed in *Down Beat*: "Possibly, Herbie Hancock has the most stimulating group playing today. Individually, each of the six men are at the very top of their respective games and none more than Benny Maupin."[60] Others responded negatively. Some jazz critics responded harshly to the elec-tronic direction of the band. Critic and former fan Leonard Feather offered a

rather ambivalent appreciation in January 1973 when he wrote: "Happy return of the year. . . . Also to Miles Davis, all of whose glorious yesterdays seem
to have been electrocuted. And to pianist/composer Herbie Hancock, Davis
alumnus, whose brilliance has been lost in a forest of percussion effects played
by sidemen who would be better off returning to—their horns."[61]

One *Down Beat* reviewer, Bill McLarney, was puzzled not by the music, but
by the negativity of his fellow critics. Having attended two Mwandishi shows,
he concluded that the listener who arrives with an open mind would be treated
to something rare: "This group has gotten a lot of strange reviews—by earnest
men, one supposes, with reasons for their reactions. . . . What matters is that
this music, these artists, have the ability to get you next to yourself and maybe
some night, even to work a transformation—if you are ready."[62] McLarney
praised the intensity and expressiveness of the band's mosaic:

> Perhaps the reviewers have all caught the band on its off nights. Or perhaps
> they haven't heeded Hancock, who told an audience, "Don't listen so hard.
> Don't worry about understanding what's going on up here." . . . Here are a
> few of the experiences of someone who stayed in the room. . . . Priester now
> the wind, with all its moods, on Hancock's sea, now a hopeful red balloon on
> that wind. . . . Henderson burning deep, a fire underground in Spain. Williams
> singing the songs only a bass can sing, great brown tree roots. Gleeson's syn-
> thesizer, sometimes one with the wind and sea, sometimes plainly man's tool,
> joining in the Afro percussion—cultures dance together . . . an impressive
> demonstration of human community without the loss of individuality.

The mixed reviews continued into June 1973, when Frankie Nemko reported about shows the band played at the Troubadour in Los Angeles:

> I found the sounds both relaxing and exciting. Maybe this is due in part to
> the instrumentation, since everyone makes use of some percussion gadget
> or other, and I always find these effects most soothing. However, the energy
> level is so high that right when I'm drifting off into that nether world, I'm
> sharply brought back by a dynamic flurry of notes from Eddie Henderson's
> pocket trumpet, and I remain riveted on that for what feels like hours.

Nemko particularly appreciated the extended soloing, accompanied by collective percussion, and was particularly impressed by Julian Priester. "It was
something I never heard before," as well as some piano trio playing "some

funky, straight-ahead playing that just blew my mind with its simplicity and earthiness."[63]

A second critic at the Troubadour, Dennis Hunt, also captured the intensity of the Mwandishi band that night, but was more critical of their approach:

> The music of the Hancock sextet is a taxing, emotional experience that conveys tension, anger and passion, as well as chaos and confusion; it is bizarrely structured and at times sounds like melodic clamor. The key to its accessibility is drummer Billy Hart, who often provides a familiar framework of uncomplicated rhythms that reorient the unsettled listeners. To appease those with more conventional tastes, Hancock, with Hart and bassist Buster Williams, even played a relatively simple trio number on acoustic instruments. One of the many memorable segments of that first set was a bass clarinet solo by Benny Maupin that sounded like a long, crazily modulated scream.[64]

What seemed most troubling to some critics were some of the strongest points of the band, its intensity, freshness, unpredictability, and passion. Where familiar handles could be found, those critics could appreciate what they were hearing.

Playing the Troubadour Presages the End of the Band

A final West Coast swing began at the Troubadour in Los Angeles from May 15 to 20. The double bill was opened by the Pointer Sisters, who were also managed by David Rubinson and were preparing to break onto the commercial scene. Hunt describes the Pointer Sisters as

> a unique, campy, often sensational quartet of singers [who] have built an act around 40s-style jazz . . . four effervescent young black singers [who] were dressed in marvelously tacky 40s outfits. . . . [The Pointer Sisters gave] a powerhouse set. . . . [T]heir act has some flaws, but all are the kind that generally disappear with experience. . . . They are the most unusual and exciting group that I have seen in quite some time.[65]

The contrast drawn between what Hunt describes as Mwandishi's "melodic clamor," despite Hart's "uncomplicated rhythms," and the palpable excitement of the Pointer Sisters wasn't lost on Hancock, as much as he loved the Mwandishi band.

Some band members saw the booking at a commercial venue to be a nega-tive direction for the Mwandishi band. Crowds of Mwandishi aficionados had been attending their shows. Due to an inherent conflict between the con-servative nature and acoustic limitations of jazz clubs and the kind of music the band was playing, they had gradually been playing other kinds of venues. Jazz clubs also did not offer an avenue for this music to reach a larger pub-lic. *San Francisco Examiner* writer Philip Elwood alluded to this in his highly positive review of a show a full year earlier, at the Both/And: "With such in-ternationally acknowledged artistry with such a large local following, with such instant communication in the finest jazz sense, why should the Hancock group be playing under such restricted and limited nightclub circumstances where less than half the necessarily small audience can see more than half the performers."[66] When the band played a San Francisco folk-rock club, Elwood commented: "The engagement was inevitable since Hancock's music has long since outgrown 'jazz-blues' clubs . . . and, in turn, the Boarding House needs occasional stimulation from musical artistry that transcends the current ultra-rock scene."[67] The idea of moving into other venues appealed to Hancock, who had noted as early as 1971:

> Oddly enough, the rock listeners can often get to my music easier than the jazz people, who come in expecting something specific and perhaps don't get it. A guy can come in high, drunk, or even sober, with maybe a book of tran-scendental meditation under his arm and [a] couple of tickets to a Bob Dylan concert in his pocket, and he can sometimes get into it more easily.[68]

The Troubadour was arguably the most mainstream, commercial club the band had ever played, and the contrast between their intense and complex music with the populist aspirations and polished presentation of the Pointer Sisters magnified the differences. Already, the experience of playing rock and popular music clubs added to a building frustration and wounded personal pride felt by members of the band. It was difficult for jazz musicians of this caliber and experience to share bills with musicians they viewed as well be-low their level. Buster Williams articulates a sentiment echoed by others: "We got this great band and we all had a personal pride in this and its music. And now we had to shave it all down. We had to underplay ourselves." Patrick Gleeson recalls a different kind of conflict felt by Hancock: "When I joined the band, he had all the elements he needed, but people weren't getting it. Herbie wanted to play in big concert halls, but he was playing small concert halls and jazz clubs and was not where, he felt, the music belonged. And he was frustrated about that."

The Troubadour show was followed by shows in Berkeley[69] and an early June concert in San Rafael, which may have been the Mwandishi band's final show.[70] Eddie Henderson describes the ending poignantly: "And through God's grace it came to that pinnacle and it vanished. It just vanished."

11

Endings and Unexpected Recordings

During spring 1973, the closing period for the Mwandishi band, the group's shows were growing in intensity and depth. Eddie Henderson recalls:

> The music was really crystallizing. It was self-evident that we had come to a pinnacle in our development. I didn't know it was going to end at the peak, at the apex. Everybody had adjusted [to Pat Gleeson's joining the band]. . . . We were all growing musically, personally, spiritually, so a lot of prejudices we had about this or about that, about music or whatever, we were growing [beyond].

But the business model on which the band was sustained was not viable. While they were on tour in Denver, the band held a crucial meeting with Hancock's management about how dire their financial situation was. Billy Hart recounts: "Herbie admitted how he was losing money. And to keep the band together we need to get into other venues." Pat Gleeson recalls an additional meeting in the Empire State Building in New York City, shortly before the recording of *Sextant* (1973), that included Herbie's accountant. David Rubinson describes the situation: "What paid their way was every dime Herbie Hancock had, every single sweat-dollar Pillsbury cake mix commercials and European sales of 'Watermelon Man,' and what happened was that Herbie, and those from whom he borrowed, ran out of money."[1]

Hancock had been supporting his more creative musical projects for some time with income from commercial sources, such as the Yardley men's cologne television ad for which he composed "Maiden Voyage."[2] "You'll Know When You Get There" was first composed for Eastern Airlines. John Wasserman, writing in the *San Francisco Chronicle*, concluded: "Herbie Hancock, a major figure in American popular music, pays for the privilege of bringing us his music. Literally."[3] The financial debt was substantial, and something had to change.

Rubinson's analysis was that the only solution would be for the band to become a business collective, with everyone carrying an equal share of the responsibility and burden of promotion and financing. This was a rare but not untested model. In 1965, John Coltrane, Babatunde Olatunji, and Yusef Lateef had attempted to collectively "organize an independent performance space and booking agency." It was abandoned due to Coltrane's death.[4] The Art Ensemble of Chicago[5] incorporated as the Art Ensemble of Chicago Operations and was owned equally by all five members of the group. Under that umbrella, they established their own publishing company and independent record label. "Decisions that impacted the group business were taken collectively in meetings," with Don Moye focusing on "administering the cooperative and generating work opportunities," while Lester Bowie "negotiated deals and contracts.'"[6]

Earlier models existed as well. Among them was the Society for Private Music Performances (Verein für musikalische Privataufführungen), founded by Arnold Schoenberg in 1918 in Vienna,[7] and, in the late 1840s and early 1850, the Germania Musical Society, first in Germany and then in the United States. The Germania Musical Society was a collective orchestra performing works in the existing European concert repertory, under the principle

all for one and one for all, equality in rights and in duties. Each member thus renounces freely and voluntarily all financial advantages, because laws that would not be based on these social principles would not be able to assure the liberty and the independence of the associated, considering that where there is inequality of wealth, true liberty is an illusion, or rather, a falsehood. It is the brotherhood of men, and not egoism, which is the greatest stimulant of all useful activities.[8]

But a business collective was not a model to which everyone could agree. Band members felt as if they were being asked to sacrifice their livelihoods, and Hancock felt like the burden was falling entirely on him.[9] Henderson concludes: "As far as I'm concerned, it was Herbie's band, even though we wanted to call it our band." Under these circumstances, the band could not last.

The experience at the Troubadour also moved Hancock to reflect about his own personal musical goals: "[I] saw how [the Pointer Sisters] immediately communicated with the audience. . . . I was trying to learn from them just what things would have to be done in order to help people get into our music a little easier."[10] "I suspected that my own energy needed something else. . . . I began to feel that I had been spending so much time exploring the upper atmosphere of music and the more ethereal kind of far-out, spacey stuff. Now there was this need to take some more of the earth and to feel a little more tethered, a connection to the earth. . . . I started thinking about Sly Stone and how much I loved his music and how funky 'Thank You for Letting Me Be Myself' is."[11] Hancock was changing. His Buddhist chanting practice led him to reflect, and he concluded that it was wrong to treat funk as somehow less than jazz. So, "I knew I had to take the idea seriously. Would I like to have a funky band that played the kind of music Sly or someone like that was playing? My response was, 'Actually, yes.'"[12]

Hancock desired more consistency than an experimental band allowed: "The problem with intuition is that as soon as the vibrations aren't happening nothing works anymore."[13] He felt that the Mwandishi music had run its course: "And at a certain point, my feeling was we had gone as far as we could. I just didn't feel there was any more development that I was capable of producing."[14]

Down Beat magazine ran a sensationalized announcement that Hancock had fired the band.[15] Hancock responded: "[The sextet disbanded because] I ran out of money. I could get gigs, but they wouldn't pay enough for the expenses. I always lost money. Not with every single gig but maybe I'd make a profit, and then on the next one, I'd lose more that the two put together."[16]

Simply put, all things, even the best things, come to an end. The dissolution of the band was painful for many of its members, as Hart recalls: "I was disappointed because I really thought we had something. . . . I was broken-hearted when the band broke up." Henderson adds: "I was shocked when he said he was going to break up the band. I was angry that the band broke up. I was hurt for a long time." The Mwandishi band was an unusual mix of a band with a leader, requiring a viable business model and a group that functioned like a musical collective once on the bandstand. They had lived together on a daily basis for an extended period of time as a touring band, built interpersonal bonds, felt like a family, but at the same time, were the current musical vehicle for one of the most searching, ever changing, creative souls, Herbie Hancock.

From Gleeson's perspective, while the sense of loss was painful, "Herbie is a creative artist. I had turned him on to what I was doing and now he wanted to do it [himself]." Hancock was ready to become the synthesizer soloist the world knows from *Head Hunters* (1973), a recording whose electronic approach continued an interest in electronic sounds that had already been building for nearly two decades and attained a unique level of creative expression during the Mwandishi era.

Hart understands the breakup this way:

> I think we channeled [the unusual gifts of the band members] into a creativity that could function under Herbie's guise with the attraction we all had for Herbie. For a while it was irresistible. [But] it was a distraction from what Herbie had originally had in mind in the first place. And so when it finally came to his attention that he was going a little too far out on the limb . . . Herbie's genius is: [if] it doesn't work, then make it work another way. He would get excited about whatever new ventures would come along. Except that he hadn't found it yet.

At this point, there were compelling reasons for Hancock to feel that the Headhunters band could provide the creative juice and audience for the next stage in his development. And many within the audiences that Hancock and Miles Davis had sought to attract were turning to various expressions of jazz-rock and jazz-funk, such as Davis alumni Chick Corea's Return to Forever and John McLaughlin's Mahavishnu Orchestra. As it turned out, the Headhunters band, really much more jazz-funk than funk, was able to reach a new audience as well as a substantial portion of Hancock's Mwandishi audience.

Recordings by Julian Priester and Eddie Henderson

But the work of the band was not completely done. Patrick Gleeson contributed Arp, Moog, and Oberheim synthesizers to Julian Priester's *Love, Love*, recorded on June 28 and September 1973, at Gleeson's Different Fur Trading Company studio.

Eddie Henderson recorded two LPs under his name, including most of the members of the Mwandishi band. *Realization* was the first, recorded a year earlier, in 1972, shortly after the Strata show. The tunes include Hancock's "Revelation," never included on a Mwandishi recording. The recording included the entire Mwandishi band minus Priester, and it shares the kinetic energy of the late-period band. As Henderson describes the recording: "The music . . . was how the Mwandishi band sounded live. My concept on two tunes ['Scorpio' and 'Libra'] was [based on] 'Hornets.' And 'Revelations,' that was Herbie's tune." The "Hornets"-related tunes are built on the same bass riff as the original, its driving rhythmic feel, and multilayered instrumental mix. The album also included Bennie Maupin's tune "Anua." "Revelations" was also recorded on Norman Connors's 1974 LP, *Love from the Sun*.

Henderson placed his own mark on *Realization*, his first recording, by using two drummers, Billy Hart and Lenny White, and including only two of the Mwandishi horn players. The album was recorded at Gleeson's Different Fur Trading Company studio, and produced for a rock label, Capricorn Records, by Gleeson, who also did synthesizer overdubs, and Skip Drinkwater. "As a composer," Henderson recalled, "I've learned to make a collective portrait rather than a self-portrait. But some composers write in every beat, fill up the space and stuff, I like to write little motifs and let it up to the other musicians to fill in. That collective portrait far supersedes any individual portrait. I just gave Buster free leeway because I'd become accustomed so much to it in Herbie's band."

Henderson's second recording, *Inside Out*, was recorded several months after the breakup of the Mwandishi band, around the time *Head Hunters* was released, in October 1973. The music was once again what Henderson calls "kind of like the [Mwandishi] band, with the synthesizers and stuff." Although it was done after the band broke up, "we still loved each other. It was very close; just a little time gap after the band broke up." The instrumentation was similar, with Billy Hart complemented this time by a second drummer, Eric Gravatt.

Norman Connors Recordings

Around the same time, the configuration of Herbie Hancock, Eddie Henderson, and Buster Williams also participated in drummer/vocalist Norman Connors's third recording, *Love from the Sun*, this time adding Hubert Laws on flute, singer Dee Dee Bridgewater, and Onaje Allan Gumbs, who played keyboards and arranged some of the tunes. The recording featured a new arrangement of Hancock's tune "Revelation." One of the tunes from that session, "Kwasi," with Hancock and Williams, found its way onto Connors's subsequent record, *Saturday Night Special* (1975).

Love from the Sun has a distinct Mwandishi feel in its interplay between instruments and intense pulse. At its core is the rhythm section of Hancock's Echoplexed electric piano and bassist Williams's slides and rapid interpolations. The string section recordings were made at Gleeson's Different Fur Trading Company studio. The former Mwandishi players were joined as in the past by saxophonists Gary Bartz, Carlos Garnett, and others.

Various members of the Mwandishi band had performed on Connors's first two recordings as well, both the previous year. Hancock, Henderson and Hart played on Connors's first recording, *Dance of Magic* (1972).[17] Hancock then returned, this time with Henderson, to participate in the first of three sessions on Connors's second recording, *Dark of Light*.[18] They were joined by saxophonists Gary Bartz, Carlos Garnett, and others at the Hit Factory in New York. The recordings were completed in February 1973 with the addition of Williams.[19]

A Final Mwandishi Recording: *The Spook Who Sat by the Door*

By spring 1973,[20] the Mwandishi band entered the studio for a fourth recording, the soundtrack to a film *The Spook Who Sat by the Door*. The film (now available on DVD) and soundtrack LP were each in circulation for only a brief period after their release. David Rubinson notes that each was recorded by a videographer and sound recorder during a movie theater film playback. The soundtrack recording is about thirty minutes long and consists of through-composed and improvised material, specifically for use in this black nationalist film thriller. The recording also includes dialogue. I only recently viewed the film and heard the LP sound track release, although I had read the Sam Greenlee novel on which it was based in high school or college.

Here is a published synopsis of the plot:

In order to improve his standing with Black voters, a White Senator starts a campaign for the CIA to recruit Black agents. However, all are graded on a curve and doomed to fail, save for a soft-spoken veteran named Dan Free-man. After grueling training in guerrilla warfare, clandestine operations and unarmed combat, he is assigned a meager job as the CIA's token Black em-ployee. After five years of racist and stereotyped treatment by his superiors, he quietly resigns to return to his native Chicago to work for a social services agency . . . by day. By night, he trains a street gang to be the vanguard in an upcoming race war, using all that the CIA has taught him.[21]

The most notable aspect of the recording, only some of which was used in the film as action backdrops, segues, and scene transitions, is its highly funky character. The opening track, "Revolution," is built on a series of four repeated seven-note riffs, with a slight rhythmic change in the fourth. This kind of vamp is reminiscent of other black film scores of the era. "The Pick Up" on side two repeats the same vamp, with a juke joint sax solo and horn refrain. The title track is a version of "Actual Proof," the reprise version on side one bearing strong similarities to the version recorded on the Headhunters band album *Thrust* in August 1974. In both cases, Hancock uses a synthesizer as a melody instrument and a Hohner Clavinet for funky comping. "Revenge," with its electronic washes behind a funk vamp, displays Maupin playing his hum-a-zoo. "At the Lounge" well reflects the title. "Training Day," "The Stick Up," "The Big Rip Off," and "It Begins" are variants on the "Revolution" vamp, with varying degrees of electronic textures. "The Big Rip Off" is the lengthiest and most intensely electronic of the group. "Main Theme" is pure Hollywood in its full tilt string and horns arrangement.

"Underground" opens with a talking drum sound anticipating the open-ing riff on the Headhunters version of "Watermelon Man." The tune contin-ues with a vamp and electric piano sounds that bear similarities to "Hidden Shadows" on *Sextant*. "Recruiting," set in a pool hall, features a blues-infused

Example 17. *The Spook Who Sat By the Door*, "Revolution" theme

electric guitar above a funky vamp that includes rhythm guitar. The final track is solely dialogue, which is otherwise occasionally interspersed within the rest of the tracks.

The funk vamps and the strong congruence between the title track and the Headhunter's recording of "Actual Proof" raises the question of whether there could have been a commercially viable Mwandishi band. Certainly, it is clear that the band that appears on *The Spook Who Sat by the Door* suggests that Mwandishi was more than musically capable of playing the music we know from its successor band. But I have some doubts about the viability of this option. The essential character of the Mwandishi band was its exploratory, unpredictable, and thus essentially noncommercial nature. After three years of a collaborative musical organization comprised of strong personalities, it could never have easily or happily become fully Hancock's band with him playing a conventional lead role. There were too many cooks in the kitchen.

At the same time, I also believe that *Head Hunters* has been largely misunderstood. I see it as a more exploratory recording than many seem to think and despite its unprecedented sales. Rubinson shocked Hancock when he told him about its sales reports. Although *The Spook Who Sat by the Door* was crafted specifically as a motion picture soundtrack, first and foremost a commercial venture, it included segments with wild electronics that are hardly tamed for the commercial market.

Gleeson describes the recording sessions for *The Spook Who Sat by the Door*:

> We did the *Spook* orchestral sessions quickly—one double session for fifty to sixty pieces, and another smaller session. David Rubinson produced the original, never released sessions, which were recorded at what was then Columbia Studios and which shortly thereafter became David Rubinson's Automatt. The players were mostly from the San Francisco Symphony and the Oakland Symphony, with the guys in the band assuming solo roles. Amusingly, when the charts were handed out, the copyist handed me one labeled "Synthesist," which had staves and, I believe, a treble clef, but was otherwise blank. Later that week we did small group sessions at Wally Heider's.[22]

Bennie Maupin's Recordings, and Two Reunion Shows

Bennie Maupin's *Jewel in the Lotus*, recorded in March 1974, also includes the Mwandishi band rhythm section of Hancock, Williams, and Hart. Its floating textures reflect the exploratory, meditative qualities of their former band. Maupin's subsequent album, *Slow Traffic to the Right* (1977), includes Onaje Allan Gumbs's arrangements of two tunes originally included on *Crossings* (1972), "Quasar" and "Water Torture." Gumbs notes: "There are subtle references to Herbie's originals, but these were basically a rearrangement of the songs. [And] while 'Water Torture' is pretty much Bennie, Eddie's presence on 'Quasar' gives more a sense of the Mwandishi band." Gumbs also did arrangements for Buster Williams's solo albums "Pinnacle" (1975) and "Dreams Come True" (1980).

The Mwandishi band participated in a reunion during a June 29, 1976, Hancock retrospective at the Newport Jazz Festival in New York City. The band appeared on the same bill as Hancock's other projects of that period, the acoustic *V.S.O.P.*, which featured members of the Miles Davis second Quintet, with Freddie Hubbard on trumpet; and the Headhunters band. I attended that concert, which was released in a highly edited form, on LP. During the brief reunion of the Mwandishi band, all of the horn players had electronic devices to process their sounds. Eddie Henderson recalls: "Me, Bennie Maupin and Julian Priester, we had electronic hook-ups. I had wah-wah, phase shifter, Echoplex. Julian had all pedals and stuff, echoes." While the recording that was released frustrated some members of the band due to its tight editing that shortened the length of their performances, the show offered a sense of how the band might have sounded were it more fully electronic.

In the early 2000s, most of the band[23] reunited to raise money to help Julian Priester through a medical crisis. Eddie Henderson recorded and toured on Hancock's *Gershwin's World* project in 1998 and 2000. Billy Hart and Buster Williams have played together with singer, and Hart's mentor, Shirley Horn, and others. Collaborations have continued periodically over the years between Pat Gleeson and Julian Priester and, more recently, Gleeson and Bennie Maupin. Later, Maupin reunited with Eddie Henderson and Buster Williams. The story continues.

What echoes through the years as I continue to live within the music created by Miles, Herbie and all the others from this generation (not all of it electric) was the sense that music could be a vehicle for exploration and advancement of a cultural consciousness. We're talking border-crossing machines here, fueled not only by musicians who in the wake of Coltrane and Dolphy were willing to traverse uncharted terrain, but also the energy of an audience that, on the best nights, was fully along for the ride. Of course, it got a little far out for general consumption, and as the decade retrenched culturally into narrower and more predictable genres, it became inevitable that, like the NASA space program itself, this era of exploration would give way to other concerns.

CHUCK MITCHELL, veteran music and media executive, and former president of Verve Records, 2010

Epilogue
Reminiscences and Legacy

The Mwandishi band demonstrated that it was possible to create music with a strong rhythmic element that simultaneously treated timbre as a primary musical factor. It did so in a manner that straddled the line between a post-bop sensibility and the avant-garde. Acoustical, electric, and electronic sounds could inhabit the same musical plane, broadening the sonic palette for each of those elements. The balance of all these factors was achieved through an interpersonal and musical chemistry that allowed tremendous flexibility in form. In such an environment, multiple varieties of musical dynamics could change in an instant, and every individual player could influence the entire fabric. Collective improvisation and open forms were interwoven with lyrical lines and an intense rhythmic interplay. Yet within this complex system, a visionary leader could provide strong direction, shaping the overall musical environment. This took place within a cultural context of black identity in the early 1970s, providing an important example in the history of black musical experimentalism and cultural celebration.

The work of the Mwandishi band represented the fruition of a group that remained together for an extended period of time. But it was also the product of Herbie Hancock's personal musical evolution, from his early days as a hard bop player through his increasing experimentalism with Miles Davis. It was foreshadowed by Hancock's experience with Eric Dolphy and given creative infusions by his participation on *Kawaida* (1970) and in notable sessions with Davis during Hancock's electric period and its extensions, such as the recording of *Zawinul* (1970). Hancock's discovery of the Fender Rhodes electric piano and his development of its use as a flexible and increasingly electronic instrument pointed toward his subsequent use of synthesizers as a performance instrument. For Hancock, the Mwandishi band was an apex of more than a decade of professional and musical development, but it was also a portal to his subsequent creative work. This book, I hope, will open the door to the close attention that Herbie Hancock's Mwandishi band has long deserved.

The Mwandishi band has always had a strong following among musicians. One of the highlights of researching and writing this book was talking to musicians about the ways the band provided significant inspiration in their lives. I close with reflections, first from fellow musicians, and then from members of the band.

Bobby McFerrin

My whole desire to improvise comes from two encounters I had—the first seeing Miles—and then Herbie, exactly a year later, in February 1972. I had been a composition major in music school and I was doing a lot of arranging. As I was a composer, I was trying to lead everything. I wanted to guarantee that the music would go in a particular direction, rather than letting the musicians go their own way. I was giving too much information and constricting my musicians, sometimes by writing out solos.

After I saw Miles' band play—it was at Shelly's Manne-Hole, in Los Angeles—when I left the club that night, I knew my path would be different. I was molecularly altered, physically and spiritually. I had been bathed in some new light. My eyes were really open and my ears were really open. I saw the invisible and I could think the unthinkable. . . . I was changed.

The first time I saw the Mwandishi band was in Montreal, at the Esquire Show Bar. I was a pianist touring with the Ice Follies and Herbie was in town.

I was just barely 22. There was a horrific snowstorm that night. It was a short, uphill walk to the Pub, but it was windy and cold. The snow was blinding. Later that night, it took me about two hours to get back to my hotel by cab. I also remember the evening because it was when I first met Herbie. I sat at the bar and talked to him. I thought it was generous of him to give me his time; I was interested in sharing my experiences as a pianist; I was still learning the craft. He was one of my heroes.

Half of the audience kind of knew what to expect when they walked in. I was one of the few who didn't have any expectations at all. I really didn't know what to expect. I thought they would play some tunes and that would be that. When they started playing the one tune that filled the entire set, I thought to myself, "How long is this tune going to go on?" Then finally after an hour, the set was over. I was dumb-founded. At first I didn't quite get it. I didn't understand it.

I thought it was the coolest thing that they played just one set-long tune, "Ostinato." They locked into this one thing. Even though Herbie was the leader, he let the music lead. With Herbie, it could be brilliant one moment; it could plod along for a while, and then it would happen. But here was this professional musician, one of my heroes, this mountain of a musician, just letting the music go by itself. He was a servant of the music. That made a huge impression on me and on my life. From that point on, I would let the music be and go where it would want.

I saw Herbie's band a second time, in Los Angeles. It was the same band, but with Patrick Gleeson playing synthesizer. This time, the club was close by, and it was my night off. I might have been prepared for the electronics. As a composition student, I was getting into electronic things, synthesizer music. I was aware of it and I was beginning to explore it. But this was probably the first I had seen anything like that *live* and I took to it because I was curious about that kind of stuff.

When I saw them for the second time, I got that they were playing the same material, their *Mwandishi* "album on tour." They played "Ostinato" again, but it was a completely different piece. It was so totally different. I've come to understand as an improviser that you are supposed to let everything in, all the differences, let the music take all the directions. You are allowing it to go, rather than controlling things all the time.

Through these experiences, I was actually seeing and imagining what would be possible in music—you really become servants of the music. You kind of stand above and outside of yourself and observe the music as it's coming out. You can only do that when you are so confident about your technique that you don't need to think about the audience and your technique. Standing outside your self and watching the music—that was what I saw with Miles and with Herbie. You are following the music. You have enough technique to keep things in check, to keep things together, to keep your understanding of things harmonically and theoretically, but you are really letting the music express itself on its own. Listening to those guys just blow and not being concerned with whether it worked—it simply worked because they were on stage just doing it. The work was just watching these things happen.

Trumpeter Wallace Roney

I first saw the Mwandishi band with Buster and Eddie, Bennie, Julian and Billy in 1972. I had [already] seen Miles for the first time, and Weather Report, right before that. I was twelve years old, in Junior High School. I left for the show right after school. It was a matinee, at the Aqua Lounge in South Philly. They had evening sets later, but they were playing like this show was it. They played three songs: "You'll Know When You Get There" "Ostinato," and then Buster's "Firewater." I talked to Eddie Henderson afterwards; We talked about trumpets and trumpet players. He was playing through Miles's conception via Lee Morgan and Freddie Hubbard.

What I remember about it was that I felt this was where music was supposed to go. Although Miles was my all-time favorite—and Tony Williams Lifetime was adding his genius to Jimi Hendrix's sonic palette—Herbie's band had a combination of all of it. It included some of what Miles's band was about, some of Tony's band, some of Trane's band. The band sounds like they are going into a time machine and going into the future. Buster was playing halfway between Ron Carter and funk.

But Herbie's was my favorite band of the 70s (with Miles a close second and Tony Williams a close third) because it had elements of Miles' band in it. He had elements of the best of everybody in his band. He had taken Tony Williams Lifetime, Wayne Shorter's compositions, Bennie's bass clarinet, the element that Miles brought in with his sound, and Herbie wrote and arranged all of that. It sounded like Miles's band but more arranged. It sounded like Weather Report, but with more focus. Like Coltrane's band but without Coltrane's power. Maybe Herbie was Coltrane and Buster was McCoy [Tyner]. It was like Tony's band only in the sense that they were playing jazz-rock. Bennie had a little Joe Henderson. It was like the best of everything.

The Mwandishi band shaped the kind of band I wanted for myself. I wanted the orchestral colors and flavors and the mutability of Mwandishi. But I wanted myself as a player to have the power of Miles. Miles was my own model. I liked the fact that Miles would take one song. One song could be five songs, because there were so many moods within a tune. The Mwandishi band had the same things in them. Plus they had the African drum choir and so many other aspects. It was the music of the future.

The Mwandishi band was my favorite. Miles was my favorite artist. His band was my almost second favorite. I almost can't say that because he was my idol. I also loved the early days of Weather Report, with Eric Gravett and Miroslav Vitous and of course Wayne Shorter. To me, that was the moment when they had everything. They had jazz, it was funky, it was hard, it was space age, all in one. I try to do that now in 2010.

Pianist/composer Billy Childs

When I turned fourteen,[1] I heard Herbie Hancock's Sextet at Shelly's Manne-Hole in Los Angeles. I went with my sister Joy who was six years older than me. Joy particularly liked "Fat Albert Rotunda" and the tune "You'll Know When You Get There" from *Mwandishi*, which were both out and receiving airplay. This is what Joy thought Herbie was going to play at the show.

I had already seen Herbie play at Royce Hall [at UCLA] when I was twelve.[2] It was his previous Sextet, which was playing music from *The Prisoner*. I was just getting into jazz and it was a little over my head. I was kind of like a blank slate. My sister had bought "Fancy Free" by Donald Byrd. It was that recording, Freddie Hubbard's *Red Clay*, and Herbie's *Empyrean Isles* and *The Prisoner* that introduced me to jazz. Herbie's early tune "Cantaloupe Island" had been the first tune I learned to play. I got really into the CTI and A&M recordings, including not only *Red Clay* but also Wes Montgomery's and Paul Desmond's records. Don Sebesky's arrangements—on [George Benson's] *White Rabbit* and [Freddie Hubbard's] *First Light*—had a profound effect on me. The orchestration was speaking a language of story telling and images that made perfect sense to me: "That's what the sun looks like coming up from the horizon; that's what a forest looks like to me."

At Shelly's Manne-Hole, Herbie was playing a Fender Rhodes with the top off; he had the Echoplex and maybe a ring modulator. Before starting the set, Herbie got on the mic and told the tiny audience: "A lot of you have come to hear 'Fat Albert' but we're here to take you on a trip." His appearance had changed since I saw him the first time: He was no longer wearing glasses and he was now wearing his hair in a natural. Herbie's stance on the stage seemed contentious, concerned with how his music was being received by the public at large. It was more abstract and people weren't showing up or appearing more enthusiastic. I noticed that there was hardly anybody in the audience. My fourteen-year-old self thought: "That's got to be a drag."

Then they played "Ostinato" for the entire set, and I was blown away. It was like watching a magic show. All of the sudden Bennie Maupin's sax playing would morph into the trumpet playing and then into the alto flute; the sounds keep flowing in waves and merging. One thing that was in my mind as I listened as a fourteen-year-old was that at one moment, Bennie would make the bass clarinet sound like a dying animal but next like a ghost-like whisper. Herbie had so many unusual sounds to bring into the mix. The chemistry of the band was like a magical experience, like a trip. While my sister wasn't really too into it, at one point I noticed that drummer Billy Hart looked at me, saw that I was into the music, and smiled.

After the set, I saw Herbie at the bar. He was the only one there. I asked for his autograph; he looked perplexed and said: "Yeah, sure," signed the mailer from the club very neatly. It hung on my wall for the next twenty years until my parents cleaned my room and threw everything out!

A light bulb went on for me after the Shelly's Manne-Hole gig. It wasn't like a conversion: "I've changed and now I'm going on this new thing forever." The shift was more subtle than that: I started imaging music in a different way. I realized that music could be a journey; it could be like a movie. The show started affecting how I listened to and perceived other music I heard. I started listening to music for the journey it could take me on. This music reminded me of cubist paintings or other modern art: If you look at a Picasso painting that is labeled: "This is a picture of a woman," it could be a woman or it could actually be something else. How you looked at it affected what it became and that's how I started listening to music.

It wasn't until the next year that I really got serious about playing piano, when my parents sent me to Midland, a boarding school for boys. My roommate set up a rig connecting his stereo with speakers in the shower room. They were playing Black Sabbath and I put on "Ostinato" from the *Mwandishi* album. At first this was all I played and it didn't go over too well at that school! But in turn I became influenced by what other students were listening to, especially Emerson, Lake, and Palmer, [which] took classical music and put it into a rock context.[3]

The *Mwandishi* album was the one that had the deepest effect on me. *Crossings* was great, but *Sextant* didn't seem as spiritual to me. The groove had a bit more rigidity to it; it was less flexible. Now they were writing for these synthesizers. Now the music was conceived with that in mind. Before that the music emanated out of what these cats played and the stories they were trying to tell. Now the stories had more to do with what could be done on the keyboards. To my ears, it limited the music. I could see it evolving into *Head Hunters*. *Mwandishi* seemed more purely a spiritual journey; to me, the impetus behind the album was to tell a story and this idea became more diluted later on.

Bassist Christian McBride

It has taken some forty years for the band to really become recognized as one of the seminal groups of its era. Of all the things Herbie has done in his career, it's the most overlooked. The music was so advanced texturally and in its densities, the African qualities, how experimental it was, and its role in what has become known as electronica. As progressive as the younger generation thought they were in the early 70s, I'm sure they weren't ready for that.

When I was a young musician growing up in Philly, I was so excited about all the different facets and time periods of jazz. Herbie was already a superstar. I first knew about him through his more popular music, but I came to recognize his genius as a jazz musician when I first heard Miles' *Four and More*. Then I discovered *Takin' Off* and all of Herbie's Blue Note recordings.

The recording that hit me so hard, when I was junior or senior in high school, was *The Prisoner*. I heard it when I was deeper into my development as a jazz musician and ready to appreciate it. It's got the seeds of the Mwandishi group; Joe Henderson and the band on there were just killing. I thought that *The Prisoner*, compared in the liner notes to Gil Evans, showed that influence, but it was Gil Evans up a notch. The bass trombone, alto flute, different time signatures, counter-rhythms and counter-melodies, the dissonances on "Promise of the Sun" . . . it's heavy, I thought: "Wow, he's got a lot of guts to write something like that!" It's gorgeous. The playing is just great. Joe Henderson's solo on the title track is one of my favorites from any era. It is one of the few saxophone solos I tried to learn on the bass.

The second record I heard at about the same time in high school was *Sextant*. At first I didn't get it. I knew it had to be great because of the players on it, but what I decided to do was put it aside for a later time. I listened to Herbie's earlier stuff, his playing with Miles, and *Round Midnight*. At the time, I was a high school senior, and Herbie's early recordings were out of print. But my uncle had a double album, a compilation called *Treasure Chest*. The first song I heard was "Ostinato: Suite for Angela." My first thought was "how come I never heard anybody talk about this?" People would always talk about *Head Hunters*, the Blue Note records, and "Rockit," but not this. *Treasure Chest* was my only link to the Mwandishi Sextet until I found *Fat Albert Rotunda* in a used record store in New York.

By this time, I was getting really curious about the Sextet. I had taken a bass lesson during high school with Buster Williams. Everybody knew what a legend Bennie Maupin was. I met Eddie Henderson, and I spent time hanging out with them and with Wallace Roney at a club. In the early 90s, *Sextant* became the last frontier in my personal journey of discovery of the Sextet. I found two of the recordings on vinyl. After studying "Ostinato: Song for Angela" and "Wandering Spirit Song" from *Mwandishi* and from *Crossings*, "Water Torture," I was getting hard core into the band and became more obsessed with understanding it. I also found an old *Down Beat* magazine from the early 1970s which included in a list of jazz going down in every major city, it said that in Philadelphia, Herbie will be at the Aqua Lounge with Jimmy Garrison sitting in for Buster Williams!

As I started to get really into the band, wondering about what it was like on the inside, I remember hanging out with Herbie himself at the Monk Institute. I found him to be so generous. We sat up all night talking about his career. I started asking questions about the Sextet and he got very emotional about it. It was obvious that it was something special to him. I sometimes wonder if Herbie knows how much musicians love that band? Billy Hart also talks with emotion about it: "Just as I was really getting the hang of what we were doing, we broke up."

I realized that now's the time for me to pull out *Sextant* again. After having absorbed the Warner Brothers recordings, did it ever hit me! I remember listening to it and going: "Oh, man!" To this very day I think that *Sextant* was a brilliant mix of the electronic with the acoustic. I have never had the sense that the acoustic instruments got lost. It's a good blend of the two. Everything is complementary. The song "Hidden Shadows" is seriously advanced music, which deserves to be studied—the time signatures, the way the melody is written over the time signature. When I asked Herbie about it, he smiled and said that it took a long time to rehearse that song and maybe months before they could really play it.

Every project Herbie did during that period seemed to grow in leaps. From *Speak Like a Child* to *The Prisoner*; from *Fat Albert Rotunda* to *Mwandishi*; and then *Mwandishi* to *Crossings* was truly a quantum leap. Then of course *Sextant* just put the cap on it. I sometimes wonder where that band could have gone after that and if there was much ground left to cover.

All of this started meaning more to me when I began playing with Bennie and Billy. I played a gig in Seattle with Julian Priester in the audience and he told me that he could tell how much the band impacted on me. In 2000, Julian asked me if I could play a benefit concert with the Sextet in place of Buster. I told him "You have no idea; sharing the stage with these guys is as great as playing with James Brown." As it turns out, Buster was able to make it and I was just happy to be there. Billy was in Japan, so Terri Lyne Carrington played the drums and did a great job. I got to hear the guys talk about the band and the old times.

To me Mwandishi was truly an all-inclusive world band. It was one of those kind of bands, no matter what style of music you listen to, while it's kind of out, there's something in there you could dig. These were musicians you could tell knew what they were doing. Like Weather Report, they never shed their jazz chops.

My dream was always to have a band, not one that sounded like Mwandishi, but one that, like Mwandishi, could somehow capture elements of all different kinds of music, filtered through a jazz lens. I tried very hard to have a band like that. My old band recorded a tune [released on *Sci Fi*] titled "Via Mwandishi," with Ron Blake playing tenor, James Carter on bass clarinet and David Gilmore on guitar. On a later recording, *Live at Tonic*, on that same tune, with Geoffrey Keezer on keyboards, again with Ron Blake playing tenor, Terreon Gully on drums, and me playing arco bass, we were aiming for that texture, and I think we got close.

Pianist Mitchel Forman

I remember listening to Herbie's *Crossings* album over and over again. I can picture the incredible album art in my mind. That and Miles's *Live Evil* were my daily doses of inspiration when I was in high school. I had been listening to *Miles Smiles* and I think I just stumbled onto these others. Though not aware of it at the time, I believe that there is a strong spiritual side to that music. I think it has the power to transport the listener to a heightened state. The degree of freedom coupled with the intense interplay I found and still find to be so inspiring.

I think the main concept that I got from the Mwandishi recordings is the idea of taking your time. Things seem to develop very slowly and build and build. The tension keeps mounting and when it finally breaks, it's a magnificent release. I would love to be able to incorporate this idea of using a longer form into some of my music.

Guitarist Pat Metheny

I saw the band on two different tours at the Landmark Club at Union Station in Kansas City, Missouri. The first time it was just the sextet and the second time included Patrick Gleeson as well. I went every night that I could during both weeks. By the time he came to Kansas City, I was still in high school, but by then I had been working around the city for a few years and was playing often at the Landmark and all the other places there were. It was actually quite an active scene for a few years there and I was lucky to be a part of it at such a young age.

I have always regarded Herbie as one of my major heroes, along with Miles and Tony Williams. I became a musician because my older brother (an excellent trumpet player) brought home a Miles Davis record when I was 11 (*Four and More*) and it changed my life. Of course, Herbie was the piano player. I got all of Herbie's records and learned as much as I could from him (and I still do). Musically, the most prominent sound of that time was the classic organ trio approach and many of the bands I was playing with were built around that model. But there was a group of us who were also really interested in what was happening and beginning to emerge from beyond the mainstream. Of course I had always loved Herbie, but *The Prisoner* and then later *Mwandishi* and the whole idea of really writing for a kind of modern chamber ensemble along with the incredible improvisational abilities he possessed opened up a whole world of imagination.

But even knowing the records, nothing prepared us for what it was like live. It was light years beyond anything that had ever been seen or heard in any Kansas City jazz club; that was for sure. It was simply the greatest thing I had ever seen or heard. Everything about it impacted me. And to this day, even after having heard a lot of other great stuff since, I would say that those gigs remain in the top three musical memories of my life. Whenever I think that I might be getting to something good I always reference it to what I heard on those nights. I loved it all. The second time around it was spacier, which at the time was super-hip. But on both go-arounds it was unbelievable. The whole range of potential was represented there. It was a great moment in time for all those guys; they were young guys, but experienced. They were looking for something new and fresh, but were well versed in playing lots of different ways and could make many references to many different kinds of relationships on a dime. It could be really free, it could really groove or it could really swing and all were viable in an equal way.

The Kansas City crowd was always loud and wild. They would be listening but also talking and yelling. That was just the way it was then. And with that band I just remember them being able to take this already excited crowd and keep building and building things. But as great as the whole band was, it was Herbie as a soloist who made the most impact. I remember one night him doing one of those amazing Herbie solos, where it just keeps getting more and more intense and by the time he got to the end, every person in the room (including me) was standing on their chairs, screaming at the top of their lungs. It was unbelievable.

Drummer Victor Lewis

I was in my senior year at the University of Nebraska at Lincoln. I had gotten tight with the program chair in charge of bringing entertainment to the university. He didn't know much about jazz artists, so he would always ask me whom to get. He'd also have me help assist by picking up the guys at the airport. One year, he'd ask: "Should I get this guy, or should I get Freddie Hubbard?" Another year, it was: "Should I get this guy, or should I get McCoy Tyner?" Then during my senior year, he asked about booking Herbie Hancock and I said: "Man, you've got to get Herbie."

Herbie's band flew in the day before the concert, probably arriving from some other place in the Midwest, where they were on tour. I'll never forget the image of first seeing them. This was before tight airport security. I park the car and I'm walking down the corridor towards the flight gate to meet the band. Meanwhile, they had already gotten off the plane and I see these guys walking towards me. Bennie was wearing a cape with all his horns strapped around his neck and in his arms. The cape was like an umbrella, wafting in the wind as he walked. Watching them, I'm thinking that these guys look like super heroes. Bennie being like Superman with the cape and Herbie being Batman. It was really a profound thing to experience. I introduced myself and they asked: "Hey brother, what are you doing way out here?" I told them "I'm a musician, learning drums." Billy Hart was into making health shakes, with lecithin, powered protein and other ingredients, but he didn't have a blender. He asked me if I knew anybody who had a blender. Lo and behold I happened to have one and the next thing you know, I have Billy Hart at my crib. I hung out with these guys for two days.

The sound check was when the magic started to happen. Everybody was at their instruments and Billy's adjusting his drums. Billy asked me if I could sit down and play his drums so he could go out front and hear how they sounded. First thing I think is "what should I play?" so I started laying down this rhythm from one of my tunes. All the sudden, I hear this killing bass line kick in along with me, and here's Buster looking at me and playing with me. He's right on me. It scared the living daylights out of me. I had written a little bass line to the tune, but the line Buster came up with just wiped that one out. Billy came back and said: "Yeah young blood, you sound pretty good there." Being tight with the program chair, he let my band be the warm up act for Herbie. Herbie asked whether I wanted to sit in with Billy and play two drum kits. In retrospect, I'm still glad that I politely declined and thanked them for the invite. I told them I'd rather sit my ass down and listen! I didn't want to be a wrench in the works, the gap in the link of the circle. Just the way things happened and flowed you had to be really keen and pay attention and be both ready and deep.

When Herbie's band was warming up, I couldn't tell when exactly they crossed the threshold into playing together. There was no "we're ready . . . one, two, three, four . . . " There was no announcement of "OK, let's do something together." They just fell into it. I looked up and they were right into it. I'm listening to this and saying to myself: "Oh, man . . . " At some point they had kind of merged and started to play together. My own band went on and did our set. Herbie's band had a chance to hear me and my band play, and they gave me a lot of encouragement.

The show was in February 1973, when Patrick Gleeson was part of the band. At the beginning, Herbie started off the evening by saying: "They've asked me to make an announcement to let everybody know that there will be no drugs and no booze!" This was during the era when a lot of kids in the audience were tripping. He then explained that what they'd be doing is something like a communal dialog, not necessarily one guy soloing and he's the only voice. It would be almost like they will be soloing communally; every now and then somebody will drop down and be featured for a while, then it would become communal again, and then somebody else would come down . . . most of it was not predetermined.

The band then proceeded to do exactly what he said they would do. Maybe people thought they understood what he meant, but it was more profound to hear it when it actually took place, like "this is what he means!" The band played material from *Sextant*, which had not yet been released; They started off with "Hornets." And then they did "You'll Know When You Get There," followed by "Ostinato," and maybe "Sleeping Giant." They did one long set, between an hour and a half and two hours long. It was seamless. They just flowed from one thing to the next. When the band came on and played, it was truly magical. It was totally like a cooperative contributing unit. The things that happened "off the paper" were so free. It was so much like: "calling the spirits" and I'll never forget it. Every once in a while Herbie would give a subtle cue and they would make a left turn and be in another zone. It was a truly mind blowing experience. I haven't been the same since.

I had never heard anything like what Pat Gleeson was doing. At that time, they didn't have synthesizers at the University of Nebraska, although we had heard about them. I remember Mr. Gleeson's looking like the Wizard of Oz with his patch chords and working all the gizmos, creating those atmospheric sounds. It must have been really something to deal with the spontaneity that required. What he offered ended up being deeper than just music and notes. The music was about atmosphere and texture, about images like rain and thunder and then the sun coming out. It was powerful.

A big major way the band impacted on me was helping me think past the bar lines, and about thinking of music form as separate parts, like the A section, the bridge. Any section can hover at will. Without anyone sending up a flare, they would just stay in one section for a while, or just loop the vibe of the bridge or even break the tempo, like the way they used to in "You'll Know When You Get There." Anything can happen, but you better pay attention so you know it's happening when it goes down!

The music was a little over the head of the program chair, but he appreciated and respected it. He didn't quite understand it, saying: "I don't know what it is, but it really sounds good." The students loved it. It was psychedelic for them, Herbie with his ring modulator and Echoplex, Patrick Gleeson with his patch chords. Herbie rearranged the molecules of the Student Union ballroom. Watching people walking out after the concert, they all had a dazed look as if they had seen a UFO or something—it was like wow, did you see that, did you hear that?

I got so possessed and blown away from this experience that I never went to another college class after that. Eddie Henderson always reminds me of it. I made a decision that playing music was really what I wanted to do. [I talked to my parents and] told them about the experience I had with Herbie's band, and hanging out with everybody. I had a clear vision of what I wanted to do and that I needed to get busy full fledged to pursue it. So I made a deal with my parents. "Give me a few years and if it doesn't look like it's panning out, I'll go back and finish my credits and become a band director in Stewart, Nebraska. A few months later, I hooked up a gig in Minneapolis to make money and thirty-eight years ago, I moved to New York and I haven't looked back since. As Eddie Henderson says, "They turned me out!" Bennie Maupin [said,] "Save some money and just come to New York and hang out for as long as your money lasts. While you're there you can take lessons from all the cats, hear the music, get some guys to jam with, and no matter how long you stay, short or long, you'll have 'accelerated growth.'" He gave me the right perspective to get enough nerve to go to New York. They really triggered my making that step.

Bill Bruford, John Wetton, and Robert Fripp, Members of the British Rock Group King Crimson, in Its 1973–75 Formation

Author Sid Smith writes: "In sound checks Bruford and Wetton would sometimes play riffs based on Herbie Hancock's 1971 album *Crossings*. This brand of vibrant post-*Bitches Brew* funk had a notable impact on the rhythm section, as Wetton explains: 'We were very impressed with American jazz-funk. What Herbie was doing and what Miles Davis was doing was using incredibly good players who could riff and that was a big influence on me and Bill. We brought that into the improvisations in a big way.'"[4] Robert Fripp, Bruford, and Wetton have all commented that Herbie Hancock and they attended each other's concerts while on the road in 1973 and learned from one another.[5] Bruford comments:

> John Wetton and I were deep into *Crossings*, which to this day sends hairs up the back of my neck. I knew Herbie from his work with Miles, of course, and loved it all. I also remember going to see the *Crossings* band. . . . It seemed from where I sat in 1971 that American jazz was just an infinitely superior and

more worthwhile form of music than our white Anglo-Euro confections. But I was rare among my colleagues, who knew nothing of jazz. I was intrigued because the music was so different, and I didn't understand how it was constructed, not being versed in jazz harmony or expression. I knew how we arrived at our music, but not how Herbie, for example, arrived at *Crossings*.

But it also turned out that our white Anglo-Euro confections weren't quite so worthless after all, and in fact were being listened to and noted by some of the demi-gods of the jazz universe I held in such high esteem! Herbie seemed to be backstage at Crimson shows asking a lot of questions about Mellotrons. So it may be that white progressive rock was being listened to by the demi-gods not only in an effort to figure out how we were "making all that money," but because they actually liked some of our ideas on form and arrangement and texture that could get them out of the old head-solo-solo-solo-head cul-de-sac that jazz had got itself in to. Perhaps the artistic traffic wasn't quite so one-way as I had imagined.

Band Member Reflections

Members of the band remember Mwandishi as a high-water mark in their own careers.

Drummer Billy Hart

I never enjoyed music as much, before or since [playing with Herbie Hancock]. It was almost a miracle musical experience. It's hard to put it in words. You could say it was spiritual, but it was so sensually pleasurable that I dare not put it in the same words. He's an extraordinary musician, even among extraordinary musicians. And that means that he's an extraordinary person, too. . . . His genius, to me, is his ability to accompany. To the point that he could be John Williams. . . . He could do that for you. He could do that for me. Just playing with him on the bandstand makes you feel like he's written a concerto just for you, a drum concerto. That's what the point is. He was perfect for me and for Buster.

Saxophonist Bennie Maupin

[The band was] a most fruitful and rewarding experience for me, not only musically but spiritually as well. I think this is the first time I have been in a group where there is such a tremendous contact both on and off the band-stand. We play together; also we experience a lot of things together in other areas as well. There is a real rapport with very little conflict, other than the normal. We just seem to give to each other.[6] [It] . . . was probably one of the greatest musical adventures I've ever had up until the present moment. I think the greatest one I'm having is right now. . . . We played together in situations where it was all about the music. The sextet was one of the greatest bands I've ever been in. It might not have been commercially the most successful, [but] in terms of music and musicality, and mutual respect and creativity; it was on the highest level. I'm glad we made the few recordings we did, but I never felt the recordings were in step with where we were musically. We always recorded and then went to develop the music later. The process should have been reversed, but it was just not meant to be.[7]

Trumpeter Eddie Henderson

I'd never played music like that in my life, you take your time, let it slowly evolve, you know? And just go . . . and listen to the band. That band taught me that because I'd be nervous when I'd jump the gun. I learned . . . nobody ever said anything, you know, verbally to me. I learned it myself. "Take your time, Eddie!"

It was a very unique band. It was one of a kind, musically, individually and personally and the interaction that we all had together was something that I had never experienced in my life. . . . You know, but that band was so univer-sal and so receptive to everything. You know, one time everybody was eating organic foods; at the time we were all vegetarians, and Herbie might have a plum or carrot on the electric piano he's playing. And all the sudden I saw him looking at the plum. I thought: "Oh, no, he's not going to do that!" Before he finished a note, he'd grab the plum and "errrruhhh, erruhhh!" over and down the keyboard. He looked at me and said "organic music!" You know, it was like that. I mean: everything was valid, you know, and it really shaped the way I approached the bandstand. It was almost like a sacred experience.

Trombonist Julian Priester

That was a very important period in my life in terms of mind expansion and the opportunity to go with it. There were no restrictions. And then you get those special groups who live, eat and sleep on the same schedule. And when they get together to perform, well, I call it magic, but it's uncanny that they perform as one.

Bassist Buster Williams

The thing we learned from Miles was possibilities and to think outside the box. When Herbie formed the Sextet, that's where we started from day one. It became a great exploration from that point. . . . We were not satisfied from night to night playing anything that sounded remotely familiar to what it sounded like last night. . . . We got to the point where we accepted that and we didn't try to direct the music. We all got on the bandstand every night with the willingness to be transcended and to be directed by the music itself. Which is why you'd hear us play nothing that resembled anything for an hour, before we even played the melody of the song. The music itself was very spiritual in that it left and transcended the plane of our bodies, the plane of laity. Because of the music we all felt quite spiritual, which was also one of the reasons we all became vegetarians, Bennie Maupin being the instigator of all that. It all made sense.

Synthesizer Player Patrick Gleeson

When I joined this deeply Afrocentric band I felt like I'd gone home. I felt like I'd found my place. This is where I belong. This was right.

Herbie Hancock

When we play, we're not playing for ourselves, purely. We are conscious of the fact that there are people out there. It has nothing to do with the people who are paying to hear us, or whatever it is. It's just the fact that the people are there and they are part of the surroundings that produce the music. We're just a vehicle that the music comes through, so the audience plays a definite part—we don't try to shut them out of the musical situation.[8]

Producer David Rubinson

Really, shockingly brand new; and for the audiences; and for the club owners. You know, and for the agency; I mean, everybody, every way you could look at it. It was a fantastic, shocking, fundamental, conceptual paradigm shift.

The way the music speaks, the way the music was made, the way the band traveled.

In retrospect, the wonder of the Mwandishi band was that it was perceived by its members and informed listeners as a deeply collective experience. But the band members all knew that behind the magic they felt as a group lay a single creative force, Herbie Hancock. The directions taken by the band unfolded in an organic way that could not have been predicted even by Hancock himself. Yet when viewed within the context of his personal development as a musician during the decade culminating in this time period, it all makes sense. Most of the constituent elements that represented vital ingredients in the music can be sourced in aspects of Hancock's previous work or experiences. From the abstraction of Eric Dolphy to the sound conception of Edgard Varèse, from the rhythmic concept of Horace Silver to the emotionally directed conception of the Miles Davis Quintet, from the rich harmonies of the Hi-Los and Gil Evans to the Afrocentric themes of *Kawaida*, Herbie Hancock had in his repertoire most of the musical attributes that would together form the backbone of the Mwandishi band's music. After building a reputation with Davis, Hancock was professionally prepared to launch a major solo career. But for nearly three years, he chose to undertake the far more experimental and fiscally riskier enterprise, the Mwandishi band. The music provided lifelong inspiration for all its members and for the young musicians who viewed them as a model for what profound music making could be.

Appendix

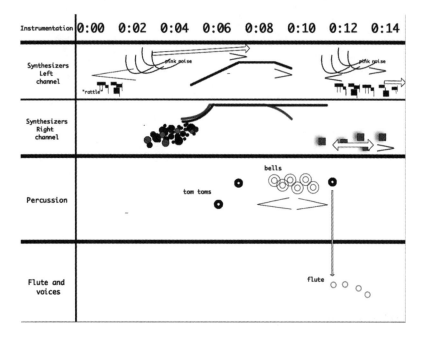

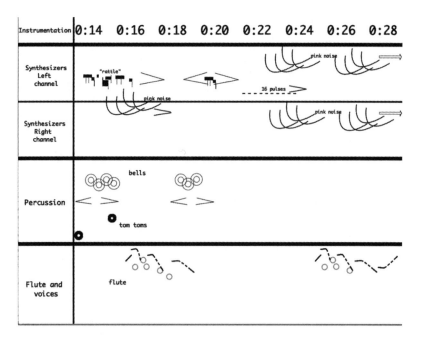

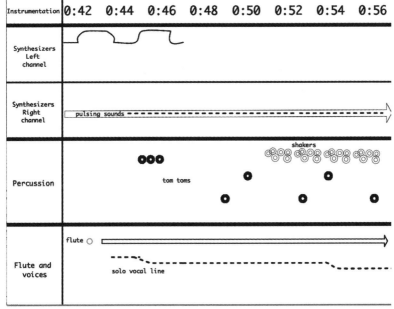

Instrumentation	0:28	0:30	0:32	0:34	0:36	0:38	0:40	0:42
Synthesizers Left channel	pink noise				"rattle"			
Synthesizers Right channel	pink noise					pulsing sounds - - - - - - - -		
Percussion						tom toms		
Flute and voices	"plaintive ... breathy, shakuhachi-like ..." flute							

Instrumentation	0:42	0:44	0:46	0:48	0:50	0:52	0:54	0:56
Synthesizers Left channel								
Synthesizers Right channel	pulsing sounds - - - - - - - - - - - - - - - - - - -							
Percussion		tom toms				shakers		
Flute and voices	flute			solo vocal line				

Instrumentation	1:00	1:05	1:10	1:15	1:20	1:25	1:30	1:35

Synthesizers Left channel — "rattle", synth tone doubles voice

Synthesizers Right channel — pulsing snds, doubles voice

Percussion — bells: hi & lo, tom toms, hi hat swish, w/cow bell on 2, flexotone bells

Flute and voices — w/tape feedback, solo vocal line

Appendix example a-e. Graphic scoring of the acoustic/electronic layering on "Water Torture"

Notes

Introduction

1. Unless otherwise noted, all interviews were conducted by the author. Detailed information is found in the reference list.

2. Hart and Iverson 2006.

3. Butters 2006.

4. Ibid.

5. Ibid.

6. M. Jones 1971.

7. Ibid.

Chapter 1

1. Zwerin 1999.

2. Williams recalls:

I was working at the Copa with Nancy [Wilson]. I had moved back to New York and I was living at the Wellington Hotel on 55th Street and Seventh Avenue. I think we started to play at 8:00 each night. And Herbie's Sextet was working at the Vanguard. Mickey Roker was the drummer with us, with Nancy Wilson, and we would finish Nancy's first show and go over to the Vanguard to hear Herbie's first show, which started at 9 o'clock. Ron [Carter] was involved in a Broadway play. Ron and I were friends, so he asked me whether I would play the first set at the Vanguard for him each night. We would finish with Nancy right at 9 o'clock and then go right over to the Vanguard, so we would start a little late. Roker would go over with me and Pete LaRoca would never be there. So Mickey and I would play the first set—me sitting in for Ron and Mickey Roker sitting in for Pete LaRoca. By the end of the week, Herbie decided that Pete wasn't going to make it. Pete told Herbie when Herbie asked him "Why can't you get here in time for the 9 o'clock set?" Pete told him that he didn't feel like playing until 10 o'clock. So that was a conflict of interest right there! Pete LaRoca didn't last more than about a week.

The drum chair settled down with the hiring of Albert "Tootie" Heath and soon with Buster Williams as bassist. By the middle of 1970, Heath, too, would leave the band, to be replaced by Billy Hart.

3. Goddet 1979.

4. The duration of this unusually long stand, set to begin on November 4, is documented in "Pianist Set for London House Debut," *Chicago Daily Defender*, November 2, 1970, 12, and Earl Calloway, "Herbie Hancock Brings a New Sound to Chicago," *Chicago Daily Defender*, November 18, 1970, 14. The November 2 article observes that Ramsey Lewis would be playing a three-week stand, followed by an additional week including New Year's Eve, suggesting that bookings of this length were not unknown at London House.

5. Recorded on December 11, 1969. Percussionist James Mtume, Tootie Heath's nephew, is given all five composing credits, although the recording is listed variously as led by Heath, Mtume, or Hancock. Mtume joined Miles Davis's band in the early 1970s.

6. Karenga 1999, 2010.

7. Hancock, Williams, and Heath were not the only members of Hancock's early Sextet to assume Swahili names. Johnny Coles was named Katumbo (Dance). Ndugu Leon Chancler, who would join as a second drummer on the recording *Mwandishi* and on a few live dates, recalls: "I had already taken on the Swahili name Ndugu in high school, maybe in 1968. This was before most of the Mwandishi band, and around when Tootie and the others involved in the 1969 Kawaida recording did so too." Mtume and Chancler were neighbors in Los Angeles.

8. G. Lewis 2008; Wilmer (1977) 1992; and Porter 2002, 210–14.

9. Chords built on intervals of the perfect fourth, rather than on thirds, and thus less characteristic of western European harmony as it evolved during the classical and romantic eras.

10. These include Umoja (unity), Kujichagulia (self-determination), Ujima (collective work and responsibility), Ujamaa (cooperative economics), Nia (purpose), Kuumba (creativity), Imani (faith). Hancock recites the explanation for Ujima.

11. Goddet 1979.

12. Carroll, Higgins, Peterson, Garner, and Shearing were pianists, Torme and Vaughan, singers, and Hall a guitarist. Tjader's presence is documented by personal reflections by band members and briefly noted in "Music from the Music Capitals of the World: Chicago," *Billboard*, November 28, 1970, 48. Reggie Willis recalls Peterson and Garner; Thurman Barker remembers Torme, Peterson, Hall, and Shearing.

13. Choice 1970.

14. Ibid.

15. Founded by Kenneth Louis Cox II and collaborators. See Melba Joyce Boyd, "Kenn Cox and Donald Walden: 'Free Jazz Radicals,'" *Solidarity*, March-April 2009, http://www.solidarity-us.org/node/2091 (accessed August 23, 2011).

16. The Buddhism of Nichiren Daishonin practiced by Soka Gakkai International (SGI) teaches that its

> practice stems from the belief that each of us already possess[es] the innate vitality, compassion and wisdom needed to live a fulfilling, contributive life. True happiness is not found in our ever-changing circumstances but is cultivated from within, through forging and maintain[ing] a vibrant state of life in which, undaunted by hardship, we can transform any circumstance into one of joy and benefit for ourselves and our loved ones. . . . By chanting Nam-myoho-renge-kyo with confidence in our innate Buddhahood, we can dispel delusion about the limits of our happiness and reveal our inherent strength, wisdom and compassion. Through chanting, studying Buddhist philosophy and taking action daily for the well-being of others, we can establish the state of absolute happiness in which we can make each moment of our lives joyful and meaningful while creating peace in our families and communities.

(*Living Buddhism* 2006) Nichiren Buddhists believe that the goal of life is peace and happiness. The philosophy is one of cause and effect. Through spiritual practice, one can create "causes" that result in "effects" that transform one's life.

17. *Billboard*, June 12, 1971.

18. O. Wilson, 1983, 1992; Douglas 1991; and Maultsby 1990.

Chapter 2

1. Black 2005, 153; Norment 1987, 136.

2. Black 2005, 154.

3. Gitler 1963.

4. J. Williams 1988.

5. Ibid.

6. Ibid.

7. Mayer 2007.

8. Heckman 2007.

9. Gitler 1963.

10. Calloway 1970.

11. Reggie Willis recalls the location as the club Bird House, across from the Playboy Movie Theatre in Chicago. In a 2011 interview with Mike Ragogna, Hancock remembers it differently: "He [Donald Byrd] hired me to play for a weekend in Milwaukee. There was a big storm that particular night, and Donald Byrd came through Chicago and was going to drive from Chicago to Milwaukee, Wisconsin—it's really not that far, like a two-hour drive or something like that. Anyway, Donald's pianist had gotten stranded somewhere, and so he needed somebody for the weekend—it was a ten day engagement. Well, Donald went to a club and asked the owner who he could get for just one weekend. I winded up getting the gig for that weekend, and Donald and the band really responded to my playing so much that they decided to fire the other piano player and hire me." Ragogna 2011.

12. He studied with noted teacher and composer Vittorio Giannini, shortly before Giannini left New York to found the North Carolina School of the Arts.

13. Hancock's employment did not include Art Blakey's Jazz Messengers, which included Horace Silver. However, Hancock played gigs and recorded with musicians who at various times were Jazz Messengers members: Donald Byrd, Lee Morgan, Wayne Shorter, and Freddie Hubbard.

14. Between 1962 and 1965, Herbie Hancock's Blue Note studio credits included several of Donald Byrd's recordings; four each with Stanley Turrentine and Wayne Shorter; two each with Grant Green, Jackie McLean, Tony Williams, and Lee Morgan; one each with Kenny Dorham, Blue Mitchell, Grachan Moncur III, Kenny Burrell, Bobby Hutcherson, Freddie Hubbard, and Sam Rivers. Additional Blue Note sessions took place with several of these musicians during 1966, 1967, and 1968. To gain a sense of his activity, in 1964, Hancock was in the studio for sessions on February 15, June 3, July 6, August 5 and 24, October 22, November 2 and 24. And in 1965: April 14, May 21, June 10 and 14, August 12, September 17–18, October 15, December 7, 8, and 22. Hancock's own Blue Note sessions included Takin' Off (May 28, 1962), My Point of View (March 19, 1963), Inventions and Dimensions (August 30, 1963), Empyrean Isles (June 17, 1964), and Maiden Voyage (March 11 and 17, 1965), with more to come. Hancock also recorded for labels other than Blue Note with Pepper Adams Quintet, Roland Kirk, Bob Brookmeyer, Donald Byrd, Sonny Rollins, and two LPs with Eric Dolphy.

15. "Boogie-woogie piano is a dynamic, colorful music form with an equally colorful history. Beginning as dance music for poor southern blacks, Boogie-woogie became a national craze when Albert Ammons, Pete Johnson, and Meade Lux Lewis performed at Carnegie Hall in 1938. It has had a major influence on blues, rock and roll, rhythm and blues, jazz, and pop, yet it has been widely neglected in the history books and is frequently misunderstood. Boogie-woogie is often confused with ragtime and stride piano. However, unlike these early jazz styles, it is defined by its blues structure, fast pace, and driving, repetitive eight-to-the-bar bass line. Although Boogie-woogie has been played by big bands and small ensembles, at its heart, it is a solo piano style." Davey 1998.

16. For background about bebop, see DeVeaux 1997.

17. It's not that blues forms did not already play a role in bebop; consider the compositions of Thelonious Monk or, from an even earlier era, Count Basie, but the new music privileged the deeper cultural moorings and melodic inflections of the blues, within a livelier rhythmic framework.

18. It should not be lost that bebop was often built on popular songs, abstracted by their performers.

19. A point well articulated by Rosenthal (1992, 62), who also offers a typology of four musical streams within hard bop (44–45).

20. Hancock's solo, however, more strongly reflects Bill Evans in its use of chords and chord fragments as melodic elements, a topic addressed later.

21. Hancock describes how what he thought of as a "funky jazz tune kind of inspired from the R&B sensibility" became a Latin jazz hit in the hands of Santamaria's musicians in Pond (2005) 2010, 59–60.

22. Davis had heard Hancock play a club date with Donald Byrd and invited him to a rehearsal. Byrd encouraged the young pianist to accept Davis's subsequent invitation to join his band as an opportunity to forward his career and musical development.

23. During Hancock's first two years with the Miles Davis Quintet, the band was constantly on the road and recorded their first two studio LPs, *Seven Steps to Heaven* (April 16 and May 14, 1963) and the stylistically transitional *E.S.P.* (January 21–22, 1965). The band's playing was also documented on several live recordings, one closing out 1965, *Miles Davis Live at the Plugged Nickel*, a club in Chicago (December 22–23, 1965).

24. Fragmentation refers to the reduction of a chord into its constituent notes, only some of which are retained.

25. Acknowledged by Hancock in Lyons (1983) 1989, 273; Coryell and Friedman 1978; and elsewhere.

26. Russell (1953) 1959. Also see http://www.lydianchromaticconcept.com (accessed August 12, 2011).

27. A notated example of Hancock's lyricism during a later point in Hancock's time with Miles, 1967–68, his solo on "Circle" from *Miles Smiles* (1967) is discussed in Yudkin 2008, 78–86.

28. Johnson 1971.

29. Flam 1995.

30. Debussy 1995.

31. Examples include Georges Braque's and Pablo Picasso's collages (e.g., Picasso's *Compotier avec fruits, violon et verre* [1912]), and Pierre Schaeffer's early *Musique concrete Etudes aux Chemins de Fer* (1948). In both cases, images and sound recordings drawn from the outside world lose any representational function. They become objects juxtaposed adjacent to one another. Arnold Schoenberg's twelve-tone music and the work of subsequent serialist composers beginning with Anton Webern (e.g., his *String Trio* [1927]), drew on mathematic models rather than harmonic or representational approaches to organize sound.

32. Goddet 1979.

33. Lyons (1983) 1989, 273. According to drummer Billy Hart, it was saxophonist Sam Rivers who bequeathed Tony Williams an "extensive knowledge of so-called 20th century harmonic movement."

34. Goddet 1979.

35. Johnson 1971.

36. On Coltrane, see Porter (1998) 2006; Price 1995. About Coleman, see Litweiler 1993. Coltrane, after briefly exploring diminished chords, began to craft melodies from permutations and combinations of note patterns, replacing scales with modes that were supported by harmonically ambiguous quartal chords. Coleman explored motivic improvisation and new ways for members of an ensemble to play together, yet maintain their own individuality. In Coleman's concept of "harmolodics," several people playing a melody in unison might play the same intervals and shapes, yet start on their own pitches. In 1958 and 1959, Miles Davis began seeking his own solutions to the constraints perceived by Coltrane and Coleman replacing chordal structures with modes, and by 1965, drawing on freer approaches to form.

37. Waters 2011 offers an extensive analysis of Hancock's work with Davis from this perspective.

38. Debussy 1995.

39. Goddet 1979.

40. Composer Henry Cowell developed a theory defining clusters as an alternate

way to construct chords, theorizing that they represented the generally inaudible upper partials of the harmonic series. Cowell (1930) 1996.

41. Several of Monk's successors more overtly utilize tone clusters, among them Cecil Taylor, Don Pullen, Andrew Hill, Marilyn Crispell, and Hancock's contemporary and successor in the Miles Davis band, Chick Corea. Corea's usage is quite substantial, particularly in his more avant-garde period, 1968–71, while playing with Davis and subsequently with Circle.

42. Jost (1974) 1994 explores how Albert Ayler's playing reflected "a pronounced discontinuity of phrasing, a result of (1) short flourishes, (2) single staccato tones, and (3) wide leaps." (123). Jost refers to Ornette Coleman's improvisational approach as "motivic chain association" (49). For an application of the term "gesture" in European classical music, see the essays in Gritten and King 2006.

43. Carr (1982) 1998, 201.

44. Mercer 2004, 113.

45. Ibid. (edited).

Chapter 3

1. For example, the Left Bank Society in Baltimore sponsored two bookings on May 23, 1965, with Ron Carter, Tony Williams, and Sam Rivers, and December 4, 1966, with Wayne Shorter, Freddie Hubbard, Ron Carter, and Jack DeJohnette. Left Bank bookings between August 16, 1964, and May 7, 1967, are listed at http://home.earthlink.net/~eskelin (accessed August 12, 2011).

2. Buster Williams recalls that once Hancock's own sextet was established, "inevitably he would always bring the little bits and pieces he had written for a commercial. Then he would bring them into the band and we'd extend them."

3. Klein (1968) 2008.

4. Davis's studio band on the tunes "Two Faced" and "Dual Mr. Anthony Tillmon Williams Process" on November 11, 1968, and on "Splash" the next day was an expansion of the second Quintet, with two electric pianists, Herbie Hancock and Hancock's replacement in the touring Quintet, Chick Corea. On November 25 and 27 and the pivotal sessions on February 18, 1969, that netted In a Silent Way, Davis added a third electric pianist, Josef Zawinul, at the time composer/pianist with Cannonball Adderley. Much of this series of sessions, completed February 22, were released in 2001 on The Complete in a Silent Way Sessions. Hancock subsequently played on several of Davis's sessions during the Bitches Brew era, including two sessions that included Bennie Maupin: November 19, 1969, which netted "Great Expectations," "Orange Lady," "Yaphet," and "Corrado"; and November 28, 1969, which included "Trevere," "The Big Green Serpent," and two takes of "The Little Blue Frog." "Great Expectations" was released on Big Fun ([1974] 2000) and the balance on The Complete Bitches Brew Sessions (2004).

5. Recorded on March 6 and 9, 1968, this was Hancock's final record on Blue Note, except for Best of Herbie Hancock, released in 1971. Hancock said that he "left after five years with the company because it was not interested in promoting jazzmen to anyone outside jazz circles. . . . I'm trying to make things better for jazz." West 1970b, 134.

6. Voce 1998.

7. March 2, 1969. Sponsored by the Newport Jazz Festival, the bill also included Clark

Terry Big Band, Newport Jazz Festival All-Stars, Thelonious Monk Sextet, and Billy Taylor Trio. Joshua Light Show provided a psychedelic display of liquid lights and photographic slides behind the performers, which was the practice at the Fillmore East and Fillmore West, in San Francisco. Six display ads for the series appeared in the *New York Times*, and the event was announced in John Wilson's column; J. Wilson 1970.

8. The Sextet played the Village Vanguard on March 27, 1969. *New York Times*, Entertainment Events listings, March 27, 1969, 53.

9. *New York Times*, display ad, April 18, 1969, 38, which notes that the band was "appearing nightly."

10. Noted in undated news clipping in Brown's personal archive.

11. Recorded on April 18, 21, and 23, 1969. Once again, Hancock uses flugelhorn in place of trumpet and includes a tenor saxophonist who can double on flute. But this time he doubles the number of trombones, adding a conventional trombone to the bass trombone. In addition, a bass clarinet and an additional flute are added to the mix.

12. A rehearsal recording was made by the Miles Davis Quintet of that tune and "Speak Like a Child," not released until *The Complete Columbia Studio Recordings* (1998).

13. Herb Wong, original liner notes to *The Prisoner* (Blue Note Records, 1969).

14. Ibid.

15. The 2000 CD release of *The Prisoner* includes alternative takes of "Firewater" and the title track, which include even more intense and abstract solos than on the original release.

16. Garnett Brown's recollection.

17. J. Wilson 1970, 33.

18. Henderson first made his mark playing with hard-bop pianist Horace Silver, organist Brother Jack McDuff, and trumpeters Kenny Dorham and Lee Morgan.

19. May 23 and 29, 1969.

20. Producer Oren Keepnews recalls that Hancock had gone out to retrieve the suits for the members of his Sextet, including Henderson, who were about to head out on the road. Liner notes, CD release of *Power to the People* (Milestone Records, 2007).

21. Their first stop was the student-run Berkeley Jazz Festival at the University of California, on April 26 at Berkeley's Greek Theater. Hancock shared the bill with James Brown, Cannonball Adderley, Nina Simone, Tony Williams, Archie Shepp, Sonny Rollins, Max Roach, and others. Six months later, the horn arrangements on *Fat Albert Rotunda* suggest familiarity with Brown, about whom Hancock had learned from Miles Davis. Next was a stand at the Both/And in San Francisco on April 29 through May 3 and again on June 3–8. The shows were announced and advertised in the *Times* (San Mateo), May 30 and June 6, 1969, and the *San Francisco Examiner*, June 5, 1969. They next played a show at Stanford University's outdoor Frost Amphitheater on Saturday, May 4, on a bill including Duke Ellington, Roland Kirk, and Smoke (R. Wilson 1969, 10EN), followed by a week at Shelly's Manne-Hole in Los Angeles, June 13–22 (Feather 1969a, E17). The Sextet was also heard on the afternoon of the 21st at the Jazz by the Bay Festival at the International Sports Arena in San Diego. Leonard Feather's preconcert announcement refers to the event as part of "a series of three programs commemorating the 200th anniversary of the city of San Diego" (Feather 1969b). Neither Siders 1969 nor Feather take note of Hancock's performance.

22. June 27. *Progress-Index*, display ad, June 22, 1969, 21. The bill included Duke El-

lington, Sly and the Family Stone, George Benson, Roland Kirk Quartet, and Young-Holt Unlimited.

23. July 6. Sources: An announcement in the *Newport Daily News*, June 23, 1969, and *Newport Mercury and Weekly News*, June 27, 1969. The *Daily News* reviewer observed: "Drawing a mixed reaction from the audience was Herbie Hancock and his group. . . . His numbers weren't on the swingy side." Nippert 1969.

24. Gitler and Morgenstern 1969; Heineman and Morgenstern 1969; Brennan 2007; Ives 2004; Gennari 2004; Gleason 1967; Wolfgang's Vault (accessed August 12, 2011).

25. Wein, Chinen, and Cosby 2004, 463–64.

26. Nicholson 1998.

27. Elwood 1969a.

28. Elwood 1969b.

29. Feather 1969b.

30. Ibid; Elwood 1969a, 1969b.

31. Elwood 1969a. The *New York Times* described the band more coolly as "occasionally brilliant, particularly in its full-group arrangements and in solos by tenor sax man Joe Henderson." Lydon 1969.

32. Gallagher, July 24, 1969.

33. Ibid.

34. J. Williams 1988.

35. *New York Times*, October 4, 1969, 26; *New York Times*, April 24, 1970.

36. Ballon 2008.

37. *Billboard*, August 28, 1970, 3.

38. Szantor 1970.

39. West, May 24, 1970, 134.

Chapter 4

1. Tingen 1991, 39.

2. Townley 1974.

3. May 17, 1968.

4. It was released on the recording *Directions* (1981). A second session with a Wurlitzer was on a February 1968 Davis session that included work by Gil Evans.

5. This listener also hears the more brittle sound of a third brand of electric piano, the RMI, on "Felon Brun," recorded on September 24, 1968, and included on Davis's 1968 recording *Filles de Kilimanjaro*. Hancock's technique on the RMI, which he also plays on the 1969 Zoller recording, is more reminiscent of his playing on acoustic piano. Two other tunes on *Filles de Kilimanjaro*, the title track and the tune "Tout de Suite," also feature the Rhodes.

6. This is the recollection of pianist Ray Bryant; see Glasser 2001, 85.

7. Ray Charles's shouts: "Baby shake that thing!" and "Come and love your daddy all night long" are a world away from "What a friend I have in Jesus," as Nelson George observes: "Charles made pleasure (physical satisfaction) and joy (divine enlightenment) seem the same thing." George 1988, 70.

8. Sun Ra played Clavioline in recordings as early as *Heliocentric Worlds*, vol. 2 (1965).

Listen, for example, to the tune "The Sun Myth," which features an eerie chromatic solo on that instrument.

9. May 17, 1968.

10. Miles himself also added an electric organ as his own second instrument toward the end of this period.

11. Davis with Troupe 1989, 295.

12. November 19 and 28, 1968.

13. Recorded on June 20, 1968.

14. Recorded on November 11–12 were "Two Faced" and "Dual Mr. Anthony Tillmon Williams Process," released later on *Water Babies* (1976), and "Splash," on *Circle in the Round* (1979).

15. Some of the tracks were released on Davis's *Directions*.

16. The Zawinul sessions took place on November 25 and 27, 1968, with "Ascent" recorded on the second date. *In a Silent Way* was recorded February 18 and 20, 1969. Hancock's appearance on Milton Nascimento's *Courage*, also during this same time period (December 19, 1968, and February 26–27, 1969), was on acoustic piano.

17. August 19, 1969.

18. On November 19, 1969.

19. November 18, 1969.

20. The sessions continue on November 28, again with Hancock and Corea, this time adding organist Larry Young to the keyboard mix. "Trevere" and "The Big Green Serpent" continue in quasi-*Bitches Brew* mode, but are fragmentary. The master take of "The Little Blue Frog" is a soloistic vehicle for Davis and saxophonist Steve Grossman, with subtle comping by Hancock and Corea. Each of them at times accentuates a musical event and at other times provides textural support. An alternate take of "The Little Blue Frog" points more toward funk influences. Layered on John McLaughlin's rhythmic funk-oriented wah-wah guitar comping is drummer Billy Cobham's suggestions of a shuffle, and then Hancock's swirling organ, on which Davis and then Grossman solo. Aside from "Great Expectations," these November recordings remained unreleased until the *Complete Bitches Brew Sessions* boxed set in 1998. Maupin, but not Hancock, appears on two additional Miles Davis sessions on January 27 and 28, 1970. Chick Corea and Josef Zawinul are the keyboard players. Miles recorded another session on the 27th, without Zawinul with music that looked ahead to *A Tribute to Jack Johnson* (1971).

21. May 23 and 29, 1969.

22. *Infinite Search* was recorded October 9–10, 1969. Note that Corea rather than Hancock was on the sessions for Wayne Shorter's *Super Nova* and Larry Coryell's *Spaces*, which are related aesthetically to the Vitous recording. This preference may have been because Corea was at the time the keyboard player in Davis's band or possibly due to Hancock's busy schedule.

23. One reviewer described the recording negatively, as a counterexample to ensemble playing: "Miroslav Vitous dominates every track from start to finish and the listener is hardly aware that there are other musicians on the album. . . . [A]lmost everything Miroslav plays is at such a fast tempo that it is as though he is trying to dazzle us with his technical virtuosity, almost as though he is saying 'Look how many notes I can play,' with the result that [the] album becomes a blur of bass notes." Davenport 1970.

24. On January 27–29, 1970.

25. Coltrane used the concept of *alap* to great effect in the opening of *A Love Supreme* (1964) and in the more abstract *Ascension* (1965), on which Hubbard performs.

26. November 16, 1970.

27. Hendrix 1999, 2010.

28. Mehegan 1964, 23.

29. Coryell and Friedman 1978, 161–62.

30. Lyons (1983) 1989, 272.

31. Coryell and Friedman 1978.

32. Chadabe 1997. Varèse's pioneering work extended to electronic music, for instance, *Poème électronique* (1958), which mixes sounds recorded, manipulated, and organized on tape with electronically generated sounds.

33. J. Williams 1988.

34. Mehegan 1964.

35. Davis with Troupe 1989, 322–23; Carr (1982) 1998, 305. Miles was listening to two Stockhausen works, *Telemusik* and *Mixtur*, in 1972, which sonically transform instrumental music using electronics.

36. Mehegan 1964.

37. George Lewis: "Extending the conception of 'listening to everyone' to 'listening to everything,' the aptly named 'little instruments' were an integral part of the multi-instrumental conception characteristic of both Art Ensemble and AACM performance practice." Lewis 2008.

38. Pond (2005) 2010, 103, includes a similar quotation.

Chapter 5

1. Highlights included shows at UCLA's Royce Hall on a January 31 bill with French violinist Jean-Luc Ponty (entertainment event announcement, *Van Nuys (CA) News*, January 8, 1970; review, *Los Angeles Times*, February 2, 1970) (this may have been the first of two concerts attended by Billy Childs, described in the epilogue); then at Civic Arts Theatre in Walnut Creek, California (press release, *Long Beach (CA) Independent*, November 19, 1969); and a two-night stand at the Both/And in San Francisco, February 13–14 (event listing, *Oakland Tribune*, February 13, 1970).

2. On March 6, 1970.

3. J. Wilson 1970. Concert listings appeared in the *New York Times*, March 1, 1970, 105; and March 6, 1970, 30.

4. On April 16, 1970.

5. Blumenthal 2000. The set list is from Blumenthal's text.

6. The show took place on April 25, 1970 (*New York Times*, April 24, 1970). By Hancock's third appearance, in June 1972, he was the Center's president.

7. The date was June 18, 1970 (television listings, *New York Times*, June 18, 1970, 72). Also see Bailey 1972; Thirteen: WNET, New York Public Media 2011a, 2011b. Hancock made an appearance on another television show, *Like It Is*, produced by Charles Hobson, on New York's ABC Television affiliate in 1969 (*Billboard*, August 16, 1969).

8. Three were to take place in Indianapolis and three elsewhere in Indiana. Two pieces

were to be included, an expansion of the title tune from *Fat Albert Rotunda* and the other a work by bassist Chuck Israels. Hancock commented: "I'm not going to try to make the orchestra swing—it's not in their bag." West 1970b. A conversation with the orchestra's archivist confirmed that the idea never went past the proposal stage. It may have been slated on a schedule of annual summer concerts by orchestra members who remained in town beyond the conclusion of the official season.

9. Milkowski 2004.

10. Session on April 7, 1970.

11. *The Complete Jack Johnson Sessions* (2003) shows Hancock's solo unfolding through takes 10a and 11.

12. Hancock's playing on "Yesternow" is sparer, offering organ swells behind John McLaughlin's guitar chords.

13. Session on May 19, 1970.

14. Several takes of all these tunes were released only on *The Complete Jack Johnson Recordings*.

15. The recordings took place on August 6, 10, and 12, and were completed on October 28, 1970. *Rolling Stone* critic Lester Bangs hailed *Zawinul* as "an absolute cathedral of an album. . . . Zawinul stretches out through a five song set [that] reveals breathtakingly the stature of the Zawinul compositional talent, and suggests that he may have had more to do with the root gestation of the New Miles Sound than anyone would have thought." Bangs 1971b.

16. Maupin 1970.

17. Arnett 1970. Arnett notes that by the end of the first set, only 200 people were in attendance, in a room with a capacity of 1500. The first set consisted of "Eye of the Hurricane," an extended version of "Maiden Voyage," and "Wiggle-Waggle." The second set included "Speak Like a Child" and Buster Williams's "Firewater." The third set opened with "The Prisoner," and continued with "Fat Albert Rotunda" and "Toys."

18. Author's recollection and display ad, *New York Times*, July 26, 1970, 62.

19. E-mail correspondence with the author, April 18, 2009.

20. Hancock reports: "I could just hear my band playing over that bass line. . . . That would definitely get us in contact with a different audience. Chances are [that] the solo work would be done by my band. Iron Butterfly sings, so that's another angle. The basic drum work would probably be done by their drummer and my drummer would work out some more complex things to fit on top." West 1970b.

21. The two had met two years earlier, when Gumbs was an eighteen-year-old college student. "I was introduced to him by Bernard Draydon who worked with a jingle house, Herman Edel Associates, providing music for commercials." Gumbs was invited by a friend of his sister to sit in on a presentation to a client. "Later, I met with Bernard at his job and he played me different examples of music that had been written for his jingle house. One of them was a theme Herbie wrote for a cigarette commercial. When cigarette commercials left TV, Herbie ended up using the song on *The Prisoner* album. The tune is 'He Who Lives in Fear.'"

22. Arnett 1970b.

23. *Hartford Courant*, August 2, 1970, 10A. "Lively Arts Calendar" prepared by the Coordinating Council for Arts.

24. See Ken Davidoff's memoirs of the show at "Shea Stadium Peace Festival," Old Rock Photo, accessed August 16, 2011, http://www.oldrockphoto.com/shea.html. The concert followed a Winter Festival for Peace staged at Madison Square Garden earlier in 1970.

25. Entertainment listings, *Van Nuys (CA) Valley News*, August 21, 1970. About concerts at the Forum, see "Inglewood Forum 1969–79," *Go-Go's Notebook* (blog), accessed August 16, 2011, http://gogonotes.blogspot.com/2010/02/forum-1969–79.html.

26. Fillmore West concert announcement card and poster; available at Wolfgang's Vault, accessed August 16, 2011, http://www.wolfgangsvault.com, and *Daily Review*, August 25, 1970.

27. Elwood 1970.

28. Graham was also proprietor of the Fillmore East, where Hancock performed on March 1969. Graham and Greenfield (1990) 2004.

29. The jazz musicians, however, were generally given second or third billing and lower salaries in comparison with the headliners. In dollars and cents terms, this made some business sense for venues and promoters since the jazz performers were less known to rock audiences. Jazz had been replaced by R&B, rock and roll, and then funk as the popular musical form that it once had been. Ideally, the new audiences would grow in their appreciation of jazz. At the same time, the equation placed jazz musicians in a second professional tier in terms of finances and status. Davis's success story may also have been an anomaly.

30. Rubinson 1974.

31. *Coda*, October 1970, 37. Singh 2006 reports that Vancouver bookings of major jazz figures began in 1964, and the next year the Cellar opened: "a club where everyone from Art Pepper to Charles Mingus played. Ornette did his first out-of-town gig there."

32. The Sextet was on a triple bill with Miles Davis and Bill Evans. The Saturday show included Cannonball Adderley, Roberta Flack, and Don Ellis. Display ad, *Seattle Times*, October 1, 1970, C7; and *Coda*, October 1970, 37.

33. Baker 1970; display ad, *Seattle Times*, October 4, 1970, F4 (advertising the band as "held over" and listing the tunes "Watermelon Man," "Fat Albert Rotunda," "Maiden Voyage," and "Speak Like a Child").

34. Butters 2006.

35. A date specifically documented is Monday, October 12.

36. West 1970a.

37. Johnson 1971.

Chapter 6

1. November 16, 1970.

2. Review of *Blues Current*, *New York Times*, December 20, 1970. John Murtaugh's son Danny Murtaugh has posted mp3s of *Blues Current* on his website, http://dannymurtaugh .com/bluescurrent/ (accessed August 17, 2011), along with these comments about his father's music: "Forming a music company, Grant & Murtaugh back in 1963, John brought so much music innovation to advertising music. The jazz influences of his soul come through clearly. John hired the greatest record musicians of the time to perform the

commercial music he would compose. . . . [My dad] was a pioneer in advertising music as one of the first true composers of music for commercials."

3. It was aired in the New York area on October 13, 1971, and on the different dates that week in other locales.

4. Engineer Fred Catero had begun working in studios

when I was sixteen, in 1959. I had been in engineering eight years before coming to Columbia [they needed a mastering guy]. My whole world was classical music and that's what I wanted to do. I studied piano and was terrible and I figured if I can't be a good musician, and who needs a mediocre piano player, what *could* I do to still be around music? I can record those who *are* good. And that's how I got into it. By the time I was eighteen, I was managing a studio in upper Manhattan called Sanders Recording, for $18 a week. Then I went to another place where we did off-the-air broadcasting. Also they had a studio there where they did recordings. And from there I applied to Columbia Records and they hired me. I was twenty-one. I started as a mastering guy, cutting discs. Very shortly after that I started doing [recording] sessions. Since I was one of the young people there, they threw me into rock and roll. Naturally I was a huge success because I was good at what I did, and because I had my youth. They were into rock and roll, so I got to do Chicago, Blood Sweat and Tears, Simon and Garfunkel and others.

5. The company covered two record companies (Fillmore Records, distributed by Columbia, and San Francisco Records, distributed by Atlantic), artist management and book-ing (Graham), production (Rubinson), and recording (Fred Catero and the Catero Sound Company). The company lasted only until November 1971. In January 1972, Rubinson set up his own production and management company, David Rubinson & Friends, Inc.

6. Herrington 1998, 34, cites the Cellar Door show as the one Rubinson first attended, but Rubinson currently believes that it was probably July 31, 1970, in New York.

7. J. Williams 1988.

8. Ibid.

9. Ibid.

10. July 13, 2010, conversation with the author.

11. The recorder console included components made by Automated Processes, Inc. (API). Founded in 1968, API is a major "audio broadcast console manufacturer for radio and television networks and high profile stations." Automated Processes, Inc., homepage, accessed August 17, 2011, http://www.apiaudio.com.

12. Rubinson to Kirk Degiorgio, e-mail message, January 2007; subsequently sent to author, June 2010.

13. Ibid.

14. Wilson defines "black music [as] . . . a shared core of conceptual approaches to the process of music making . . . reflect[ing] deeply-rooted values of this culture." Among the musical values Wilson addresses are a centrality of rhythm, cross-rhythms, antiphony, physicality, and high-information density; "rhythmic clash or disagreement of accents"; "singing or the playing of any instrument in a percussive manner"; "antiphonal or call-and-response musical structures"; and a "high density of musical events within a relatively

short musical time frame—a tendency to fill up all of the musical space." O. Wilson 1983. Pond (2005) 2010, 36, draws on Wilson's definition.

15. This was one aspect of the musical approach that Schaeffer termed *musique concrète*. Chadabe 1997, 26–28.

16. M. Jones 1971.

17. Rubinson to Kirk Degiorgio, e-mail message, January 2007; subsequently sent to author, June 2010.

18. Trumpeter and big band leader whose compositions showed an affinity to additive meters.

19. By combining two copies of the same sound, separated by a short delay, flanging creates a rapidly oscillating filter sweep across the frequency spectrum.

20. For those who cannot read musical notation, the melody travels a minor third down, back up, a half step up and back down, and then back down a minor third.

21. The term had sexual overtones.

22. "Although the bass is given a primary role in establishing the groove, it is by no means alone. Rather, the bass acts as a focus within an interlocked group of instruments, which we can conceive of as a matrix, acting as a *fixed rhythmic* group [as defined by Olly Wilson]. The matrix is constructed to set up the all-important arrival on the downbeat. The *one* beat is both prepared and commented upon: the rest of the one- or two-measure groove is either anticipatory (acting as a pickup gesture before the one) or reactive (acting as a response to the *one*). The groove, then, is made of a recurring preparation/ arrival/follow-through cycle. It is the reliability of the *one's* arrival, set up by the recurring preparatory gestures within the matrix, reinforced in the follow-through after the *one* (and signified upon through syncopation) that gives the groove power on the dance floor." Pond (2005) 2010, 66–67.

23. "Best Selling Jazz LP's," *Billboard*, May 29, 1971, 40.

24. Rubinson to Kirk Degiorgio, e-mail message, January 2007; subsequently sent to author , June 2010.

25. Another of those bands was Santana.

26. Lichtenberg 1971.

27. Ibid.

28. Bangs 1971a.

29. Ibid.

30. *New York Times*, November 21, 1971, H3. It is difficult to tell whether this was just a list of new recordings or a list of best-selling or favored recordings; also included are Mahavishnu John McLaughlin's *My Goal's Beyond*, *Miles Davis at Fillmore*, and LPs by Gary Burton, Don Ellis, and Rahsaan Roland Kirk; in other categories, one finds Stevie Wonder's "Signed, Sealed, and Delivered"; Emerson, Lake, and Palmer's *Tarkus*; Jackson Five's "ABC"; Simon and Garfunkel's *Bridge Over Troubled Water*; and James Taylor's *Sweet Baby James*.

31. Promotional review, *Billboard*, March 20, 1971, 45.

Chapter 7

1. February 15–17, 1972.

2. The large cast of musicians included, in addition to Miles Davis, tenor saxophonists

David Liebman and Carlos Garnett, sitarist Colin Walcott, bassist Michael Henderson, and guitarist David Creamer.

3. David Rubinson recalls: "This is an acoustic piano, recorded full pedal, at double speed and backwards, to get the sub harmonics, and to build to climax at that point, as the backward wave shape reaches its peak."

4. Tape feedback is a form of sound processing in which the output of the tape recorder is delayed and reinserted into its input. The amount of delayed signal can be calibrated to control the amount of resulting feedback.

5. Multiphonics is a method by which a reed instrumentalist plays chords using special finger and breath techniques.

6. Herbie Hancock, interview by Howard Reich, Knight Ridder syndicated column, published in the *Albany (NY) Times Union*, June 24, 2004.

7. J. Williams 1988.

8. Vincent 1996, 5.

9. Bernstein 2004, 2008. The center originally operated in tandem with the San Francisco Mime Troupe, the Actor's Studio, and the Anna Halprin Dance Company serving as an integral part of San Francisco cultural life.

10. On the tune "Universal Copernican Mumbles" from *Sunfighter* (1971).

11. Among these were Mark Almond, Dr. Hook, Confunktion, and bass player Larry Graham of Sly and the Family Stone.

12. Forerunners of sample players, the Chamberlain and, subsequently, the Mellotron were keyboard instruments that played back short-tape loops of prerecorded instrumental sounds, particularly strings. These instruments were used at the time by rock groups King Crimson, Yes, and the Moody Blues.

13. The recording opens with ascending watery electronic sound, joined by bells, a single tom-tom, and then flute, treated with reverb. Additional electronic sounds enter shortly after the thirty-second mark and in the left channel, a vocal sound (maybe electronic) a few seconds later, which then pans right, ending at just after 1:00. Bells and other percussion continue, and a pulse begins, takes further shape with hi-hat, and then cowbell. A vocal sound returns in the left channel, increasing in amplitude and pans right, and then back left, and fades.

At this point, the pulse continues on cowbell, tom-tom, and hi-hat, shifting to the tune's melody, set up by a bass riff above which the melody is played on bass clarinet and electric piano. Some atmospheric trumpet sounds enter around 2:00. A repetition of the melody repeats and concludes with an explosion of brass (four notes, the final one held). The textural mix that follows for several minutes is described in the main body of the text.

A trumpet burst is followed by a downward synthesizer glissando reminiscent of a Theremin, returning us to the twice-repeated melody, which concludes with a burst of horns, drums, and synthesizer, followed at 4:30 by collective free improvisation, out of which a trumpet solo emerges. Shortly before 6:00, a melodic theme in the Mellotron and electric piano appears, one that I've taken to calling "Hollywood." The main melody returns, repeats, and concludes with another horn and synthesizer burst, extended by high trumpet and electric piano, and even further with quiet electric piano sounds, bass, and, in the distance, altissimo trumpet.

The hi-hat motif that prefaced the initial appearance of the melody returns shortly after 7:00, joined by bass, synthesizer, and high-register trumpet. A spare free improvisation unfolds, with quasi-tonal yet very funky wah-wah electric piano comping. A fine line divides solo from accompaniment. The improvisation continues, briefly including a kazoo-like wind instrument, and then the brass instruments make use of extended techniques. At 8:30, Maupin begins an abstract bass clarinet solo, at times up in the altissimo range. The other players add sparse figures and occasional glissandi, accompanied by Hancock's funky, wah-wah electric piano, which continues even when the bass clarinet drops out for half a minute. As 10:00 approaches, rising chromatic figures briefly appear, followed by sustained long chords and shapes on the Mellotron, synthesizer, and other instruments. The closing section is described in the main text.

14. Rubinson 1974.

15. Zak 2009, 2010.

16. David Rubinson to Kirk Degiorgio, e-mail message, January 2007; subsequently sent to author, June 2010. Portions of the discussion that follows are also addressed by Pond (2005) 2010, 134–45.

17. J. Lewis 1994, 21; quoted in Tingen 1991.

18. David Rubinson to Kirk Degiorgio, e-mail message, January 2007; subsequently sent to author, June 2010.

19. Ibid.

20. A test pressing of the album is marked with the date April 24.

21. Display advertisement, *New York Times*, June 18, 1972.

22. *Billboard*, May 27, 1972, 15.

23. *Billboard*, June 17, 1972, 56.

24. John A. Davlin, "What's Happening," *Billboard*, June 4, 1972, 31.

25. Presumably either the entire album or a single compiled from a series of highlights. "FM Action," *Billboard*, July 15, 1972, 48, representing twenty-seven "leading progressive radio stations" in major population centers of the United States.

26. Welding 1972.

27. Butters 2006.

28. *Las Cruces (NM) Sun-News*, January 11, 1973.

Chapter 8

1. The show took place on May 25, 1972, and Field (1972) describes the venue: "Ear deafening amplification hampers the appreciation of even a consummate artist like Herbie. I personally won't visit the Whisky again until I hear that the loudness has been lowered; it would be an injustice to the artist for me to review under those conditions."

2. R. Williams 1971.

3. Elwood 1972b.

4. *Jazz* (France), #201, June 1972, notes Gleeson's presence in the band at the time, but doesn't offer a specific date or venue.

5. J. Williams 1988.

6. See Pinch and Trocco 2002, 261–62.

7. This was achieved through the synthesizer's ability to control the number and depth of overtones, essentially building a waveform by choosing its components.

8. Gleeson describes his approach in technical terms:

It's really all about the overtone series and what you do with it. . . . I think "harmonic richness" and "timbral depth" become different names for the same thing. . . . So when you start with a pitched sound, which, despite all the "noisy" elements was almost invariably where I started, often using noise, though, as one of the FM sources, and subject it to bandwidth restriction and increased overtone density, especially overtones not congruent with the usual series for pitched sounds, then you've still got a limited number of overtones, but their density—how far apart they are—has increased. . . . When you band pass [limit the frequencies within a particular frequency range] a waveform you're restricting its overtone series. If, at the same time, you introduce frequency modulation you're now stacking up overtones within that restricted area that wouldn't normally be there. If you take a look at the harmonic series for a stretched circular membrane (formally called drum) you'll see that there's a different series there, and its constituents aren't congruent with, for instance, any of the usual musical scales, whereas the usual harmonic series gives us an octave, then a fifth, then a fourth, then a major third (nearly) and then a minor third, etc. That's why train whistles almost always sound like seventh chords. And of course that's what distinguishes a drum (which we "hear" as being non-pitched) from a whistle.

As computer music composer Jean-Claude Risset (2009) describes this phenomenon:

Synthesis allows us to compose sounds themselves, just as one composes a chord; composing spectra helps impart to timbre a functional role and not only a coloristic one. Harmony can be prolongated into synthetic timbres—such as certain bell-like tones or the slowly gliding tones that evoke the flight of planes—or it can be the root of melodic textures, through spectral analyses of chords, such as in the harmonic arpeggios opening of the piece [Risset's *Computer Suite from Little Boy*, 1968]. Here, instead of being heard simultaneously, the harmonics of the notes forming the chord are scanned in succession from top to bottom.

9. Gormley (1971) includes Hancock as one of the "notables," along with Archie Shepp and Rahsaan Roland Kirk, who "have visited the city," including Strata Gallery.

10. Afuche is a circular Latin hand percussion instrument. The performer turns a wooden handle, rotating and spinning metal beads, to make rhythmic scraping sounds.

11. *Billboard*, June 2, 1973, 13.

12. *Billboard*, August 11, 1973, 37; one behind was Donald Byrd's *Black Byrd*.

13. *Billboard*, November 17, 1973, 28. By week thirty-four, it remained in the top forty, at number thirty-five, yet Hancock's recently released *Head Hunters* was now number twelve in the same charts, in its third week. *Billboard*, June 25, 1973, 47. What topped the charts that week was Billy Cobham's *Spectrum*. Return to Forever's inaugural fully electric recording, *Hymn of the Seventh Galaxy*, opened at number twenty-five that week.

14. Pond (2005) 2010, 124–25, also notes this anecdote.

15. Butters 2006.

Chapter 9

1. The term "free jazz" has often been used interchangeably with "new thing" to refer to new musical approaches arising from jazz traditions in the 1960s, particularly associ-

ated with John Coltrane, Archie Shepp, Ornette Coleman, and others. A brief retrospective consideration of free jazz is found in "Music: The New Thing," *Time*, April 16, 1970, and is discussed extensively in Wilmer (1977) 1992, Jost (1974) 1994, among others.

2. A term initially associated with the AACM and adopted by Karl Berger, Ingrid Sertso, and Ornette Coleman, founders of the Creative Music Studio in the 1970s, first in New York City and then in Woodstock, New York.

3. G. Lewis 1996; G. Lewis 2008; Wilmer (1977) 1992, 213–15; Porter 2002, 191–239. The JCO is in some ways distinct from the others due to its racial integration and the power issues that arose as a consequence, and because of the challenge of maintaining an organization in economically competitive New York City.

4. G. Lewis 1996, ix; Anderson 2007, 92–152.

5. Curran and Teitelbaum 1989; Curran 2000.

6. Floyd 1995, 228.

7. Baker 1970.

8. Goddet 1979.

9. "The Magical Journey: An Interview with Wayne Shorter," *Jazz Improv* 2, no. 3 (2000): 75.

10. Lichtenberg 1971.

11. Mithen 2006.

12. Johnson 1971.

13. Herbie Hancock tells a parallel story about playing with Miles Davis, from whom he learned about the role of mistakes (Primack 1996):

> I was playing with Miles and we were doing this concert in Stuttgart. This was one of the nights when the band was hot. The stuff was burning, Tony Williams was smoking, Wayne was . . . sweating. And Miles was just playing like God-like stuff that he played. It was just smoking. And then, at this one point, which was like a peak in Miles' solo, I hit this chord that was so wrong. It was just awful. It was in the wrong place and it was like boom, I just felt like I destroyed the music. And Miles took his breath and played some notes that made my chord right.
>
> I don't know where he found these notes but he just wiped away the chord being wrong. He made this chord fit. I was dumbfounded. I couldn't even play for about two minutes. He just blew me away and what it taught me was that Miles didn't hear it as a mistake. He just heard it as an event. He just trusted it and did his musician thing and found the notes that fit that thing. I said, wait a minute, this is a lesson not just for music but for life. Things that happen to you are events. It's what you do with them that determine whether they're going to be problems or solutions. This is the kind of thing that I hope to develop more in my life and spread. And it's not something for just musicians, it's something that everyone can spread.

14. Jagajivan 1973.

15. For example, listen to *Live at the Fillmore East, March 7, 1970: It's About That Time* (1997) and *Miles Davis at Fillmore: Live at the Fillmore East* (1970). See Tate 1992, 68–85; Veal 2002, 2009; Tingen 1991.

16. For instance, *The Paris Concert* (1971). Circle also included Anthony Braxton and Barry Altschul.

17. Many of these are bootlegged recordings, with the exception of *Weather Report:*

Live in Tokyo (1972), excerpts from which are included the same year on *I Sing the Body Electric* (1972).

18. Norddeutscher Rundfunk (NDR).

19. A musette is a mouth-blown wind instrument, related to the recorder but capable of playing more than one note at a time. Its origins may date to a Baroque era French bagpipe.

20. Shepp 1966, 39–42, 44.

21. Steinbeck 2008a, 415–16.

22. G. Lewis 1998, 76, similarly describes an Art Ensemble of Chicago performance of Joseph Jarman's tune "Erika": "Eventually, the music began to move toward a kind of furious texture vamp, which at that time was described as 'intensity' within which the saxophones had primacy." For a more detailed analysis, see Steinbeck 2008b, 155–71.

23. Pond (2005) 2010, 126; Maupin interview, March 12, 1998.

24. Oliveros 2010.

25. Pharoah Sanders and Tony Williams were among the few; their appearances occurred by happenstance.

26. Mercer 2004. For more information about Nichiren Buddhism, see Ikeda 2001.

27. Johnson 1971.

Chapter 10

1. On January 29 and 30, 1971, the Sextet shared a bill with the New Generation Singers and singer David T. Walker at the Harding Theater in San Francisco. The shows began early, at 6:30 p.m. ("Herbie Hancock Plans Concert," *San Mateo Times*, January 28, 1971, 5; Russ Wilson, "Kenton, Tjader to Play," *Oakland Tribune*, January 29, 1971, 42). The *Tribune* referred to the New Generation Singers as "a fresh and stimulating gospel group that has appeared at the Newport Jazz Festival, U.C. Jazz Festival, and New York's Apollo Theater as well as in concert" (*Long Beach [CA] Independent and Press-Telegram*, January 22, 1971). The Sextet next appeared for a pair of two-week engagements in February, first at the Lighthouse in Hermosa Beach, near Hollywood, California (*Long Beach [CA] Independent and Press-Telegram*, February 11, 1971, B6). There were also announcements posted in the *Press-Telegram* on February 5 and 12, 1971, and a review by Leonard Feather of the show at the Lighthouse in the *Los Angeles Times*, February 5, 1971. After that came shows at the Both/And in San Francisco (closing on the February 19, *Oakland Tribune*, February 19, 1971), and the band completed their stay in California with a week at El Matador in San Francisco, where "there have been changes in the group, personnel- and music-wise" (Phillips 1971). The gig is mentioned again in the *Tribune* on February 26, 1971, followed on February 28 by a return to the Both/And, where the band shared the bill with Freddie Hubbard's quintet (*Oakland Tribune*, February 28, 1971); stands at Old Town Theater in Los Gates, March 23–28 (*Oakland Tribune*, March 19, 1971); two weeks at Shelly's Manne-Hole; and an appearance at a jazz festival at the California State University at Los Angeles on April 7 (*Los Angeles Times*, April 4, 1971). *Pasadena News*, April 18, 1971, lists an appearance by Herbie Hancock on *The Jazz Show*, hosted by Billy Eckstein. Sarah Vaughan also appeared. *Billboard*, April 24, 1971, 52, reviewed the April 6 Sextet show. This is likely the second show attended by Billy Childs as a child (discussed in the epilogue).

2. Source of the set list from an evening at the Both/And is Elwood 1971. Elwood's column misnames "Ostinato" "Aftinado."

3. Ndugu Leon Chancler adds: "A few months later, I got the gig with Miles [playing in the band that included Keith Jarrett and Michael Henderson] from having been playing with Herbie and on Walter Bishop Jr.'s recommendation. I didn't think about any parallels between Miles and Herbie's band until ten years ago. When I look at it now, I was involved, with the exception of Return to Forever, with three giants that spearheaded that era, Miles, Herbie, and Weather Report, plus of course George Duke. But I didn't think about it at that time."

4. Feather, 1971b.

5. *Billboard*, May 8, 1971, 34, also lists Hancock playing "a one-nighter" with Freddie Hubbard at the Taft Theater, Cincinnati, on Saturday, May 1, probably without the Sextet. Also see *Billboard*, May 1, 1971, 34. In early May, Billy Hart appeared with pianist Kenny Barron at Muse, in Brooklyn. *New York Times*, May 8, 1971, 16.

6. Eliot Tielgel, "Herbie Hancock Sextet" review, *Billboard*, April 24, 1971, 52. Note that the Los Angeles venue is incorrectly listed as being in New York.

7. Willis alternated with Rufus Reid; both were in college at the time.

8. Mr. Henry's Capitol Hill, May 18–23. "Pianist-composer Herbie Hancock, whose music has easily absorbed the influence of Debussy and big city blues, says he doesn't want to become bored with his art." West 1971.

9. At Kiosque International. *Coda*, August 1971, 35.

10. *Coda*, October 1971, 36.

11. Lichtenberg 1971. The context was a review of the *Mwandishi* recording, which also touched on this show.

12. The shows took place in Arhus, Denmark, at Folkets Park on July 15; in Finland, at the Pori Jazz Festival, July 16–17; and at the Jazz Festival Juan-Les-Pins, on July 21, in Nice, France. Returning to Denmark, the band may have played a show at Vejlby-Risskovhallen in Arhus, Denmark, which was followed by a night at the Copenhagen club Montmartre on July 24. Wrapping up the tour, the band embarked on a two-week run at Ronnie Scott's in London, July 26–August 3; a date at Jazzhaus in Hamburg, Germany, August 4; and at the Molde Jazz Festival in Norway (August 2–7). A brief film documentary of the latter festival that has circulated on the Internet shows a clip of the performance and band members enjoying their time around town. The shows at Nice and Arhus were radio broadcast and recorded, as was an undated performance from the same period, from Kristianstad, Sweden. The Nice set list included "You'll Know When You Get There," "Toys," and something titled "Be What," which appears to be a version of "Ostinato." *Orkester Journalen Tidskrift för jazzmusik* (Kristianstat, Sweden); Concert announcement, Nr. 6, June 1971; Radio broadcast announcement, Nr. 7, July/August, 1971; Concert review, *Jazz* (France) #192. A recording also exists of a show at Tivoli, in Copenhagen, Denmark, that includes tunes that would appear on *Crossings*, the band's upcoming studio album. It may have come from this tour. The set list includes "Maiden Voyage," a nearly twenty-six-minute performance of "Toys," a more than half-hour version of "Sleeping Giant," and "Water Torture," twenty minutes in duration.

13. R. Wilson 1971; further *Oakland Tribune* notices appeared September 12 and 17, 1971. Wilson described "Ostinato" as "evocative of a forest scene," with Buster Williams

on electric bass, Bennie Maupin on wooden flute, and the others on percussion. "Then came a shift as Maupin used his bass clarinet to create sound effects, Hancock moved to electric piano, and Hart began playing loudly on his drums. . . ."

14. October 17–22. Also in October, the Sextet's performance on the *Soul!* television show was broadcast throughout California on various dates: *Long Beach (CA) Independent and Press-Telegram*, October 13, 1971, and *Lima (OH) News*, October 13, 1971. Multiple sources document additional broadcasts throughout the United States, in July 1972, one of which was in Tennessee, *Kingsport Times*, July 26, 1972.

15. In early October, Hancock, maybe without the band, performed at a weekend Black Expo in Chicago. *Chicago Daily Defender*, September 25, 1971, 36. Other performers on the Sunday, October 3, bill included Bill Cosby, Ramsey Lewis, the Staple Singers, Isaac Hayes, and Gloria Lynne.

16. E-mail correspondence with the author, May 7, 2008.

17. The club was open and operated by Roger Bohn, 1971–75, during which time Krivda played opposite a roster of jazz notables. See Mosbrook 2000.

18. E-mail correspondence with the author, May 7, 2008.

19. The Kansas City show might instead have taken place during the previous spring. Metheny's recollections are in the epilogue.

20. Correspondence with the author, November 6, 2011; e-mail correspondence with the author, November 11, 2010.

21. Facebook messaging and e-mail correspondence with the author, July 14–15, 2010.

22. The Sextet appeared opposite soul singer Wilson Pickett.

23. On December 26.

24. Buster Williams and Bennie Maupin joined Harold Land on his *A New Shade of Blue* (Mainstream 1971); Williams on Joe Farrell's *Outback* (CTI 1971; King Japan 2006). Toward the end of 1971, Hancock played on three more CTI recordings, including a folk record by singer Victoria Domagalski (piano on "Now You're Gone"), who would appear the following year in the postproduction of *Crossings*. Hancock also recorded sessions for bassist Terry Plumeri's *He Who Lives in Many Places* (GMMC Records [1971] 2007).

25. Feather 1971b.

26. Ibid.

27. Heckman 1971.

28. *Coda*, October 1971, 37, also notes the length but not the exact dates of the gig. About the club, see "Ronnie Scott's in London Is Europe's Leading Club," *Billboard*, June 13, 1973, 61. *Melody Maker* gave the Sextet two reviews by Richard Williams and a feature article; Jones 1971.

29. R. Williams 1971. The week prior, Williams wrote a shorter review of one of the shows.

30. Feather 1971b.

31. R. Wilson 1971; returning to Russ Wilson's observation in footnote 13, this critic continues: ". . . Hancock moved to electric piano and Hart began playing loudly on his drums. . . . Sound built up until it seemed like a madhouse."

32. "Best Albums of 1971," *Time*, January 3, 1972.

33. G. Lewis 1996; G. Lewis 2001/2002.

34. There were two shows at the Carnival Bowl in St. John, Antigua, on Saturday and Sunday, January 1 and 2, 1972; other performers included singer Roberta Flack and trumpeter Lee Morgan (Ed Ochs, "New York," *Billboard*, January 2, 1972). A weeklong stand at the Esquire Show Bar in Montreal followed on January 31–February 5, and then shows at the Aqua Lounge in Philadelphia (noted without the date in *Coda*, April 1972, 33). The Montreal set list, as remembered by Canadian Broadcast Company (CBC) jazz show host Katie Malloch, at the time a college student at McGill University, included "Ostinato," "Wandering Spirit Song," "You'll Know When You Get There," "Firewater," "Toys," and most likely "Speak Like a Child" (e-mail communication with the author, May 6, 2008). Wallace Roney's reminiscence about the Philadelphia show may be found in the epilogue (the show is also mentioned in *Coda*, August 1972). The Sextet played the Village Vanguard in New York City, February 8–13, 1972.

35. Including an evening at the Both/And in San Francisco, on February 18; followed by shows at In Your Ear in Palo Alto, February 21–23 (February event calendar for the venue); a benefit for imprisoned political activist Angela Davis at the Berkeley Community Theater on February 28 (Ed Ochs, "New York," *Billboard*, January 2, 1972; Staska and Mangrum 1972; *Billboard*, January 29, 1972, 20, lists the date incorrectly as February 25); and a stand at the Lighthouse in Hermosa Beach, March 9–12 (event listings, *Pasadena Star-News*, March 9, 1972).

36. Elwood 1972a, who reports that the set list included "Toys," Buster Williams's "Firewater," and other tunes.

37. The set list in Baden, Switzerland, included "You'll Know When You Get There," "Toys," "Water Torture," "Firewater," and "Maiden Voyage."

38. The tour began with a concert at Maison de la Culture in Rennes, France, March 15 (*Jazz* [France] #198, March 1972); continued with shows at Kantonsschulein, Baden, Switzerland, at the Gaetano Donizetti Opera House; as part of the festival Rassegna Internazionale Jazz Bergamo, Italy, on May 17–19 (*Jazz Forum* #18, 1972; *Ciao 2001* [Italy, August 29, 1976]); at Jazzhus Montmartre in Copenhagen, Denmark, on March 21 (*Coda*, August 1972); and then with two shows in Sweden, Örebro and at Studentkaren in Göteborg (*Orkester Journalen*, May 1972; *Jazz Wereld* #38, April/May 1972). There may have been additional dates on this tour, which wrapped up at Studio de Joinville le Pont in Paris, on March 25; at De Doelen in Rotterdam; and back in Paris at Salle Pleyel (March 29) (*Jazz* [France], #200, May 1972; also see *Jazz* [France] #201, June 1972). The Baden and Copenhagen concerts were audio recorded. A partial recording exists of the Rotterdam performance, opening with an extended bass solo that leads into the tune "Toys" played by Hancock on acoustic piano and then the opening minutes of "Sleeping Giant." *Jazz Forum* reported that the Sextet was "one of the highlights of the festival and probably one of the highlights of contemporary jazz in general," but worried that the "old" acoustic Hancock might "be lost forever." The Paris studio set was also the scene of a photo shoot by Jean-Pierre Leloir, images from which were published in the *Wire* (Herrington 1998, 34).

39. Boland Baggenaes, review of Copenhagen concert, *Coda*, August 1972, 37.

40. Savy 1972.

41. A full week at Paul's Mall, which Gleeson believes included a Sunday matinee, plus two sets that same evening. A test pressing of *Crossings* includes the handwritten phrase:

"opens: Jazz Workshop Boston May 1–8, 1972." Gleeson recalls that it was at Paul's Mall, not Jazz Workshop.

42. May 25. Noted in J. Coleman 1972, 22, without specific dates.

43. Field 1972.

44. They played a concert on Monday, June 19, at St. Thomas Church on Fifth Avenue at 53rd Street (*New York Times*, "Who Makes Music" June 18, 1972, D28; *New York Times*, "Events Today," June 19, 1972, 38). Hancock, probably alone, also played his second bene- fit for the Harlem Music Center, an all-night Jam Session Party featuring Herbie Hancock, Max Roach, Airto Moreira, and Dane Belany of Senegal, an all-woman West Indian Steel Band (Richard F. Shepard, "Going Out Guide," *New York Times*, June 24, 1972, 18).

45. July 5. John S. Wilson simply noted: "Mr. Hancock brought three bags of exotic percussion instruments on stage with which his sextet colored and accented a long work that was largely a journal through areas of sound." (J. Wilson 1972a). Hancock's appearances were also announced in a *New York Times* display ad for the entire festival (May 7, 1972, D6). Heckman 1971 notes that Hancock participated in a jam session at the Festival, two nights prior. Later that month, the 1971 *Soul!* TV show on which the band performed was rebroadcast nationally including in Des Moines, Iowa; several cities in Texas; Blytheville, Arkansas; Syracuse, New York; Bennington, Vermont; Morgantown, West Virginia; Chicago; and Kingsport, Tennessee.

46. At some point in late July or early August, the Sextet played a one-hour concert at Funky Quarters in San Diego, one in a series of shows featuring jazz and rock musicians and a comedian, designed for radio broadcast on KGB-AM-FM ("Funky Quarters & KGB in Tie," *Billboard*, August 12, 1972, 19). The band was in Seattle, August 8–13 (Elwood 1972b; Baker 1972). The shows were also noted in the *Hayward (CA) Daily Review*, August 10, 1972. Berkeley shows included the Keystone (event listings, *Hayward [CA] Daily Review*, September 14, 1972, 54) and, as Pat Gleeson recalls, Freight and Salvage. A Monterey Jazz Festival set took place Saturday evening, September 16, 1972. The festival took place September 15–17, 1972. Calloway 1972 reported that the bill was titled "Giants of Jazz" and also included Thelonious Monk, Art Blakey, Clark Terry, and others. Harvey Siders, "Monterey Memo," *Down Beat*, November 23, 1972, 12–14. Other sources for the dating and locations of these shows: *The News*, Van Nuys, California, Friday, September 8, 1972; *The Press-Courier*, August 24, 1972, Oxnard, California; and *Fresno Bee*, Fresno, California, Sunday, July 30, 1972, D5; *Oakland Tribune*, September 9, 1972; *San Mateo Times*, September 4, 1972; and the *Reno Evening Gazette*, Tuesday, September 5, 1972, 6). The column "Nostalgia and Good Jazz" in the *Tucson Daily Citizen*, September 16, 1972, 15, quotes Leonard Feather: "Criticized by some fans last year for insufficient representa- tion of current events on the jazz scene, Lyons consulted with his musical director, John Lewis of the Modem Jazz Quartet. As a result, Herbie Hancock, conspicuous by his 1971 absence, will report for duty, as will the quartet of drummer Elvin Jones."

47. Elwood 1972b. The shows were also noted in the *Hayward (CA) Daily Review*, August 10, 1972. At times during that time period, one finds Maupin's name spelled "Benny."

48. Including shows in Baltimore; Washington, D.C.; St. John, Antigua; and various other East Coast locations.

49. Gumbs recalls the Revilot: "All the great musicians on tour would play there: Fred-

die Hubbard, Rahsaan Roland Kirk, Ahmad Jamal, Herbie, George Benson, Eddie Harris. Pharaoh Sanders played there the week after Herbie. It is now a diner with no evidence that the Jazz club was ever there with its rich musical history."

50. West 1972.

51. J. Wilson 1972b, 53.

52. On December 30 and 31, the band played a stand at Lion's Share in San Anselmo, California, at Francisco (concert listings, *Hayward [CA] Daily Review*, December 29, 1972), followed by dates at the Boarding House, in San Francisco (*San Francisco Examiner*, January 20, 1973). The date of a show at Tulagi's in Boulder, Colorado, is unknown ("Denver," *Billboard*, January 20, 1973, 14).

53. In early March, Hancock, performing without the Mwandishi band, joined Freddie Hubbard and Stanley Turrentine, with Ron Carter, guitarist Eric Gale, and drummer Jack DeJohnette for two nights of concerts, at the Civic Opera House in Chicago, March 3, 1973 (Calloway 1972), and Ford Auditorium in Detroit, March 4, 1973. The set included Hancock's "Hornets" and tunes by Hubbard. Both concerts were recorded and released by CTI. *Freddie Hubbard / Stanley Turrentine in Concert*, vol. 1 (CTI, 1974); *Freddie Hubbard / Stanley Turrentine in Concert*, vol. 2 (CTI, 1975). Rereleased on one CD as *Herbie Hancock—Live: Detroit/Chicago* (Hudson Street, 2005).

54. *Down Beat*, May 10, 1973.

55. Track list is from the recorded radio broadcast.

56. Including Gilly's in Dayton, Ohio, April 2–8; the Smiling Dog Saloon in Cleveland, Ohio, April 9–15; and Landmark Restaurant, located in Kansas City, Missouri's Union (Railroad) Station, Thursday, April 19–Sunday April 22, followed by an evening at Hancher Auditorium at the University of Iowa, in Iowa City, Thursday, April 26 (*Iowa City Press-Citizen*, March 28, 1973; *Cedar Rapids Gazette*, March 25, 1973; display ad, *Waterloo [IA] Sunday Courier*, April 8, 1973, 48; also see "Campus Dates," *Billboard*, April 14, 1973, 28). The tour wrapped up with a series of shows at Ebbets Field in Denver, Colorado, April 30–May 5 (Flyer with schedule for Ebbets Field).

57. Now a professor of percussion at the Berklee School of Music in Boston, Hadden appeared on Weather Report's recording *Mysterious Traveler* (1974). See http://www.skiphadden.com (accessed August 22, 2011).

58. E-mail correspondence with the author, May 7, 2008.

59. Edelman 1973.

60. Meadow 1973.

61. Feather 1973.

62. McLarney 1972.

63. Nemko 1973.

64. Hunt 1973. The show is noted in *Hamilton [OH] Journal News*, July 22, 1973. There is a preconcert announcement in *Hayward [CA] Daily Review*, May 25, 1973.

65. Hunt 1973.

66. Elwood 1972a.

67. Elwood 1972b.

68. M. Jones 1971.

69. Including at the University of California at Berkeley's Zellerbach Auditorium (display ad, *Oakland Tribune*, May 20, 1973, 10-EN; *Fremont [CA] Argus*, May 18, 1973; both list the band as a Septet) and a stand at the Great American Music Hall in San Francisco,

May 23–27 (*Hayward [CA] Daily Review*, May 12, 1973; *Fremont [CA] Argus*, May 25, 1973). Another multiple bill, again with the Pointer Sisters and with Jerry Garcia, took place at Keystone Berkeley, in Berkeley, California, May 29–31 ("Bay Sounds," *Oakland Tribune*, May 30, 1973), and on June 2, the band appeared on a bill headed by Jerry Garcia with Merle Saunders, and also the Pointer Sisters, at the Marin Civic Auditorium, in San Rafael (The Jerry Site, http://thejerrysite.com/shows/show/952 [accessed August 22, 2011]).

70. Hancock appeared on Saturday, June 16, at the Santa Monica Civil Center, but this was likely no longer the Mwandishi band. Ernie Kreiling described the event: "Another black station, KJLH (Compton) takes its first step in the concert business at the Santa Monica Civic by showcasing such stars as Alice Coltrane, Herbie Hancock, Monk Montgomery, Jimmy and Vella and the Young Hearts plus special guests Smokey Robinson and Syreeta to raise funds for the Transcendental Meditation Center on Saturday with the show getting under way at 730 p.m., reports station manager Rod McGrew who will emcee the event." ("A Closer Looook" column, *Van Nuys [CA] Valley News*, June 14, 1973, C-13). That same week, on June 21, Hancock participated in a panel discussion "on the future direction of jazz" (press release for the Bay Area Jazz Festival, June 16–23, 1973), along with John Hendricks and *San Francisco Examiner* critic Philip Elwood. This followed a free noon concert, as part of the Bay Area Jazz Festival, held at San Francisco City College.

Chapter 11

1. Rubinson 1974. Hancock had also done commercials for Chevrolet, Virginia Slims cigarettes, Standard Oil, and a shaving lotion company. *Chicago Daily Defender*, November 2, 1970, 12.

2. Lyons (1983) 1989, 275.

3. John Wasserman, *San Francisco Chronicle*, August 20, 1972.

4. G. Lewis 2008, 91.

5. The Art Ensemble of Chicago was affiliated with the Association for the Advancement of Creative Musicians.

6. Steinbeck 2008b, 267.

7. G. Lewis 2008, cites Robert P. Morgan, *Twentieth-Century Music: A History of Musical Style in Modern Europe and America* (New York: W. W. Norton, 1991), 197.

8. Principles written by founding member Henry Albrecht, quoted in Newman 1999, 96. Also see Newman 2010.

9. Herbie Hancock was not alone in footing the bill for a leader's band tours. Quincy Jones mounted a series of successful European big band tours in 1956–1960, that resulted in over $145,000 in personal debt, which took him seven years of work to repay, producing jazz and pop stars as an Artist and Repertoire (A&R) professional and subsequently Vice-President of Mercury Records. Jones 2008.

10. Townley 1974.

11. Hancock 1996, liner notes to *Head Hunters*, Columbia Records.

12. Ibid.

13. Townley 1974.

14. Ibid.

15. Gaer 1973.

16. Townley 1974.

17. Recorded on June 26–27, 1972. These are just a few of the recordings that included members of the band. A year earlier, Eddie Henderson, Billy Hart, and Buster Williams (listed exclusively as Mchezaji) played on saxophonist Buddy Terry's *Pure Dynamite* (Mainstream, 1972). At various others point in that year, combinations of band members appeared on a handful of other recordings. Patrick Gleeson recorded on the Philadelphia fusion band Catalyst's second LP *Perception* (Cobblestone, 1972). Billy Hart had appeared on two of their other recordings from this time period, as well. Buster Williams, Eddie Henderson and Billy Hart joined Kenny Barron, Stanley Clarke and Dom Um Ramao on *Dance of Allegra* (Mainstream, 1972), a recording by saxophonist Pete Yellin, who had subbed for Joe Henderson in the Herbie Hancock Sextet in 1969. Ramey 1973 describes *Dance of Allegra* as "mid-60s Blue Note avant garde, with Henderson playing the Freddie Hubbard role and Yellin as James Spaulding . . . "

18. On December 13–14, 1972.

19. On February 25, 1973. The pianist/arranger, Onaje Allan Gumbs, hired by Connors to work on the recording, was the same young man whom Hancock met in 1968 through an advertising agency connection. They met a second time after the Sextet's July 1970 show in Central Park, New York and yet again during the Mwandishi band's engagement in Buffalo, New York, in October 1972. Gumbs recalls: "Herbie was still in town on the Monday before Pharoah started his shows at the Revilot Lounge Norman Connors came into the club talking about his vision for his upcoming album. He wanted to do a tune that would be Brazilian in flavor, with strings. I jumped into the opportunity because I loved Brazilian music and had gained experience arranging, in college. Norman told me that Herbie, Eddie, and Buster would be on the album. But when I got to New York with the finished piece, his producer Skip Drinkwater thought that Norman had lost his mind; Skip didn't know me but wasn't aware that all the musicians on the date knew me. He saw me as a new kid on the block doing his first recording, having only done one gig at Baker's Keyboard Lounge with Kenny Burrell. But when I got on the podium to conduct the piece, he saw that Herbie and the others were consulting me about my chart. He realized that while I might have been a 22 year-old guy all of the cats already knew me, and he was so impressed. He asked whether I had a publishing company and suggested that I start my own company."

20. On March 10, Hancock appeared without his band as part of a CTI/Kudu records Winter Jazz Festival concert joining Hancock with Eric Gale, Johnny Hammond, Hank Crawford, Stanley Turrentine, Ron Carter, and Jack DeJohnette. Earl Calloway, "Heads really together," *Chicago Defender*, March 10, 1973, 32.

21. The Internet Movie Database (IMDb), http://www.imdb.com/title/tt0070726/plotsummary. Accessed August 1, 2010.

22. E-mail correspondence with the author, July 26, 2010.

23. Terri Lyne Carrington replaced Billy Hart, who was unable to attend.

Epilogue

1. Most likely a show during the first week of April 1971.

2. This may have been the January 30, 1970, show. An alternate possibility is a show in 1969 for which I have not found documentation.

3. Childs adds: "I started really getting into various kinds of musical fusion, attempts to put together different musical disciplines at an organic level—Scott Joplin's opera *Treemonisha*, the friendship between Vladimir Horowitz and Art Tatum, George Gershwin, ELP, and others."

4. Smith 2001, 175.

5. Ibid.; Fripp 2007.

6. Meadow 1973.

7. Butters 2006.

8. Johnson 1971.

References

Unless otherwise noted, all interviews were conducted by the author, including Thurman Barker (November 15 and December 1, 2010); Garnett Brown (November 11 and 12, 2010); Fred Catera (March 1, 2008); Ndugu Leon Chancler (November 1, 2010); Billy Childs (October 20, 2010); Alvin Fielder (November 30 and December 18, 2010); Mitchel Forman (March 12, 2008 and November 11, 2010); Patrick Gleeson (on several occasions, October 2007—January 2008 and May—July 2008); Onaje Allan Gumbs (November 18, 2010); Herbie Hancock (December 19, 2008 and August 9, 2010); Billy Hart (June 17, 2008); Eddie Henderson (March 29, 2008); Bennie Maupin (January 7, 2008); Christian McBride (November 6, 2010); Bobby McFerrin (October 2, 2010); Pat Metheny (November 27, 2010); Wallace Roney (September 25, 2009 and October 7, 2010); David Rubinson (January 29, 2008); Richard Teitelbaum (April 12, 2008); Buster Williams (February 23 and July 3, 2008); Reggie Willis (November 10 and December 17, 2010); e-mail consultation with George Lewis (several dates, September 2007–November 2010). In most cases, conversations by telephone or in person were followed by additional e-mails. Additional, shorter interviews conducted by e-mail are cited in the notes.

Anderson, Iain. 2007. *This Is Our Music: Free Jazz, the Sixties, and American Culture*. Philadelphia: University of Pennsylvania Press.

Arnett, Earl. 1970. "Jazz Commentary: Concert Reveals State of the Art." *Baltimore Sun*, August 7, B1.

Baker, Ed. 1970. "After Dark: Hancock Stays to Play." *Seattle Times*, October 9, F3.

———. 1972. "After Dark." *Seattle Times*, August 11, B4.

Baggenaes, Boland. 1972. Review of Copenhagen concert. *Coda*, August, 37.

Bailey, Peter. 1972. "Black Excellence in the Wasteland." *Ebony*, March, 44ff.

Ballon, John. 2008. Review of *Fat Albert Rotunda*. MustHear.com, October 4. http://www.musthear.com/reviews/fatalbert.html.

Bangs, Lester. 1971a. Review of *Mwandishi*. *Rolling Stone*, September 2.

———. 1971b. Review of *Zawinul*. *Rolling Stone*, August 5.

Bernstein, David. 2004. Program notes to "Wow and Flutter," a SFTMC retrospective at Rensselaer Polytechnic Institute, Troy, New York, sponsored by the Curtis R. Priem Experimental Media and Performing Arts Center (EMPAC).

———, ed. 2008. *The San Francisco Tape Music Center: 1960s Counterculture and the Avant-Garde*. Berkeley: University of California Press.

Billboard. 1969. "Soul Sounds in the Marketplace." August 16, 26.

———. 1971. "Musician a Technician Who Picks Up, Expresses Environment: Hancock." June 12, 31, 44.

Black, Timuel. 2005. "Wayman Hancock Sr." In *Bridges of Memory: Chicago's First Wave of Black Migration*, 153. Evanston, IL: Northwestern University Press.

Blumenthal, Bob. 2000. Liner notes to Herbie Hancock, *The Prisoner*, Blue Note Records.

Brennan, Matt. 2007. "Failure to Fuse: The Jazz-Rock Culture War at the 1969 Newport Jazz Festival." *Jazz Research Journal* 1 (1): 73–98.

Butters, Rex. 2006. "Bennie Maupin: Miles Beyond." *All About Jazz*, September 12. http://www.allaboutjazz.com/php/article.php?id=22723.

Calloway, Earl. 1970. "Herbie Hancock Brings a New Sound to Chicago." *Chicago Daily Defender*, November 18, 14.

———. 1972. "Chicago Talent Soars to Top." *Chicago Defender*, September 16, 21.

———. 1973. "Heads Really Together." *Chicago Defender*, March 10, 32.

Carr, Ian. (1982) 1998. *Miles Davis: The Definitive Biography*. New York: Thunder's Mouth Press.

Chadabe, Joel. 1997. *Electric Sound: The Past and Promise of Electronic Music*. Upper Saddle River, NJ: Prentice Hall.

Chicago Daily Defender. 1970. "Pianist Set for London House Debut." November 2, 12.

———. 1972. "Here's a New Breed of Jazzman: The Man, Herbie Hancock." February 12, A15.

Choice, Harriet. 1970. "Jazz by Choice." *Chicago Tribune*, November 13, B15.

Coleman, Julian. 1972. *Soul Sauce*, June 3, 22.

Coryell, Julie, and Friedman, Laura. 1978. "Herbie Hancock." In *Jazz-Rock Fusion: The People, the Music*, 159–64. New York: Dell.

Cowell, Henry. (1930) 1996. *New Musical Resources*. Cambridge: Cambridge University Press.

Curran, Alvin. 2000. "Improvisationspraxis der Musica Elettronica Viva." *MusikTexte*, November. English translation: "From the Bottom of the Soundpool," August 6, http://www.alvincurran.com/writings/soundpool.html.

Curran, Alvin, and Richard Teitelbaum. 1989. "Musica Elettronica Viva: Program Notes, New Music America Festival," Knitting Factory, New York City. http://www.alvin curran.com/writings/mev.html.

Daily Review (Hayward, California). 1970. "Big Names Soon at Fillmore West," August 25.

Davenport, Mike. 1970. "The Jazz Scene." *Van Nuys (CA) News*, March 31, 25A.

Davey, Colin. 1998. "Boogie Woogie Piano: From Barrelhouse to Carnegie Hall." Oregon Festival of American Music, program booklet, August. http://www.colindavey.com/ BoogieWoogie/articles/ofamart.htm.

Davis, Miles, with Quincy Troupe. 1989. *Miles: The Autobiography*. New York: Simon and Schuster.

Degiorgio, Kirk. 2008. "Herbie Hancock." *Wax Poetics*, June/July.

DeVeaux, Scott. 1997. *Bebop: A Social and Musical History*. Berkeley: University of California Press.

Douglas, Robert L. 1991. "Formalizing an African-American Aesthetic." *New Art Examiner*. June/Summer, 18–24.

Edelman, Mark. 1973. "Real Live Hancock." *University News*, University of Missouri, Kansas, April 19.

Elwood, Philip. 1969a. "Hancock Probing New Areas." *San Francisco Examiner*, May 1.

———. 1969b. "Herbie's Sophisticated Sound." *San Francisco Examiner*, June 5.

———. 1970. "Musical Whirlwinds Fly Through Fillmore West." *San Francisco Examiner*, August 28, 29.

———. 1971. Concert review. *San Francisco Examiner*, February 18.

———. 1972a. "Hancock Carves Out New Sounds." *San Francisco Examiner*, February 19, 6.

———. 1972b. "Hancock Seven Plus an Engineer." *San Francisco Examiner*, August 9.

Feather, Leonard. 1962. Liner notes to Herbie Hancock's *Takin' Off*, Blue Note Records.

———. 1969a. Concert review. *Los Angeles Times*, June 13, E17.

———. 1969b. Concert review. *Los Angeles Times*, June 24, C12.

———. 1971a. "Hancock Worth Waiting For." *Los Angeles Times*, September 24, F17.

———. 1971b. "Herbie Hancock." *Melody Maker*, March 13.

———. 1973. "Fame Plays No Part: Awards Given in Jazz." *Tucson Daily Citizen*, January 6.

Field, Vic. 1972. "Viewing the Rock Scene . . . " *Van Nuys (CA) Valley News*, May 26.

Flam, Jack D., ed. 1995. "Interview with Jacques Guenne, 1925." In *Matisse on Art*, 80. Berkeley: University of California Press.

Floyd, Samuel A., Jr. 1995. *The Power of Black Music: Interpreting Its History from African to the United States*. New York: Oxford University Press.

Fripp, Robert. 2007. "Robert Fripp's Diary." Discipline Global Mobile, October 27. http://www.dgmlive.com/diaries.htm?entry=8170.

Gaer, Eric. 1973. "Herbie Hancock Fires His Band," *Down Beat*, August 16.

Gallagher, Joe. 1969. Concert review. *Down Beat*, July 24.

Gennari, John. 2004. "Hipsters, Bluebloods, Rebels, and Hooligans: The Cultural Politics of the Newport Jazz Festival, 1954–1960." In *Uptown Conversation: The New Jazz Studies*, edited by Robert G. O'Meally, Brent Hayes Edwards, and Farah Jasmine Griffin. New York: Columbia University Press.

George, Nelson. 1988. *The Death of Rhythm & Blues*. New York: Pantheon Books.

Gitler, Ira. 1963. Liner notes to Herbie Hancock, *My Point of View*, Blue Note Records.

Gitler, Ira, and Dan Morgenstern. 1969. "Big Crowds, Bad Vibes." *Down Beat*, August 21, 25–31, 45.

Glasser, Brian. 2001. *In a Silent Way: A Portrait of Joe Zawinul*. London: Sanctuary.

Gleason, Ralph. 1967. "Like a Rolling Stone." *Jazz and Pop*, September 14.

Goddet, Laurent. 1979. Herbie Hancock interview. *Jazz Hot*, July–August, 363–64. Translation by Mark Dermer, 2010.

Gormley, Michael P. 1971. "From the Music Capitals of the World: Detroit." *Down Beat*, May 13, 55.

Graham, Bill, and Greenfield, Robert. (1990) 2004. *Bill Graham Presents: My Life Inside Rock and Out*. New York: Da Capo Press.

Gritten, Anthony, and King, Elaine, eds. 2006. *Musical Gesture*. London: Ashgate.

Hancock, Herbie. 1996. Liner notes to *Head Hunters*, Columbia Records.

Hart, Billy, and Iverson, Ethan. 2006. "Let's Call It the Jazz Tradition—That Huge World That Is a Sociological Development Demonstrated through Music." January. http://www.billyhartmusic.com/interview.htm.

Heckman, Don. 1971. "Soul Artist on Bill with the Herbie Hancock Sextet." *New York Times*, November 7, 83.

———. 2007. "Pianist Dazzled Jazz World with Technique, Creativity: Oscar Peterson, 1925–2007." *Los Angeles Times*, December 25.

Heineman, Alan, and Dan Morgenstern. 1969. "Rock, Jazz, and Newport: An Exchange." *Down Beat*, December 25, 22–23.

Herrington, Tony. 1998. "Tomorrow People." *Wire*, August.

Hunt, Dennis. 1973. "At the Troubadour: A Double Helping of Jazz." *Los Angeles Times*, May 17, H17.

Ikeda, Daisaku. 2001. *For the Sake of Peace: Seven Paths to Global Harmony, a Buddhist Perspective*. Santa Monica: Middleway Press.

Ives, Bill. 2004. "The Original Newport Jazz Festival: 1969–1971." *Portals and KM* (blog), August 29. http://billives.typepad.com/portals_and_km/2004/08/the_original_ne_1.html.

Jagajivan. 1973. "Musing with Mwandishi." *Down Beat*, May 24, 4–15, 38.

Johnson, Brooks. 1971. Interview with Herbie Hancock. *Down Beat*, January 21.

Jones, Max. 1971. "Jazzscene: Hancock's Heritage." *Melody Maker*, August 7.

Jones, Quincy. 2008. *The Complete Quincy Jones: My Journey & Passions*. San Rafael, CA: Insight.

Jost, Ekkehard. (1974) 1994. *Free Jazz*. New York: Da Capo Press.

Karenga, Maulana Ron. (1993) 2002. *Introduction to Black Studies*. Los Angeles: University of Sankore Press.

———. 1999. "Philosophy, Principles and Program." Organization Us. http://www.us-organization.org/30th/ppp.html.

———. 2010. "Forty-Five Years of Service, Struggle and Institution-Building." Organization Us. http://www.us-organization.org/30th/30yrs.html.

Lewis, George E. 1996. "Improvised Music after 1950: Afrological and Eurological Perspectives." *Black Music Research Journal* 16 (1): 91–122.

———. 1998. "Singing Omar's Song: A (Re)construction of Great Black Music." *Lenox Avenue: A Journal of Interarts Inquiry* 4:69–92.

————. 2001/2002. "Experimental Music in Black and White: The AACM in New York, 1970–1985." *Current Musicology*, Spring, 71–73.

————. 2008. *A Power Stronger than Itself: The AACM and American Experimental Music.* Chicago: University of Chicago Press.

Lewis, Joel. 1994. "Running the Voodoo Down." *Wire*, December, 21.

Lichtenberg, James. 1971. "Higher Order of Energy." *New York Times*, July 25, D24.

Litweiler, John. 1993. *Ornette Coleman: A Harmolodic Life.* New York: William Morrow.

Living Buddhism. 2006. "The SGI-A Global Community of Nichiren Buddhists." Inside cover page statement, November–December.

Lydon, Michael. 1969. "At Berkeley, a Joyous Two Days of Jazz." *New York Times*, May 10.

Lyons, Len. (1983) 1989. *The Great Jazz Pianists: Speaking of Their Lives and Music.* New York: Da Capo Press.

Maultsby, Portia K. 1990. "Africanisms in African-American Music. In *Africanisms in American Culture*, edited by Joseph E. Holloway, 191–92. Bloomington: Indiana University Press.

Maupin, Bennie. 1970. Liner notes to the CD release of *Lee Morgan: Live at the Lighthouse*, Blue Note Records (1970) 1996. Excerpts posted at http://www.shout.net/~jmh/articles/lee01.html. Accessed August 23, 2011.

Mayer, Andre. 2007. "An Interview with Jazz Legend Herbie Hancock." CBC Radio-Canada, June 18. http://www.cbc.ca/arts/music/hancock.html.

McLarney, Bill. 1972. "Caught in the Act." *Down Beat*, May 10.

Meadow, Elliot. 1973. "Meet Benny Maupin." *Down Beat*, January 18.

Mehegan, John. 1964. "Discussion: Herbie Hancock Talks to John Mehegan." *Jazz*, September, 23ff.

Mercer, Michelle. 2004. *Footprints: The Life and Work of Wayne Shorter.* New York: Penguin.

Milkowski, Bill. 2004. Liner notes to Miles Davis, *The Complete Jack Johnson Sessions*, Columbia Records.

Mithen, Steven. 2006. *The Singing Neanderthals: Origins of Music, Language, Mind, and Body.* Cambridge: Harvard University Press.

Mosbrook, Joe. 2000. "Jazzed in Cleveland." WMV: Web News Cleveland, January 3. http://www.cleveland.oh.us/wmv_news/jazz49.htm.

Nemko, Frankie. 1973. "High-Energy Hancock." *Melody Maker*, June 9.

Newman, Nancy. 1999. "Gleiche Rechte, gleiche Pflichten, und gleiche Genüsse: Henry Albrecht's Utopian Vision of the Germania Musical Society." *Yearbook of German–American Studies* 34:83–111.

————. 2010. *Good Music for a Free People: The Germania Musical Society in Nineteenth–Century America.* Eastman Studies in Music. Rochester, NY: University of Rochester Press.

Nicholson, Stuart. 1998. *Jazz Rock, a History.* Munich, Germany: Schirmer Mosel.

Nippert, Jane. 1969. "Rock Group Closes Festival." *Newport Daily News*, July 7, 1, 5.

Norment, Lynn. 1987. "Walking the Tightrope Between Jazz and Pop." *Ebony*, March, 136.

Oliveros, Pauline. 2010. Description of "Deep Listening." Deep Listening Institute. http://deeplistening.org/site/content/about.

Phillips, Perry. 1971. "Night Sounds." *Oakland Tribune*, February 19, 33.

Pinch, Trevor, and Frank Trocco. 2002. *Analog Days: The Invention and Impact of the Moog Synthesizer*. Cambridge, MA: Harvard University Press.

Pond, Steven F. (2005) 2010. *Headhunters: The Making of Jazz's First Platinum Album*. Ann Arbor: University of Michigan Press.

Porter, Eric. (1998) 2006. *John Coltrane: His Life and Music*. Ann Arbor: University of Michigan Press.

———. 2002. *What Is This Thing Called Jazz? African American Musicians as Artists, Critics, and Activists*. Berkeley: University of California Press.

Price, Emmett, III. 1995. "The Development of John Coltrane's Concept of Spirituality and Its Expression in Music." *McNair Journal*. McNair Scholars Program, University of California, Berkeley.

Primack, Bret. 1996. "A Conversation with Herbie Hancock & John McLaughlin." *Jazz Times*, May. Available at http://www.cs.cf.ac.uk/Dave/mclaughlin/art/hancock.html. Accessed August 23, 2011.

Ragogna, Mike. 2011. "Tribute to Miles: A Conversation with Herbie Hancock." *Huffington Post*, June 24. http://www.huffingtonpost.com/mike-ragogna/tribute-to-miles-a-conver_b_883658.html.

Ramey, Guthrie P., Jr. 1973. Review of Pete Yellin, *Dance of Allegra*. *Down Beat*, January 18.

Reich, Howard. 2004. Interview with Herbie Hancock. Syndicated column, Knight Ridder newspapers. Published in *Albany (NY) Times Union*, June 24.

Risset, Jean-Claude. 2009. "Max Mathews's Influence on (My) Music." *Computer Music Journal* 33 (3): 27.

Rosenthal, David H. 1992. *Hard Bop: Jazz and Black Music 1955–1965*. New York: Oxford University Press.

Rubinson, David. 1974. Liner notes to Herbie Hancock, *Treasure Chest*, Columbia Records.

Russell, George. (1953) 1959. *Lydian Chromatic Concept of Tonal Organization*. New York: Concept.

Savy, Michel. 1972. Review of March 29, 1972, concert at Salle Pleyel, Paris. *Jazz* (France) #200, May. Translated from the French by Françoise Chadabe.

Shepp, Archie. 1966. "A View from the Inside." *Music '66/Down Beat Yearbook*, 39–42, 44.

Shorter, Wayne. 2000. "The Magical Journey: An Interview with Wayne Shorter." *Jazz Improv* 2 (3): 75.

Siders, Harvey. 1969. Concert review. *Down Beat*, September 4.

———. 1972. "88 Divided by 4: A Round Table Discussion with Herbie Hancock, Roger Kellaway, Joe Sample and Toshiko Akiyoshi." *Down Beat*, November 9.

Singh, Taran. 2006. "Gregg Simpson: Avant-Garde from Vancouver." *All About Jazz*, August 15. http://www.allaboutjazz.com/php/article.php?id=22604.

Smith, Sid. 2001. *In the Court of King Crimson*. London: Helter Skelter.

Staska, Katie, and Mangrum, George. 1972. "Pamela Polland Great on Soon-to-be-Released Album." *Hayward (CA) Daily Review*, February 17.

Steinbeck, Paul. 2008a. "'Area by Area the Machine Unfolds': The Improvisational Performance Practice of the Art Ensemble of Chicago." *Journal of the Society for American Music* 2 (3): 397–427.

———. 2008b. "Urban Magic: The Art Ensemble of Chicago's Great Black Music." PhD diss., Columbia University.

Szantor, Jim. 1970. Review of *Fat Albert Rotunda. Down Beat*, August 8.

Tamarkin, Jeff. 2010. "Energy in the Environment." *Jazz Times*, September, 35–40.

Tate, Greg. 1992. *Flyboy in the Buttermilk: Essays on Contemporary America*. New York: Simon and Schuster.

Thirteen: WNET, New York Public Media. 2011a. "About the Show" (WNET's *Soul!*). http://www.thirteen.org/soul/about-soul/series-description.

———. 2011b. "*Soul!* Episode List, 1968–1973." http://www.thirteen.org/soul/about-soul/soul-episode-guide-1968–1973/.

Tingen, Paul. 1991. *Miles Beyond: The Electric Explorations of Miles Davis, 1967–1991*. New York: Billboard Books.

Townley, Ray. 1974. "Hancock Plugs In." *Down Beat*, October 24.

Varèse, Edgard. 1966. "The Liberation of Sound." *Perspectives on New Music* 3 (Fall/Winter): 11–19.

Veal, Michael. 2002. "Miles Davis and the Unfinished Project of Electric Jazz." *Raritan* (Summer).

———. 2009. Review of Miles Davis, *The Complete On the Corner Sessions. Jazz Perspectives* 3 (3): 265–73.

Vincent, Rickey. 1996. *Funk: The Music, the People, and the Rhythm of the One*. New York: St. Martin's/Griffin.

Voce, Steve. 1998. Interview with Herbie Hancock. *London Independent*, January 2.

Wasserman, John L. 1972. "Hancock's Unusual Music That You Know Is Right." *San Francisco Chronicle*, August 11.

Waters, Keith. 2011. *The Studio Recordings of the Miles Davis Quintet, 1965–68*. New York: Oxford University Press.

Wein, George, Nate Chinen, and Bill Cosby. 2004. *Myself Among Others*. New York: Da Capo Press.

Welburn, Ron. 1971. "The Black Aesthetic Imperative." In *The Black Aesthetic*, edited by Addison Gayle Jr., 132–49. New York: Doubleday.

Welding, Pete. 1972. Review of *Crossings. Down Beat*, November 23.

West, Hollie I. 1970a. "Jazz with Art and Appeal." *Washington Post, Times Herald*, October 14, B9.

———. 1970b. "Jazz with Comfort." *Washington Post, Time Herald*. May 24, 134.

———. 1971. "Herbie Hancock Views." *Washington Post*, May 20, C17.

———. 1972. "Color It Contemporary Jazz." *Washington Post, Times Herald*, October 27, B13.

Williams, Joy. 1988. "Herbie Hancock Interview." *Jazz Forum: The Magazine of the International Jazz Federation* 111 (Poland). Available at JoyZine, http://www.artistwd.com/joyzine/music/hancock/hancock.php. Accessed August 23, 2011.

Williams, Richard. 1971. "Herbie Hancock." *Melody Maker*, August 7.

Wilmer, Valerie. (1977) 1992. *As Serious as Your life: John Coltrane and Beyond*. London: Serpents Tail.

Wilson, John S. 1969. "Unruly Newport Fans Upset Newport Jazz Festival." *New York Times*, July 7, 28.

———. 1970. "Hancock Gives Jazz a New Dimension." *New York Times*, March 7, 33.

———. 1972a. Review of Newport Jazz Festival's Third Connoisseur Concert. *New York Times*, July 6, 45.

———. 1972b. "3 Jazz Styles Give a Colorful Pattern to Bill at Beacon." *New York Times*, December 11, 53.

Wilson, Olly. 1983. "Black Music as an Art Form." *Black Music Research Journal* 3:1–22.

———. 1992. "The Heterogeneous Sound Ideal in African-American Music." In *New Perspectives on Music: Essays in Honor of Eileen Southern*, edited by Josephine Wright, 327–38. Warren, MI: Harmonie Park Press.

Wilson, Russ. 1969. "Black Musicians Raise Employment Issue." *Oakland Tribune*, April 27, 10EN.

———. 1971. "Volume Builds in 'Ostinato.'" *Oakland Tribune*, September 10.

Wolfgang's Vault. Description of James Brown's performance at the 1969 Newport Jazz Festival. http://www.wolfgangsvault.com/james-brown/concerts/newport-jazz-festival-july-06–1969.html. Accessed August 23, 2011.

Yudkin, Jeremy. 2008. *Miles Davis, Miles Smiles, and the Invention of Post Bop*. Bloomington: University of Indiana Press.

Zak, Albin J., III. 2009. "Mitch the Goose Man, Mitch Miller and the Invention of Modern Record Production." American Musicological Society, November 12–15, Philadelphia.

———. 2010. *I Don't Sound Like Nobody: Remaking Music in 1950s America*. Ann Arbor: University of Michigan Press.

Zwerin, Mike. 1999. "Sons of Miles: Streamlines Herbie . . . Sight and Sound." Culturekioque, April 1. http://www.culturekiosque.com/jazz/miles/rhemile37.htm.

Discography

Art Blakey and the Jazz Messengers. (1961) 2004. *Buhaina's Delight*. Blue Note Records, audio compact disc.

Byrd, Donald. (1961) 2004. *Free Form*. Blue Note Records, audio compact disc.

Circle. (1971) 2001. *The Paris Concert*. ECM Records, audio compact disc

Coleman, Ornette. (1960) 1992. *Change of the Century*. Atlantic Records, audio compact disc.

Coltrane, John. (1964) 2003. *A Love Supreme*. Impulse! Records, audio compact disc.

———. (1965) 2000. *Ascension*. [Impulse! Records] Polygram Records, audio compact disc.

———. (1965) 1994. *Live in Seattle*. [Impulse! Records] Grp Records, audio compact disc.

Connors, Norman. (1972) 1976. *Dance of Magic*. Cobblestone/Buddha, audio LP.

———. 1973. *Dark of Light*. Cobblestone/Buddha, audio LP.

———. 1974. *Love from the Sun*. Buddah, audio LP.

———. 1975. *Saturday Night Special*. Buddah, audio LP.

Davis, Miles. (1956) 1987. *Relaxin' with the Miles Davis Quintet*. Prestige, audio compact disc.

———. (1957) 2008. *Bag's Groove*. Prestige, audio compact disc.

———. (1957) 1997. *Miles Ahead*. [Columbia Records] Sony, audio compact disc.

———. (1958) 2001. *Milestones.* [Columbia Records] Sony, audio compact disc.

———. (1958) 1997. *Porgy and Bess.* [Columbia Records] Sony, audio compact disc.

———. (1959) 2000. *A Kind of Blue.* [Columbia Records] Sony, audio compact disc.

———. (1960) 2000. *Sketches of Spain.* [Columbia Records] Sony, audio compact disc.

———. (1965) 1998. *E.S.P.* [Columbia Records] Sony, audio compact disc.

———. (1967) 1998. *Miles Smiles.* [Columbia Records] Sony, audio compact disc.

———. (1967) 1998. *Nefertiti.* [Columbia Records] Sony, audio compact disc.

———. (1967) 2008. *Sorcerer.* [Columbia Records] Sbme Special Mkts, audio compact disc.

———. (1968) 2008. *Miles in the Sky.* [Columbia Records] Sbme Special Mkts, audio compact disc.

———. (1968) 2008. *Filles De Kilimanjaro.* [Columbia Records] Sbme Special Mkts, audio compact disc.

———. (1969) 2002. *In a Silent Way.* [Columbia Records] Sony, audio compact disc.

———. (1970) 2010. *Bitches Brew.* [Columbia Records] Sony Legacy, audio compact disc.

———. (1970) 1997. *Black Beauty: Miles Davis at Fillmore West.* [Columbia Records] Sony, audio compact disc.

———. (1970) 1997. *Get Up with It.* [Columbia Records] Sony, audio compact disc.

———. (1971) 1997. *Live Evil.* [Columbia Records] Sony, audio compact disc.

———. (1970) 1997. *Miles Davis at Fillmore: Live at the Fillmore East.* [Columbia] Sony, audio compact disc.

———. (1971) 2000. *A Tribute to Jack Johnson.* [Columbia Records] Sony, audio compact disc.

———. (1972) 1997. *In Concert: Live at Philharmonic Hall.* [Columbia Records] Sony, audio compact disc.

———. (1972) 2010. *On the Corner.* [Columbia Records] Sony, audio compact disc.

———. (1974) 2010. *Big Fun.* [Columbia Records] Sony, audio compact disc.

———. (1974) 1997. *Dark Magus.* [Columbia Records] Sony, audio compact disc.

———. (1975) 2009. *Agharta.* [Columbia Records] Sony, audio compact disc.

———. (1975) 1990. *Pangaea.* [Columbia Records] Sony, audio compact disc.

———. (1976) 2002. *Water Babies.* [Columbia Records] Sony, audio compact disc.

———. (1979) 1990. *Circle in the Round.* [Columbia Records] Sony, audio compact disc.

———. (1981) 2001. *Directions.* [Columbia Records] Sony, audio compact disc.

———. (1982) 1995. *The Complete Live at the Plugged Nickel,* vol. 1. Columbia Records/ Columbia Legacy, audio compact disc.

———. 1997. *Live at the Fillmore East, March 7, 1970: It's About That Time.* Sony, audio compact disc.

———. (1998) 2004. *Miles Davis Quintet, 1965–'68.* Sony, audio compact disc.

———. 2001. *The Complete in a Silent Way Sessions.* Sony, audio compact disc.

———. 2004. *The Complete Bitches Brew Sessions.* Sony, audio compact disc.

———. 2005. *Cellar Door Sessions 1970.* Sony, audio compact disc.

———. 2005. *The Complete Jack Johnson Sessions.* Sony, audio compact disc.

———. 2007. *The Complete on the Corner Sessions.* Sony, audio compact disc.

Debussy, Claude. 1995. *La Mer, Nocturnes, Jeux, Rhapsodie pour clarinette et orchestre.* The

Cleveland Orchestra / Pierre Boulez. Deutsche Grammophon Gesselshaft, audio compact disc.

———. 1995. *Préludes*, vol. 1, *Images*. Arturo Benedetti Michelangeli, piano. Deutche Grammophon Gesselshaft, audio compact disc.

Dolphy, Eric. (1963) 1999. *Illinois Concert*. Blue Note Records, audio compact disc.

Eric Dolphy Quintet with Herbie Hancock. 2007. *Gaslight 1962*. Get Back, audio compact disc.

Hancock, Herbie. (1962) 2007. *Takin' Off*. Blue Note Records, audio compact disc.

———. (1963) 2005. *Inventions and Dimensions*. Blue Note Records, audio compact disc.

———. (1963) 1999. *My Point of View*. Blue Note Records, audio compact disc.

———. (1964) 1999. *Empyrean Isles*. Blue Note Records, audio compact disc.

———. (1965) 1999. *Maiden Voyage*. Blue Note Records, audio compact disc.

———. (1968) 2005. *Speak Like a Child*. Blue Note Records, audio compact disc.

———. (1969) 2005. *The Prisoner*. Blue Note Records, audio compact disc.

———. (1969) 2001. *Fat Albert Rotunda*. Warner Brothers, audio compact disc.

———. (1971) 2003. *Mwandishi*. Warner Brothers, audio compact disc.

———. (1972) 2001. *Crossings*. Warner Brothers, audio compact disc.

———. (1973) 2008. *Sextant*. [Columbia Records] Columbia Legacy, audio compact disc.

———. 1973. *The Spook Who Sat by the Door—Original Motion Picture Soundtrack*. United Artists Records, audio LP.

———. (1974) 1997. *Head Hunters*. [Columbia Records] Sony, audio compact disc.

———. (1974) 1998. *Thrust*. Columbia Records. [Columbia Records] Sony, audio compact disc.

———. (1977) 2007. *V.S.O.P.* [Columbia Records] Sony / Bmg Japan, audio compact disc.

———. 1994. *Mwandishi: The Complete Warner Brothers Recordings*. Warner Brothers, audio compact disc.

Heath, Albert Tootie. 1970. *Kawaida*. O'Be Records, audio LP.

Henderson, Eddie. 1973. *Realization*. Capricorn, audio LP.

———. 1974. *Inside Out*. Capricorn, audio LP.

———. 2003. *Anthology*, vol. 2, *The Capricorn Years*. Soul Brother, audio compact disc.

Henderson, Joe. (1969) 2007. *Power to the People*. Milestone, audio compact disc.

Hendrix, Jimi. 1999. *Jimi Hendrix: Live at Woodstock*. Experience Hendrix, audio compact disc.

———. 2010. *Blue Wild Angel: Jimi Hendrix Live at the Isle of Wight*. Legacy Recordings, audio compact disc.

Hubbard, Freddie. (1962) 1998. *Hub-Tones*. Blue Note Records, audio compact disc.

———. (1970) 2002. *Red Clay*. [CTI Records] Sony, audio compact disc.

———. (1971) 2008. *Straight Life*. [CTI Records] Sbme Special Mkts, audio compact disc.

Klein, Jonathan. (1968) 2008. *Hear O Israel*. [Union of American Hebrew Congregations] Trunk Records, audio compact disc.

Maupin, Bennie. (1975) 2007. *Jewel in the Lotus*. ECM, audio compact disc.

———. 1977. *Slow Traffic to the Right*. Mercury Records, audio LP.

McLean, Jackie. (1963) 2000. *Vertigo*. Blue Note Records, audio compact disc.

Messiaen, Olivier. 1992. *Turangalila-Symphonie, for orchestra* (1946–48). Myung-Whun Chung (conductor), Bastille Opera Orchestra. Deutsche Grammophon, audio compact disc.

Monk, Thelonious. (1957) 1991. *Monk's Music*. [Riverside] Ojc, audio compact disc.

Pendereski, Krzysztof. 1991. *Threnody for the Victims of Hiroshima* (1959–61). Krzysztof Penderecki (composer), Polish Radio National Symphony Orchestra. EMI Classics, audio compact disc.

Peterson, Oscar. (1945) 2007. *I Got Rhythm*. Prism Leisure Corp, audio compact disc.

———. (1962) 2003. *Night Train* [Verve] Universal Japan, audio compact disc.

Powell, Bud. (1958) 1990. *The Amazing Bud Powell, Time Waits*. Capitol Records, audio compact disc.

Ra, Sun. (1965) 1999. *Heliocentric Worlds*, vol. 2 [Saturn] Get Back, audio compact disc.

Ravel, Maurice. 1995. *Daphnis et Cloe, La Valse*. Pierre Boulez (conductor), Berliner Philharmoniker. Deutsche Grammaphon, audio compact disc.

Rivers, Sam. (1965) 2004. *Contours*. Blue Note Records, audio compact disc.

Roach, Max. (1960) 2006. *We Insist! Max Roach's Freedom Now Suite*. Candid Records, audio compact disc.

Schaeffer, Pierre. 1990. "Etudes aux Chemins de Fer" (1948). *L'Oeuvre Musicale*. EMF Media, audio compact disc.

Silver, Horace. (1955) 2005. *Horace Silver and the Jazz Messengers*. Blue Note Records, audio compact disc.

———. (1959) 1999. *Blowin' the Blues Away*. Blue Note Records, audio compact disc.

———. (1961) 2006. *Doing the Thing*. The Horace Silver Quintet at the Village Gate. Blue Note Records, audio compact disc.

Stockhausen, Karlheinz. 1991. "Gesang der Jungling" (1956). *Elektronische Musik 1952–1960*. Stockhausen-Verlag, audio compact disc

———. 1993. *Mixtur for orchestra, sine wave generators and ring modulators*. Stockhausen-Verlag, audio compact disc

———. 1995. *Mikrophonie I, Mikrophonie II, Telemusik*. Stockhausen-Verlag, audio compact disc.

Strauss, Richard. 2007. *Elektra*. Georg Solti (conductor), Vienna Philharmonic Orchestra. Decca, audio compact disc.

Stravinsky, Igor. 1991. *Firebird Suite, Pulcinella Suite*. Pierre Boulez (conductor), BBC Symphony Orchestra, New York Philharmonic, and Ensemble InterContemporain. Sony, audio compact disc.

———. 1995. *Petrushka, Rite of Spring (Le Sacre de Printemps)*. Pierre Boulez (conductor), Cleveland Orchestra, and New York Philharmonic. Sony, audio compact disc.

Taylor, Cecil. (1956) 1991. *Jazz Advance*. Blue Note Records, audio compact disc.

———. (1958) 1991. *Looking Ahead*. [Contemporary] Original Jazz Classics, audio compact disc.

Varèse, Edgard. 1990. "Poème électronique" (1958). *Electro Acoustic Music: Classics*. Neuma Records, audio compact disc.

———. 1998. "Integrales" (1926), "Equatorial" (1934). *The Complete Works*. Ricardo Chailly (conductor), Royal Concertgebouw, Asko Ensemble. London Decca, audio compact disc.

Vitous, Miroslav. (1972) *Mountain in the Clouds*. Atlantic. Also released as *Infinite Search*. [Embryo 1974] Collectables 2001, audio compact disc.

Wagner, Richard. 1997. *Tristan und Isolde* (1859). Deutsche Grammophon, audio compact disc.

Weather Report. (1972) 1990. *I Sing the Body Electric*. [Columbia Records] Sony, audio compact disc.

———. (1972) 1998. *Weather Report: Live in Tokyo*. [Sony Japan] Columbia Europe, audio compact disc.

Webern, Anton. 1995. "String Trio" (1927). *Webern: Works for String Quartet, String Trio op. 20*. Emerson String Quartet. Deutsche Grammophon Gesselschaft, audio compact disc.

Williams, Buster. (1975) 1998. *Pinnacle*. [Muse] 32 Jazz, audio compact disc.

———. (1980) 1998. *Dreams Come True*. [Buddha] 32 Jazz, audio compact disc.

Wonder, Stevie. (1972) 2000. *Music of My Mind*. Motown, audio compact disc.

———. (1972) 2000. *Talking Book*. Motown, audio compact disc.

———. (1973) 2000. *Innervisions*. Motown, audio compact disc.

———. (1974) 2000. *Fulfillingness' First Finale*. Motown, audio compact disc.

Zawinul, Josef. (1970) 2007. *Zawinul*. [Atlantic Records] Mosaic, audio compact disc.

Index

Lincoln, Nebraska, 195; at 1976 reunion performance, 181; within quadraphonic soundboard, 126; on recorded and NDR live performance of "Ostinato," 151–52; on Strata Art Gallery live performance of "You'll Know When You Get There," 131

electric piano: Miles Davis's interest in the Rhodes, 64; design of the early Rhodes models, 65; development of Herbie Hancock's technique on *Fat Albert Rotunda*, Freddie Hubbard's *Red Clay*, 68–70; Herbie Hancock's aesthetic interest in the Fender Rhodes, 61–62; Herbie Hancock's first experience of, in the studio with Miles Davis, 62; Herbie Hancock playing more than acoustic piano, 14; 46; multiple electric piano recordings and Herbie Hancock's appearance on Miles Davis's "Dual Mr. Anthony Tillmon Williams Process," 50; processed Fender Rhodes as a precursor to synthesizers, 60, 71; on "Stuff" from *Miles in the Sky*, 62–63; prior use of Wurlitzer electric piano on "Water on the Pond," 63; as sound design instrument in Herbie Hancock's hands, 70–75, 127; RMI on 1968 Miles Davis Quintet session, 212. *See* wah-wah pedal

electric bass: Ron Carter on Joe Henderson's *Power to the People*, 54–55; Jerry Jermott on "Wiggle Waggle," 68; Jermott on John Murtaugh's *Blues Current*, 87; about September 1971 live performance, 224–25; Buster Williams at Both/And show reviewed by Leonard Feather, 162; Buster Williams playing, 14; on "Hornets," 135–36; on "Sleeping Giant," 108

electronic music, 2, 89

Ellington, Duke: Julian Priester's membership in the Orchestra, 10–11; Wallace Roney compares Herbie Hancock with, 157

energy, 183; Herbie Hancock describes his changing musical needs in 1973, 175; "intensity," 154; 160–61; Archie Shepp's term "energy-sound," 154; term to describe level of intensity within performance, 24, 41, 101, 132, 134, 146; term used by critics to describe Mwandishi performances in 1972–73, 166–68, 177

Evans, Bill, 41; early influence on Herbie Hancock, 29; harmonic influence on Herbie Hancock, 73; *Waltz For Debby* (1961), 39

Evans, Gil, 200; in audience at Patrick Gleeson's first performance with the Mwandishi band, 127; harmonic influence on Herbie Hancock, 73; influence on Herbie Hancock's *Speak Like a Child*, 17, 50; Christian McBride compares work with Herbie Hancock's *The Prisoner*, 189; orchestration model influences Miles Davis interest in Fender Rhodes, 64; Wallace Roney comparison with Herbie Hancock, 157

Farnon, Robert: influence on Herbie Hancock's orchestration, 73

Fat Albert Rotunda (1970), 3, 37; commercial success and negative critical response, 60; 67; Bill Cosby invitation to record, 58; lyrical compositions, 59; R&B features of, 59, 68–69; "Tell Me a Bedtime Story," 50, 59, 69; 79, 87, 88, 89; "Wiggle Waggle," 68, 70

Fender Rhodes (Rhodes). *See* electric piano

Fielder, Alvin: Mwandishi band stand at London House, 18; playing with young Herbie Hancock in Chicago, 32

Fillmore East, 81; Herbie Hancock Sextet appearance in Sunday jazz series, 52; ownership by Bill Graham, 89, 216

Fillmore West: example of Herbie Hancock's interest in rock venues, 83–84; ownership by Bill Graham, 89; site where Billy Hart rejoins band, 83

Fischer Clare. *See* Hi-Lo's

flange. *See* postproduction

Floyd, Samuel: observation about the collective within black music, 144

Forman, Mitchel, ix, 191

Four Freshmen: influence on Herbie Hancock's harmonies, 73

fragmentation: chord fragments, 29, 39, 45, 46, 65, 208; definition, 209; melodic fragments, 36, 43–44, 68, 100; noise fragments, 86; of a riff, 151–52

free jazz, 54, 142–43, 145, 147, 207; Ornette Coleman's recording titled *Free Jazz*, 142, 144; definition, 221–22

early Sextet, 53–56; *Power to the People,*
Herbie Hancock electric piano on "Black
Narcissus," 67; Schaefer Music Festival,
82; Sextet departure, 9; Miroslav Vitous
Infinite Search, 67; "Wiggle Waggle" solo,
68; Pete Yellin as one of his subs, replacement by Bennie Maupin, final appearance
with the band, 80

Hendrix, Jimi, 186; Herbie Hancock sees
recordings in Miles Davis's apartment,
109; sonic distortion with guitar, "Star
Spangled Banner," portamenti in "Sgt.
Pepper's Lonely Hearts Club Band," 71

Hi-Lo's, 200; influence on Herbie Hancock's
harmonies, 73. *See also* Fischer, Clare

Horn, Shirley: Billy Hart's association with,
7–8

Hubbard, Freddie, 7; on John Coltrane's
Ascension, 214; influence on and contact
with Eddie Henderson, 11; Victor Lewis
refers to, 193; Julian Priester recording on
sessions and joining Hubbard's Quintet,
10; *Red Clay* as example of Herbie
Hancock's emerging funky style, 68–70;
Red Clay, 3; *Red Clay* referenced by Billy
Childs, 187; *Straight Life,* 70, 87

Hyde Park High School: Herbie Hancock's
attendance, 29–30

impressionism. *See* abstraction, and Debussy,
Claude

improvisation. *See* collective

intuitive musical forms, 2; collective building of tension and release, 153–55;
Miles Davis Quintet models of intuitive
forms applied to Mwandishi band,
146–49; Herbie Hancock's description
of Mwandishi band's musical approach,
16–17; Julian Priester's description of
Mwandishi band upon joining, 10–11;
Jullian Priester's memory that "everyone
was of the same mind," 22–23; spiritual
practice, 155–57

Iron Butterfly: rock band sharing billings
with the Sextet and Mwandishi band,
81, 83

Jazz Workshop (Boston club): Mwandishi
band performances, 77, 130–31, 162,
166, 227

Jones, Harold: drummer with a band in
Chicago that included young Herbie
Hancock, 32

Jordan, Clifford: with first Sextet at the
Village Vanguard and other initial
performances, 51; replacement by Joe
Henderson, 53

Karenga, Maulana Ron, 15, 206; title of
composition on *Kawaida,* 16

Kawaida (1969), 14, 15–17, 85; 200; influence of AACM upon, 19; 59; use of "little
instruments," 74

Kelly, Wynton: comparison to Herbie Hancock's playing on "Yams," 36. *See* McLean,
Jackie

Krivda, Ernie: memories of Mwandishi band
shows in Cleveland, 161, 225

Kwanzaa: influence of Maulana Ron Karenga
on Kawaida, and *the recitation of its principles on its final tune,* 15–16. *See* Karenga,
Maulana Ron

Lewis, Victor: reminiscences about Herbie
Hancock and Mwandishi band, 193–96

locked groove, 91–92, 150, 154. *See* Schaeffer,
Pierre; *see also* riff; vamp

London House (Chicago restaurant): 2, 15,
31, 85–87, 206; Mwandishi band November 1970 month–long stand, 17–23;
ownership by the Marienthal brothers, 17

lyricism/lyrical, 3, 14, 30–31, 37–39, 47,
53–54, 59, 61, 70, 85, 97, 98–99, 102, 108,
131, 152, 154, 166, 183, 209

McLaughlin, John: on Miles Davis's "Car-
rado," 66; on Davis's "Honky Tonk," 79;
on Davis's "The Little Blue Frog," 213; on
Davis's "Yesternow," 215; *New York Times*
to five jazz LP list includes McLaughlin's
My Goal's Beyond alongside *Mwandishi,*
218; on Miroslav Vitous's *Infinite* Search,
67

Macero, Teo: use of Echoplex in postproduction of Miles Davis's *Bitches Brew,* 71;
contrast with David Rubinson's approach
to studio techniques, 106, 117–18

Marienthal brothers, 17

Maupin, Bennie (Mwile): 1976 reunion
concert, 181; Thurman Barker hears play